Compagno · Intelligente Glasfassaden / Intelligent Glass Façades

Andrea Compagno

Intelligente Glasfassaden

Material

Anwendung

Gestaltung

Intelligent Glass Façades

Material

Practice

Design

Birkhäuser Verlag
Basel·Boston·Berlin

Translation German – English:
Ingrid Taylor / English Experts, Munich
Gestaltung / Design: Urs Berger-Pecora
Umschlagphoto/Cover photo:
Studio Holger Knauf, Düsseldorf

Alle in diesem Buch enthaltenen Angaben, Daten,
Ergebnisse usw. wurden vom Autor nach bestem
Wissen erstellt und von ihm und dem Verlag mit
größtmöglicher Sorgfalt überprüft. Dennoch sind
inhaltliche Fehler nicht völlig auszuschließen.
Daher erfolgen die Angaben usw. ohne jegliche
Verpflichtung oder Garantie des Verlags oder des
Autors. Beide übernehmen deshalb keinerlei
Verantwortung und Haftung für etwa vorhandene
inhaltliche Unrichtigkeiten.

Die Deutsche Bibliothek – CIP-Einheitsaufnahme

Compagno, Andrea:
Intelligente Glasfassaden : Material, Anwendung,
Gestaltung = Intelligent glass façades / Andrea
Compagno. [Transl. German – Engl.: Ingrid
Taylor]. – 2., unveränd. Nachdr. – Basel ;
Boston ; Berlin : Birkhäuser, 1996
 Text dt. und engl.
 ISBN 3-7643-5547-6

Zweiter, unveränderter Nachdruck 1996
Second uncorrected reprint 1996
© 1995 Birkhäuser – Verlag für Architektur,
P.O. Box 133, CH-4010 Basel, Switzerland
Printed on acid-free paper produced from
chlorine-free pulp. TCF ∞
Printed in Germany
ISBN 3-7643-5547-6
9 8 7 6 5 4 3

Publiziert mit Unterstützung von /
Supported by:

GARTNER

Josef Gartner & Co.
Werkstätten für Stahl- und
Metallkonstruktionen
Gundelfingen/Donau, Deutschland

Glas Trösch AG
Bützberg, Schweiz

HL⁄Technik

HL-Technik AG
Beratende Ingenieure
Hauptverwaltung München/Berlin, Deutschland
HL-Technik AG, Zürich, Schweiz

HTP ▲ HOCHTIEF
PROJEKTENTWICKLUNG GMBH

HOCHTIEF Projektentwicklung GmbH
Essen, Deutschland

Kapillarglas GmbH
Marktheidenfeld-Altfeld, Deutschland

⟨ VEGLA

Vereinigte Glaswerke GmbH
Aachen, Deutschland

Inhalt

Contents

Einleitung   Introduction

Eine «intelligente» Glasfassade kann sich auf dynamische, gleichsam lebendige Weise durch selbstregelnde Wärme- und Sonnenschutzmaßnahmen den wechselnden Licht- und Klimaverhältnissen anpassen, um den Bedürfnissen der Benutzer und Benutzerinnen gerecht zu werden und zugleich den Verbrauch an Primärenergie eines Gebäudes zu senken. Durch eine optimale Nutzung von natürlichen, erneuerbaren Energiequellen wie Sonnenstrahlung und Windströmungen kann sie wesentlich dazu beitragen, unsere Umwelt zu schonen.

Eine «intelligente» Fassade ist insbesondere bei großflächig verglasten, bisher vollklimatisierten Büro- und Verwaltungsgebäuden ökologisch wie ökonomisch von Bedeutung: Immissionen und der damit verbundene Treibhauseffekt können weitgehend verhindert, Investitions- und Betriebskosten bei der Gebäudetechnik so niedrig wie möglich gehalten werden.

Bei vollverglasten Gebäuden sind nicht nur die Wärmeverluste ausschlaggebend, sondern auch der Energieaufwand für Lüftung, Kühlung und Belichtung. Durch die vermehrte Nutzung der natürlichen Luftströmungen, des einfallenden Tageslichts oder der Speicherfähigkeit der Gebäudemasse kann der Energieverbrauch maßgeblich gesenkt werden.

Seit den 20er Jahren sind transparente, filigrane Glasbauten ein Merkmal der modernen Architektur, nachdem zu Beginn des Jahrhunderts die industrielle Produktion von Glasscheiben mit dem Ziehverfahren nach der Erfindung von Emile Fourcault (1904) und Irwin W. Colburn (1905) wesentlich erleichtert worden war und das aufwendige Gießverfahren in dieser Beziehung überholt hatte.

Bald traten allerdings die Nachteile einer Glasfassade zutage: Überhitzung und Wärmeverlust. Zu deren Beseitigung schlug Le Corbusier schon um 1930 zwei Gegenmaßnahmen vor: «la respiration exacte» und «le mur neutralisant», womit

An "intelligent" glass façade makes use of self-regulating thermal protection and solar control measures to adapt in a dynamic, "living" way to changing light and weather conditions. In this way it meets the requirements of the building's users and at the same time reduces energy consumption levels. By optimum use of natural, renewable energy sources such as solar radiation and air flows, it can play a major part in protecting our environment.

Intelligent glass façades are of particular ecological and economic importance in the kind of fully glazed office buildings which until now needed full air-conditioning. Intelligent façades are capable of achieving a significant reduction in emissions and thus do not contribute to the greenhouse effect in the earth's atmosphere; investment and operating costs for the relevant building systems are kept as low as possible.

In fully glazed buildings not only the heat losses are critical, but also the energy consumption of systems for ventilation, cooling and lighting. By increased utilisation of natural air movements, incident daylight or the thermal storage capacity of the building mass, total energy consumption levels can be considerably reduced.

Transparent, filigree glass buildings have been a feature of modern architecture since the 1920s; at that time new industrial production methods for sheet drawn glass, based on inventions by Emile Fourcault (1904) and Irwin W. Colburn (1905), replaced the traditional, more complicated pouring process and greatly simplified the manufacture of flat glass.

However, with the increasing use of glass in façades came also a realisation of the disadvantages: overheating and heat loss. Already in 1930 Le Corbusier suggested two measures for counteracting these problems: "la respiration exacte" and "le mur neutralisant", thus marking the start of mechanical air conditioning systems.

die mechanische Klimakontrolle ihren Anfang nahm.

Das Ende der 50er Jahre von Alastair Pilkington entwickelte Floatverfahren ermöglichte die Produktion von noch größeren Mengen an Glas zu tieferen Preisen.

Etwa zur selben Zeit aber wurde die Kritik an der Energieverschwendung bei vollflächigen Glashüllen unüberhörbar. 1969 äußerte Reyner Banham in «The Architecture of the Well-Tempered Environment» seine Vorbehalte gegen den zunehmenden, von der Klimaregelung verursachten Aufwand an Energie und gegen die Loslösung der Architektur von klimatischen und regionalen Gegebenheiten. Seine Gedanken waren eben veröffentlicht und rezipiert, als die Energiekrise der Jahre 1973/74 dringender denn je nach einer Lösung rief.

Da sowohl die Nachteile als auch die Vorteile einer Glasfassade in ihrer Strahlungsdurchlässigkeit liegen, stellte der englische Architekt Mike Davies 1981 in seinem Artikel «Eine Wand für alle Jahreszeiten» die Entwicklung einer Verglasung mit veränderbaren Eigenschaften zur Diskussion, die den Energiefluß von außen nach innen und umgekehrt je nach Bedarf dynamisch steuern könnte.

Diese «polyvalente Wand» stellt die Reduktion der Außenhaut auf ein mehrschichtiges Verbundelement dar, welches durch selbstregelnde Steuerungssysteme Sonnen- und Wärmeschutz gewährleistet und zugleich den dazu notwendigen Strom erzeugt. Davies' Idee stützte sich auf bereits vorhandene Errungenschaften bei Produkten aus anderen Bereichen der Technik, wie selbstverdunkelnde Brillengläser oder Solarzellen der Weltraumkapseln, und versuchte sie auf die Glasproduktion für die Bauwirtschaft zu übertragen. Da er das sich ständig verändernde Aussehen der «polyvalenten Wand» mit der Haut eines Chamäleons verglich, führte das in der Folge zum Begriff der «intelligenten» Fassade.

Verbunden mit dem Bemühen um ein ökologisches, umweltgerechtes Bauen, hat in den 80er Jahren die Entwicklung der Glasarchitektur, nach dem Rückschlag durch die Energiekrise der 70er Jahre, wieder an Bedeutung gewonnen.

Der Wendepunkt lag im Erkennen des großen Energiepotentials der Sonnenstrahlung, die auf eine Fassadenfläche auftrifft, und in der Absicht, dieses Potential zu nutzen. Die Sonnenstrahlung wurde als ideale Energieform erkannt, weil sie die Umwelt nicht belastet und überall zu allen

The float glass process developed at the end of the 1950s by Alastair Pilkington enabled the production of even larger quantitites of glass at lower prices.

At about the same time, however, criticism was growing of the energy waste associated with a fully glazed building skin. In 1969, in "The Architecture of the Well-Tempered Environment", Reyner Banham spoke out against the high energy requirements of artificial air conditioning systems and against the separation of architecture from local climatic and regional conditions. Soon after the publication and general recognition of his views the 1973/74 oil crisis added a new level of urgency to the search for a solution. As the radiation transmission properties of a glass façade represent both an advantage and a disadvantage, the English architect Mike Davies, in his article on "A Wall for all Seasons" published in 1981, proposed the development of a multiple-performance glazing which could dynamically regulate the energy flow from outside to inside and vice versa.

This "polyvalent wall" is a reduction of the outer skin of a building to a multi-layered compound element which makes use of self-regulating control mechanisms to provide heat insulation and solar protection, while at the same time generating the necessary electrical energy needed for the operation of these systems. Davies's idea is based on principles already exploited in other areas of technology, such as automatically darkening photochromic glass used in the manufacture of spectacles, or the solar cells used in space capsules. He advocated using these achievements in the manufacture of glass for building. His comparison of the ever-changing appearance of the "polyvalent wall" with the skin of a chameleon led to the coining of the phrase "intelligent" façade.

After the setbacks of the 1970s, developments in glass architecture regained significance in the 1980s, at the same time as pressure was mounting for more ecological, environmentally-friendly building techniques.

The turning point lay in recognising the enormous energy potential of the solar radiation striking the façade of a building, and in determining to utilise this potential. Solar radiation was seen as the ideal form of energy because it does not pollute the environment and is present everywhere in more or less abundant quantities at all times of the year.

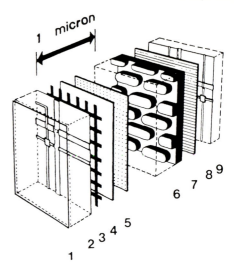

Vorschlag von Mike Davies für eine «polyvalente Wand»:

1 Silikat-Wetterhaut und Schichtenträger
2 Sensor- und Steuerungslogik außen
3 Photoelektrisches Gitter
4 Wärmestrahlende Schicht / Selektiver Absorber
5 Elektroreflektierende Schicht
6 Feinporige gasdurchströmte Schicht
7 Elektroreflektierende Schicht
8 Sensor- und Steuerungslogik innen
9 Silikat-Innenhaut und Schichtenträger.

Proposal of Mike Davies for the "polyvalent wall":

1 Silica weather skin and deposition substrate
2 Sensor and control logic layer – external
3 Photoelectric grid
4 Thermal sheet radiator / selective absorber
5 Electro-reflective deposition
6 Micro-pore gas flow layers
7 Electro-reflective deposition
8 Sensor and control logic layer – internal
9 Silica deposition substrate and inner skin.

Jahreszeiten mehr oder weniger ergiebig zur Verfügung steht.

Im Winter und in der Übergangszeit führt die Sonnenstrahlung zu Wärmeenergie- und Tageslichtgewinnen, welche, neben der Senkung der Wärmeverluste durch eine geeignete Verglasung, zu einer Verminderung des Verbrauchs an Primärenergie führen.

Im Sommer sind solche Gewinne weniger erwünscht und müssen durch wirksame Sonnenschutzmaßnahmen kontrolliert werden. Lichtumlenkende Elemente können hingegen weiterhin den Bedarf an künstlicher Beleuchtung reduzieren, die im Sommer einen großen Teil der Kühllasten verursacht.

Die Umsetzung von Davies' Grundidee bedingt nicht nur die Entwicklung neuer Glasprodukte für eine hochwertige Gebäudehülle, sondern auch fortschrittliche Energiekonzepte, welche die Interaktion der Fassade mit der Gebäudetechnik gewährleisten. Dies führt zu einer zunehmenden Komplexität der Entwurfsaufgabe, die nur durch eine integrale oder ganzheitliche Planung bewältigt werden kann.

In den einzelnen Kapiteln der vorliegenden Monographie werden die Gebäudehüllen nach der Anzahl Glasschichten beschrieben und mit Anwendungsbeispielen illustriert. Zu Beginn werden einzelne Scheibentypen in ihrer Zusammensetzung und der Behandlung ihrer Oberfläche vorgestellt. Dann folgen der mehrschichtige Aufbau der Verbund-, Isolier- und Mehrfachisoliergläser und die zahlreichen Möglichkeiten der Füllungen des Zwischenraums, von dünnen Folien bis zu dickeren Elementen mit wärmedämmenden oder lichtumlenkenden Eigenschaften. Schließlich werden die Einsatzmöglichkeiten im ein- und mehrschaligen Fassadenaufbau beschrieben, wobei zusätzliche Maßnahmen für den Sonnenschutz zur Anwendung kommen. Zuletzt werden die «intelligenten» Glasfassaden behandelt, die nicht nur durch einen besonderen Aufbau gekennzeichnet sind, sondern vor allem durch die Interaktion zwischen Fassade und Gebäudetechnik.

Die vorliegende Publikation will also die neuen Glasprodukte und ihre Anwendungsmöglichkeiten anhand von technischen Steckbriefen und von ausgeführten Beispielen dem Leser näherbringen. Sie will so auch eine gemeinsame Ausgangslage für das Gespräch zwischen Architekten, Fassadenplanern und beratenden Fachingenieuren schaffen.

In winter and in spring or autumn solar radiation gives rise to gains in terms of heat and light, both of which, given suitable glazing with little heat loss, lead to a reduction in energy consumption levels.

In summer such gains are less desirable and have to be controlled by appropriate solar control devices. Light-deflecting elements, on the other hand, can contribute to a reduction in the need for artificial lighting, which in summer is the cause of a large part of the cooling load.

In order to realise Davies's basic idea, not only new glass products for a high-quality building skin have to be developed, but also advanced energy concepts to guarantee the interaction of the façade with the building services. The design stages thus become increasingly complex, and can only be resolved successfully through an integrated or holistic planning.

The individual chapters of this monograph divide the building skins according to the number of layers of glass in the façade, each type being illustrated with carefully chosen examples. At the begin the composition and surface treatments of the different types of glass pane are described. Following this is a description of the multi-layered assemblies of laminated and insulating glass, together with a look at the options available for filling the cavity, from thin films to thicker integrated units with insulating or light-deflecting properties. The final chapter deals with the various ways of using the different types of glass in single-skin and multi-skin façades, in conjunction with additional solar control measures. This chapter finishes with a close look at intelligent glass façades, notable not only for their special construction, but for the interaction between façade and building services.

The present work seeks to acquaint the reader with the new glass products and, by means of technical summaries and built examples, to illustrate possibilities for their use. As such it also aims to present a joint basis for a dialogue between architects, façade planners and building engineers.

Glas ist ein anorganisches Schmelzprodukt, welches durch eine kontrollierte Kühlungstechnik ohne Kristallisation vom flüssigen in den festen Zustand übergeht. Deshalb wird es auch als erstarrte Flüssigkeit definiert. Verschiedene chemische Stoffe haben die Fähigkeit, Glas zu bilden: unter den anorganischen hauptsächlich die Oxide von Silizium (Si), Bor (B), Germanium (Ge), Phosphor (P) und Arsen (As). Da die Hauptkomponente praktisch aller Glasprodukte Siliziumdioxid ist, spricht man allgemein von Silikatgläsern.

Normales Floatglas enthält Sand (SiO_2, 71 bis 75%), Natron (Na_2O, 12 bis 16%), Kalk (CaO, 10 bis 15%) und einige Prozente an anderen Stoffen, die die Farbe bestimmen (z.B. Fe_2O_3).

Die besonderen Eigenschaften von Glas bezüglich Lichtdurchlässigkeit, thermischen Verhaltens, Festigkeit u.a. sind bedingt durch den Strukturzustand und die Zusammensetzung. Sie sind unabhängig von der Richtung, in der sie gemessen werden, weil Glas wegen des fehlenden Kristallgitters isotrop ist.

Optische Eigenschaften

Die «Transparenz» des Glases ist das wichtigste Merkmal bei seiner Verwendung im Bauwesen. Die Eigenschaften bezüglich Durchlässigkeit und damit Durchsichtigkeit sind auf den unterkühlten Zustand zurückzuführen. Da die kristalline Struktur fehlt, kommen die Lichtstrahlen durch, ohne gestreut zu werden.

Das sichtbare Licht bildet lediglich einen Teil der auf die Erde auftreffenden elektromagnetischen Sonnenstrahlung, da das menschliche Auge nur Strahlen mit Wellenlängen von 380 nm bis 780 nm wahrnehmen kann. Nicht sichtbar für uns sind die ultraviolette Strahlung (UV; mit Wellenlängen kleiner als 380 nm) und die infrarote Strahlung (IR; mit Wellenlängen größer als 780 nm).

Glass is an inorganic product of fusion which is cooled to a rigid state without crystallizing, and thus is also defined as a super-cooled liquid. Various chemical substances can form glass: among the inorganic ones are principally the oxides of silicon (Si), boron (B), germanium (Ge), phosphorus (P) and arsenic (As). Generally glass is of the soda-lime-silica type, as the main component of almost all glass products is silicon dioxide.

Normal float glass contains silica sand (SiO_2, 71 to 75%), soda (Na_2O, 12 to 16%), lime (CaO, 10 to 15%) and a small percentage of other materials which have an effect on the colour (e.g. Fe_2O_3).

The particular properties of glass in terms of light transmittance, thermal behaviour, strength etc. are determined by its structure and composition. These properties are independent of direction of measurement, as glass is isotropic due to its lack of a crystal lattice.

Optical Properties

The transparency of glass is its most important property for use in building. Its properties of light transmission, and thus transparence, are a result of the super-cooled state.

The lack of a crystalline structure means that the light rays pass through it without being scattered.

Visible light forms just one part of the solar electromagnetic radiation reaching the Earth; the human eye is only capable of detecting light in the 380 nm to 780 nm wavelength interval. We are unable to see ultraviolet radiation (UV; with wavelengths less than 380 nm) and the infrared range (IR; wavelengths longer than 780 nm).

The spectral intensity of the solar radiation reaches a peak at approx. 550 nm. The human eye's sensitivity corresponds to this maximum range of solar radiation.

Linke Seite: Die Verglasung mit geschraubten Eckhalterungen, sogenannten «patch fittings», zeigt die Festigkeit von Glasscheiben in hängenden Konstruktionen.
Verwaltungsgebäude für Willis, Faber und Dumas, Ipswich, England, 1971–75, Sir Norman Foster und Partner.
Left page: The glazing system with bolted corner plates, or "patch fittings", demonstrates the strength of glass in suspended constructions.
Headquarters for Willis, Faber und Dumas, Ipswich, England, 1971–75, Sir Norman Foster and Partners.

Die spektrale Verteilung der Intensität der Sonnenstrahlung ist durch ein Maximum bei etwa 550 nm gekennzeichnet. Die Empfindlichkeit des menschlichen Auges korrespondiert mit dem Maximum der solaren Strahlung.

Der relative Energiegehalt der Sonnenstrahlung beträgt im UV-Bereich 3 %, im sichtbaren Bereich 53 % und im nahen IR-Bereich 44 %. Durch ein Silikatglas gelangen Strahlen mit einer Wellenlänge von 315 nm bis 3000 nm. Sie erstrecken sich vom ultravioletten Bereich von 315–380 nm über den sichtbaren Bereich (von 380–780 nm) bis zum nahen IR-Bereich von 780–3000 nm. Dabei werden der UV-Bereich unter 315 nm und der langwellige IR-Bereich oberhalb 3000 nm fast völlig absorbiert. Letzterer wird in der Regel nur bis 2500 nm ausgewertet, weil die Intensität der Sonnenstrahlung größerer Wellenlängen sehr klein ist.

Aufgrund der Undurchlässigkeit für die langwellige Strahlung läßt sich der Treibhauseffekt einer Verglasung erklären. Die durchgelassene sichtbare und die nahe infrarote Strahlung wärmen die Gegenstände im Raum auf, aber kommen danach als längerwellige Strahlung zurück, die nicht mehr durch die Verglasung nach außen gelangen kann. Die Absorption der Strahlen im Glas produziert ebenfalls Wärme, welche vom Material an der Oberfläche durch Wärmestrahlung, Wärmeleitung und Konvektion abgegeben wird.

Thermische Eigenschaften

Beim normalen Floatglas ist der Wärmedurchgang ausschlaggebend für den Wärmeverlust und den damit verbundenen Heizaufwand. Während der Wärmewiderstand infolge Wärmeleitung nur unwesentlich mit der Scheibendicke zu beeinflussen ist, können die Wärmestrahlung durch Beschichtungen und die Konvektion durch konstruktive Maßnahmen verändert werden.

In bezug auf die Wärmedehnung des Glases hängt der spezifische Koeffizient von der chemischen Zusammensetzung des Glases ab: Bei normalem Floatglas bewirkt die Zuführung von Substanzen wie Alkalien einen Koeffizienten von 80–$90 \cdot 10^{-7}$/K, was eine Wärmedehnung von ca. 0.5 mm/m bei Temperaturen zwischen $-20\,°C$ und $+40\,°C$ zur Folge hat. Sie nähert sich derjenigen von Stahl oder Stahlbeton und muß somit bei der Kombination mit anderen Materialien berücksichtigt werden.

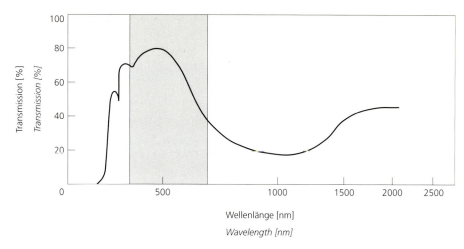

Die spektrale Verteilung der Intensität der Sonnenstrahlung weist ein Maximum bei etwa 550 nm auf.
Spectral energy transmission curve with a dominant peak at 550 nm in the visible band.

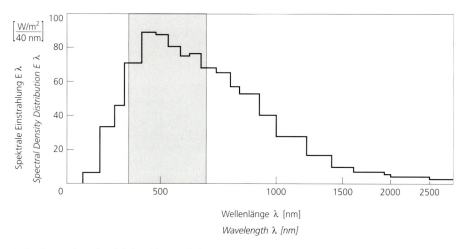

Spektrale Verteilung der Globalstrahlung nach der Commission Internationale de l'Eclairage (CIE).
Spectral energy distribution according to the Commission Internationale de l'Eclairage (CIE).

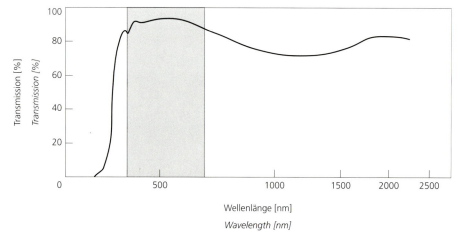

Spektrale Transmission eines üblichen Floatglases.
Spectral transmission of standard float glass.

Allerdings weisen reinere SiO_2-Gläser, wie Kiesel- und Quarzgläser, wesentlich kleinere Wärmedehnungskoeffizienten auf, die bei $5 \cdot 10^{-7}$/K liegen und sich beispielsweise für die Herstellung von Herdplatten eignen.

Technische Kenngrößen

Zahlreiche Kenngrößen stehen zur Verfügung, um die licht-, strahlungs- und wärmetechnischen Eigenschaften zu beurteilen. Mit den Begriffen der Reflexion, Absorption und Transmission beschreibt man die Strahlungsdurchlässigkeit einer oder mehrerer Glasscheiben. Sie werden als prozentualer Anteil des gesamten Strahlungseinfalls ausgedrückt. Die absorbierte Strahlung bewirkt die sekundäre Wärmeabgabe, indem sie in Wärme umgewandelt wird, welche durch Abstrahlung und Konvektion an den Scheibenoberflächen weitergegeben wird.

Die wesentlichen physikalischen Größen für die Bewertung des Lichteinfalls und der Wärmegewinne und -verluste sind die Faktoren der Tageslichttransmission τ (= «Lichtdurchlässigkeit») und der Gesamtenergietransmission g, sowie der Wärmedurchgangskoeffizient k.

Sie sind wie folgt definiert:

— Die Tageslichttransmission τ gibt den prozentualen Anteil an direkt durchgelassener, senkrecht einfallender Strahlung, bezogen auf das Helligkeitsempfinden des Auges, wieder.

— Der Gesamtenergietransmissionsgrad, g-Wert, ist die Summe des direkt durchgelassenen Strahlungsanteils (Energietransmission τ_E) bei senkrechtem Einfall und der sekundären Wärmeabgabe q_i der Verglasung nach innen infolge Wärmestrahlung, Wärmeleitung und Konvektion.

— Der Wärmedurchgangskoeffizient k, der sogenannte k-Wert, ist der Wärmestrom, der in

The relative energy content of solar radiation is 3 % in the UV range, 53 % in the visible range and 44 % in the near IR range.

Radiation with wavelengths in the range from 315 nm to 3000 nm can pass through soda-lime-silica glass. This range extends from ultraviolet at 315–380 nm across the visible range at 380–780 nm to the near infrared range at 780–3000 nm. The UV radiation with wavelengths below 315 nm and the radiation in the far infrared range above 3000 nm are almost completely absorbed. The latter is generally only recorded up to 2500 nm, because the intensity of solar radiation in the longer wavelengths is very low.

The non-transmission of radiation in the longer wavelengths explains the heating-up effect behind glazing. The visible and near infrared light passing through the glass heat up the objects in the room, and are returned as longer wavelength radiation, which can no longer pass through the glass to the outside. The absorption of radiation in the glass also produces heat which is then dissipated from the surface by radiation, conduction and convection.

Thermal Properties

In normal float glass thermal transmission is a critical factor in heat loss and thus also in associated heating expenditure and requirements. While thermal resistance as a result of conduction can only marginally be affected by the thickness of the glass, radiation can be changed by applying coatings, and convection can be controlled by modifying the construction.

With reference to the thermal expansion of glass, the specific coefficient is dependent on the composition of the glass: in normal float glass the addition of substances such as alkalines can produce coefficients from $80–90 \cdot 10^{-7}$/K, which in turn produces a thermal expansion of approx. 0.5 mm/m at temperatures between $-20\,°C$ and $+40\,°C$. It approaches the values of steel and reinforced concrete, and as such must be taken into account when combining it with other materials.

Purer SiO_2 glass, such as fused silica or quartz glass, has noticeably lower coefficients of thermal expansion, at around $5 \cdot 10^{-7}$/K; this makes it suitable for use in the manufacture of cooking surfaces.

Technical parameters

Many parameters are available for assessing

Gesamte Sonneneinstrahlung
Total Solar Radiation

Lichttransmission τ_L
Light Transmission τ_L

τ_L

Reflexion
Reflection

Transmission τ_e
Transmission τ_e

+

sekundäre Wärmeabgabe nach aussen q_a
Absorption dissipated outside q_a

sekundäre Wärmeabgabe nach innen q_i
Absorption dissipated inside q_i

=

Gesamtenergietransmission g-Wert
Total Solar Energy Transmission g-factor

Strahlendurchgang bei einer Glasscheibe: Reflexion, Absorption, Transmission und Gesamtenergietransmission (g Wert).

The solar radiation received by a pane of glass: reflection, absorption, transmission and total solar energy transmission (g-factor).

einer Stunde durch einen 1 m² großen Bauteil fließt bei einem Temperaturunterschied der an den Bauteil angrenzenden Luftschichten von 1 Kelvin.

Festigkeit

Der hohe Anteil an Siliziumdioxid ist für die Härte und die Festigkeit maßgebend, aber auch für die unerwünschte Sprödigkeit des Glases.

Die Sprödigkeit führt bei einer minimalen Überschreitung der Grenze der elastischen Verformung zum Bruch einer Glasscheibe, weil im Bereich der Bruchdehnung praktisch keine plastischen Verformungen möglich sind.

Die theoretische Zugfestigkeit des Glases liegt bei Werten um 10^4 N/mm². Die praktische Erfahrung zeigt aber, daß die effektive Zugfestigkeit maximal 30–80 N/mm² erreicht, also Festigkeitswerte bis knapp 1 % der theoretischen Werte. Bei Dauerbelastungen sind sogar nur 7 N/mm² bei Berechnungen zulässig. Die Verminderung ist auf die Tatsache zurückzuführen, daß Glas kein völlig gleichmäßiger Werkstoff ist, sondern Fehl- und Störstellen aufweist. Dieselbe Auswirkung haben kaum sichtbare Oberflächenrisse, die sowohl im Fertigungsprozeß als auch durch mechanische oder korrosive Beanspruchungen während der Nutzung entstehen.

Die niedrige Zugfestigkeit kann durch eine geeignete Nachbehandlung der Oberfläche, wie thermische oder chemische Vorspannung, bis auf ca. 5.10^2 N/mm² erhöht werden.

Bei der thermischen Vorspannung wird die Glasscheibe auf ca. 685 °C erwärmt und dann mit kalter Luft angeblasen. Durch die rasche Abkühlung verfestigt sich die äußere Schicht zuerst und wird durch das langsame Zusammenziehen der inneren Schicht unter Druck gesetzt. Die Zugkräfte in der Kernzone und die Druckkräfte in der Oberflächenschicht bewirken einen Vorspannungszustand.

Neben der erhöhten Zugfestigkeit hat eine thermisch vorgespannte Scheibe den Vorteil, beim Zerbrechen in viele Krümel ohne scharfe Kanten zu zerfallen. Auf diese Eigenschaft weist die Bezeichnung Einscheiben-Sicherheitsglas (ESG) hin.

Ein ähnlicher Kräftezustand wird bei der chemischen Vorspannung durch eine Änderung in der Zusammensetzung der Glasoberfläche erreicht. Die Scheiben werden in elektrolytische Bäder eingetaucht, wo die außenliegenden Natriumionen durch Kaliumionen, die einen 30 % größe-

light, radiation and thermal properties. Reflection, absorption and transmission are used to describe permeability to radiation of one or more glass panes. These values are expressed as a fraction (in per cent) of the total incident radiation. Absorbed radiation is converted to heat (secondary heat transmission) which is then dissipated from the surfaces of the glass by radiation or convection. The main physical parameters in the evaluation of incident light and thermal gain or loss are the factors of light transmittance τ and total solar energy transmission, g-factor, as well as the thermal transmittance coefficient, the U-value.

They are defined as follows:

– Light transmission, τ, refers to the fraction of directly transmitted light as perceived by the human eye.

– Total solar energy transmission, g-factor, is the sum of directly transmitted incident radiation (energy transmission τ_E) passing trough the glass, and the secondary heat transmission q_i from the glass to the inside of the room as a result of radiation, conduction and convection.

– Thermal transmittance, the U-value, is the rate of loss of heat per hour and per square metre, for a temperature difference of one degree Kelvin between the inner and outer environments separated by glass.

Strength

The high silicon dioxide content is significant for the hardness and strength of glass, but also for its undesired brittleness.

The structure of glass cannot accommodate plastic deformation so that it deforms elastically under stress up to the point where it suddenly breaks. The theoretical tensile strength of glass is 10^4 N/mm². Experience shows, however, that the effective tensile strength reaches a maximum of 30–80 N/mm², in other words, it values barely 1 % of the theoretical figures. When glass is subject to longer strain, values of only 7 N/mm² can be expected. The reduction is due to the fact that glass is not a completely uniform material, but instead contains flaws and weak points. The same effect is produced by microcracks on the surface, which can arise during the manufacturing process or through mechanical stress or corrosion during use.

Its low tensile strength can be improved up to approx. $5 \cdot 10^2$ N/mm² by an appropriate surface

ren Radius aufweisen, ausgetauscht werden. Damit bildet sich eine außenliegende Druckzone. Die Vorteile der chemischen Vorspannung gegenüber der thermischen sind: keine Formänderung der Glasscheibe infolge des Aufwärmungsprozesses sowie die wesentlich weniger tiefe (ca. 0.1 mm) Oberflächenschicht, was die Härtung von dünnen Scheiben ermöglicht.

Verglasungssysteme

Für den Einsatz von Glas im Fassadenbau bietet sich heute eine Vielzahl von Systemen an, die dem Bestreben entsprechen, eine maximale Transparenz durch die Reduktion der nichttransparenten tragenden Konstruktion zu erreichen. Die Arbeit einiger Architekten hat sich, in engem Zusammenwirken mit der Glasindustrie, intensiv mit den technischen Möglichkeiten des Werkstoffs Glas auseinandergesetzt, so daß einfachere Systeme wie Rahmen- und Pfosten-Riegel-Konstruktionen zu mehrgeschossigen hängenden Nur-Glas-Konstruktionen weiterentwickelt werden konnten.

Normale Verglasungssysteme basieren auf Glashalteleisten, die die Scheiben von innen gegen den äußeren Profilanschlag anpressen. Bei einer geschoßhohen Verglasung wird die Ansichtsbreite wegen des Glaseinstands, der Toleranzspielräume und der Breite der tragenden Profile selten weniger als 70 mm erreichen.

Verglasungssysteme mit Preßleisten ermöglichen Ansichtsbreiten von 50 mm. Da die Preßleisten aus Aluminium oder Stahl von außen angebracht werden und das Glas an die tragende Unterkonstruktion anpressen, sind hier nur Glaseinstand und Toleranzen maßgebend. Die Unterkonstruktion ist meistens als Pfosten-Riegel-Konstruktion

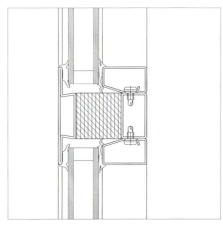

Detail einer Verglasung mit Glashalteleisten.
Detail of a bead glazing.

treatment after manufacture, such as thermal or chemical toughening.

In the case of thermal toughening the glass pane is heated to approx. 685 °C and then exposed to a stream of cold air. This rapid cooling has the effect of first consolidating the outer layer, which is then subjected to compression by the contraction of the inner layer. The tensile forces in the core zone and the compressive forces in the surface layer prestress the material.

In addition to increased tensile strength, a thermally toughened pane of glass has the advantage that on breakage it disintegrates into many small pieces without sharp edges, the dice. Therefore toughened or strengthened glass is indicated by the term safety glass.

A similar pattern of forces is achieved in chemical toughening by changing the composition of the surface of the glass. The panes are dipped into electrolysis baths where the external sodium ions are exchanged for potassium ions, which have a 30 % larger radius: this creates an external layer under pressure. The advantages of chemical toughening over thermal toughening are: no deformation of the glass pane as a result of the heating process, and the shallower depth of the surface layer (approx. 0.1 mm), which permits the toughening of thinner layers of glass.

Glazing Systems

Many systems are now available for the use of glass in façades, all aimed at achieving maximum transparency by reducing the non-transparent support structure. In close collaboration with the glass industry, some architects have carried out much work on the possibilities of glass for use in building, and this has led to the development of simpler systems, from frame systems and mullion and transom structures to curtain walls several floors high, made entirely of glass.

Normal glazing systems are based on glazing beads which press the panes from the inside against the outer frame structure. In a curtain wall the visible face of these bars is seldom less than 70 mm, due to glazing rebate, the tolerances and the width of the support profiles.

Pressure glazing systems enable the use of 50 mm wide panes of glass. As the pressure caps of aluminium or steel press the glass from the outside onto the internal support structure, only the insertion depth of the glass and the tolerances are critical. The support frame is generally a post

ausgeführt, was zu einem gleichmäßigen filigranen Erscheinungsbild führt.

Selten werden Preßleistensysteme aus EPDM-Profilen verwendet, wie beim IBM-Gebäude in Cosham (England), 1971, einem frühen Beispiel der Architektur von Sir Norman Foster und Partnern.

Mit dem Begriff «structural glazing» wird in der Regel ein Nur-Glas-System bezeichnet, bei dem die Glasscheiben mit hochbelastbaren Silikonen auf die tragende Konstruktion der Fassade geklebt sind. Dabei handelt es sich um eine Variation der Rahmen- oder Pfosten-Riegel-Konstruktion, welche nur das Erscheinungsbild von außen betrifft, ohne daß die tragende Struktur wesentlich verändert wird. Daher sollte eher von «geklebter Fassade» die Rede sein. Um diesen optischen Eindruck – ein Erscheinungsbild, das nur vom Glas bestimmt wird – zu erzielen, werden gefärbte oder verspiegelte Glasscheiben eingesetzt. Wenn aber das Licht von innen kommt, verliert sich das kristalline Erscheinungsbild.

Wie bei Schaufenstern üblich, kann eine Verglasung aus aufgeständerten oder aufgehängten großformatigen Scheiben mit Silikon-gedichteten Stoßfugen bestehen, die nach Bedarf mit Glasstreifen gegen die Windkräfte stabilisiert werden. Diese Konstruktion kommt sowohl für Einfachverglasungen als auch für Isolierverglasungen in Frage.

Ein Beispiel bietet das Wohnhaus in Almere (Niederlande), 1984 von den Architekten Benthem

and beam structure which creates an even, filigree appearance.

Systems based on EPDM (synthetic rubber) gasket fixing systems are seldom used; one such example is the IBM office building in Cosham (England), built in 1971, an early work of Sir Norman Foster and Partners.

The term structural glazing generally refers to an all-glass system in which the glass panels are bonded to the façade support structure using high stress silicone. Here a variation of the frame or mullion and transom structure is used, which affects only the overall appearance from the outside, without significantly altering the support structure. For this reason it would be more accurate to speak of a "bonded glazing". To heighten

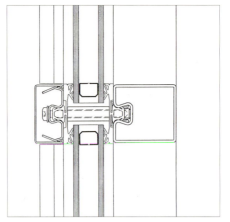

Detail einer Verglasung mit Preßleisten.
Detail of a pressure cap glazing.

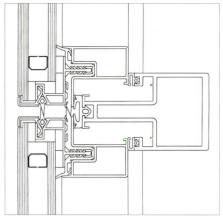

Detail eines «structural glazing»-Systems.
Detail of a structural glazing system.

Verglasung mit Preßleisten aus EPDM-Profilen.
Verwaltungsgebäude IBM, Cosham, England, 1971,
Sir Norman Foster und Partner.
Glazing with EPDM gasket fixings.
IBM office building, Cosham, England, 1971,
Sir Norman Foster and Partners.

und Crouwel erbaut. Die Glaswand des Wohn-
raums besteht aus vorgespannten, 12 mm dicken
Scheiben mit Silikon-Versiegelung, die mit
15 mm dicken Glasstreifen beim Glasstoß stabilisiert sind und als Auflager für das in leichter
Bauweise hergestellte Dach dienen.
Wesentliche Schritte in der Entmaterialisierung
der Glashaut sind die Reduktion der Befestigung
auf punktförmige Halterungen und die Nutzung
der Tragfähigkeit des Glases für Hängekonstruk-
tionen. Dieses Vorgehen setzt aber die Erhöhung
der Biegebruchfestigkeit der Scheibe durch die
Vorspannung voraus. Hier findet der Begriff
«structural glazing» seine treffende Anwendung,
da die Glasscheiben Teile der tragenden Struktur
zur Aufnahme der vertikalen und horizontalen
Kräfte werden.
Einen Vorläufer des punktförmigen Halterungs-
systems bildet die Verglasung mit geschraubten
Eckhalterungen, den sogenannten «patch fittings», welche Sir Norman Foster und Partner zusammen mit dem Glashersteller Pilkington für
das Verwaltungsgebäude Willis, Faber und
Dumas in Ipswich (England) 1971–75 angewen-
det haben. Die vorgespannten, 2 x 2.5 m großen
und 12 mm dicken Scheiben – die Dimension
wurde damals von der Größe der Vorspannöfen
begrenzt – sind mit geschraubten, 165 x 165 mm
großen Eckbeschlägen aus Messing an der jeweils nächsthöheren Scheibe aufgehängt, so daß
die rund 15 m hohe Fassade an der obersten
Geschoßdecke abgehängt ist. Die horizontale
Windaussteifung erfolgt im Gebäudeinneren mit

the optical impression that the façade is all glass,
coloured or reflecting glass panes are often used.
However, when the light comes from the inside of
the building, this crystalline illusion disappears.
As in normal practice for shop windows, glazing
can consist of large span panes supported from
below in a frame structure, or suspended; joints
are butted and sealed with silicone, and where
necessary the glass panes are also stabilised with
glass fins against wind loads. This type of structure can be used both for single glazing and insulated glazing.
One example is the house in Almere (Netherlands), built by the architects Benthem and Crouwel in 1984. The glass wall of the living room
consists of 12mm thick prestressed panes of
glass with joints sealed with silicone and stabilized with 15 mm thick glass fins; the lightweight
roof construction also bears on this glass wall.
A major step in the "dematerialisation" of the
glass skin is the reduction of bead or cap fixing
systems into bolted fixing systems, and the uti-
lization of the load-carrying capacity of the glass
itself in suspended glass wall systems. This
method relies on the higher bending strength of
toughened glass. The term structural glazing is
thus appropriate for this type of application, as
the glass panes carry vertical and horizontal
forces as part of the overall load-carrying structure.
A forerunner of bolted supports is the use of
glazing with bolted corner-plate fixing points, so-
called patch fittings, used by Sir Norman Foster

Verglasung mit aufgeständerten großformatigen
Glasscheiben und aussteifenden Glasstreifen.
Wohnhaus, Almere, Niederlande, 1984, Benthem-
Crouwel.
Large-span glazing, supported from below, and
stabilizing glass fins.
House, Almere, The Netherlands, 1984, Benthem-
Crouwel.

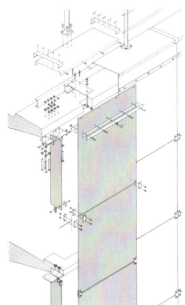

Glasschwertern, die an den jeweiligen Geschoßdecken abgehängt sind.

Wesentlich bei diesem Befestigungssystem ist, daß die vertikale Lastabtragung noch auf der Glasoberfläche durch Anpreßdruck und Reibung der verschraubten Eckhalterung erfolgt.

Die Weiterentwicklung dieses Systems hat zum punktförmigen Befestigungssystem Planar®-Fittings geführt, wo eine mit einer Kunststoffhülse versehene Schraube gleichzeitig als Halterung und Auflager dient. Dabei wird der Schraubenkopf in eine Senkbohrung eingelassen, so daß eine flächenbündige Verschraubung der Glasscheibe resultiert. Die Befestigung kann sowohl direkt auf der tragenden Unterkonstruktion als auch mit Verbindungsteilen für eine hängende Verglasung erfolgen.

Das Planar®-System wurde von Sir Norman Foster und Partnern zusammen mit Pilkington Glass entwickelt und zum ersten Mal 1982 für die Fassade aus Einfachglas des Renault Centre in Swindon (England) eingesetzt. Dort sind die vorgespannten, 1.8 x 4 m großen und 10 mm dicken Scheiben an Federteller geschraubt, welche ihrerseits an den Riegeln der Fassadenkonstruktion befestigt sind. Aus diesem «Typ 902» wurde der «Typ 905» entwickelt, wo die geschraubten Beschläge in Konsolen aus den tragenden Pfosten der Fassadenkonstruktion eingehängt werden. Beide Befestigungssyteme eignen sich auch für Fassaden mit Isoliergläsern.

Das punktförmige Befestigungssystem mit Kugelgelenk RFR wurde 1986 für die Gewächshäuser des Museums für Wissenschaft und Technik in

and Partners in collaboration with Pilkington glass manufacturers for the headquarters for Willis, Faber and Dumas in Ipswich (England), built between 1971 and 1975. The toughened, 2 x 2.5 m large and 12 mm thick glass panels – the dimensions were determined by toughening capabilities at the time – are suspended from the panels above by means of patch fittings, brass plates, 165 x 165 mm in size; the 15 m high façade is thus suspended on one bolt from the uppermost floor. The lateral restraint against wind loads is achieved by means of glass fins inside the building, suspended from the intermediate floors.

A significant feature of this fixing system is that vertical in-plane forces are resisted by friction and pressure at the interface of the bolted patch fittings with the glass panes.

Further development of this system produced the countersunk "Planar® Fittings" fixing system, in which bolts with plastic bushes serve both as fixing and bearing points. The head of the bolt is countersunk, flush with the glass pane. This fixing can either be used to attach the glazing directly to the support frame or, by means of additional connecting elements, to create a suspended glazing structure.

The Planar® system was developed by Sir Norman Foster and Pilkington Glass and used for the first time in 1982 for the single-glazed façade of the Renault Centre in Swindon (England). Here the toughened, 1.8 x 4 m size, 10 mm thick panes are bolted to spring plates attached to the transoms of the façade structure. From

Hängende Verglasung und ihr Konstruktionsprinzip. Verwaltungsgebäude Willis, Faber und Dumas, Ipswich, England, 1971–75, Sir Norman Foster und Partner.

Suspended glazing and detail of the wall assembly. Headquarters for Willis, Faber and Dumas, Ipswich, England, 1971–75, Sir Norman Foster and Partners.

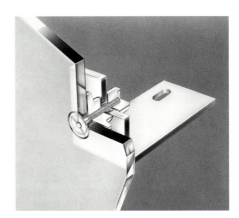

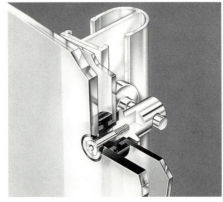

Planar®-System: «Typ 902» und «Typ 905».
Planar®-System: "Type 902" and "Type 905".

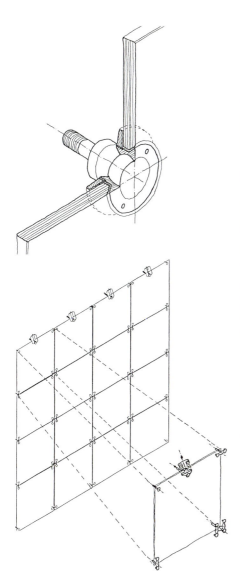

Das punktförmige Befestigungssystem RFR mit Kugelgelenk; die Unterteilung in quadratische Felder mit den Federbeschlag-Glasplatten und den darunterliegenden, wie ein Kettenhemd abgehängten Platten; Gesamtansicht.
Museum für Wissenschaft und Technik, Paris, 1986, Adrien Fainsilber mit Rice-Francis-Ritchie RFR.
The RFR bolted fixing system with swivel joints; the subdivision into square façade sections: the uppermost panes with spring connections, the remaining panes suspended below; general view.
Museum of Science and Technology, Paris, 1986, Adrien Fainsilber with Rice-Francis-Ritchie RFR.

Paris von Adrien Fainsilber und den Spezialisten für Glaskonstruktionen Rice-Francis-Ritchie entwickelt. Die Verglasungen bestehen aus vorgespannten, 2 x 2 m großen und 12 mm dicken Scheiben, die quadratische Felder von ca. 8 m Seitenlänge bilden. Die oberen vier Platten sind jeweils mit einem Federbeschlag an den Riegeln des tragenden Gerüsts aufgehängt, während die übrigen untereinander abgehängt sind. Diese hängende Glaswand ist mit einer räumlichen Hinterspannung gegen die Windkräfte stabilisiert. Da die gespannte Seilkonstruktion sich den Windkräften gegenüber elastisch verhält, könnten große Drehmomente um das Bohrungsloch auftreten. Um das zu verhindern, wurden in die Befestigungsknoten Kugelgelenke eingebaut, die in der Glasachse liegen.
Heute sind verschiedene Produkte auf dem Markt erhältlich, die eine punktförmige Befestigung ermöglichen, wie Multipoint®, Megatech® usw. Deren Erfolg ist nicht nur auf die Entmaterialisierung der tragenden Unterkonstruktion zurückzuführen, sondern auch auf das glatte Erscheinungsbild der Glasoberfläche bei der Gestaltung einer Fassade.

this "902 Type" a later version, the "905 Type", was developed, whereby the bolt fittings were suspended in pins projecting from the support posts of the façade structure.
Both countersunk bolt fixing systems are also suited to façades with insulated glazing.
A bolted fixing system with swivel joints RFR® was developed in 1986 by Adrien Fainsilber and the glass construction specialists Rice-Francis-Ritchie for the greenhouses of the "La Villette" Museum of Science and Technology in Paris.
The glazing consists of 2 x 2 m size, 12 mm thick toughened glass panels, grouped to form 8 m square façade sections. The four uppermost panes are each suspended by means of a spring connection to the transom of the support frame, while the remaining panes are all suspended one below the other. This suspended glass wall is stabilised against wind loads by a prestressed cable construction of wind bracing behind the glass. As the system is designed to move slightly when subject to wind loads, this would give rise to great torsional stress around the milled hole in the glass, and so to avoid this, a system of swivels was built into the in-plane fixing points.
Today various products are available which enable this kind of bolted fixing – for example, Multipoint®, Megatech®, etc. Their success is not only due to the "dematerialisation" of the load-bearing frame, but also to the smooth surface of the glass of today's façade design.

Die Glasscheibe

The Glass Pane

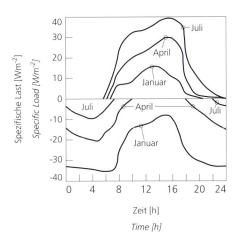

Gegenüberstellung der Wärmegewinne und -verluste verschiedener Monate des Jahres.
Comparison of heat gains and losses for different months of the year.

Linke Seite: Die «Dichroic Glass Spine» ist eine gespannte Konstruktion mit rot reflektierenden und blau transmittierenden dichroitischen Glasscheiben, die James Carpenter für den Haupteingang eines von Sir Norman Foster und Partner projektierten Gebäudes entworfen hat.
Bürogebäude «Chiswick Park», London, 1989–91, Sir Norman Foster und Partner.
Left page: The "Dichroic Glass Spine" is a tensile structure with red-reflecting and blue-transmitting dichroic glass panes, designed by James Carpenter for the main entrance of a building by Sir Norman Foster and Partners.
Chiswick Park office building, London, 1989–91, Sir Norman Foster and Partners.

Eine Glashülle bestimmt sowohl den Einfall an Licht- und Wärmestrahlung in ein Gebäude als auch deren Austritt. Die für die Heizlast maßgebenden Wärmeverluste werden bei Bürobauten allmählich unbedeutender, weil einerseits der Wärmedurchgangskoeffizient mit der fortschreitenden Glastechnologie laufend gesenkt werden kann, andererseits die im Raum selber entstehende Abwärme durch Personen, Beleuchtung und Geräte den Wärmeverlust oft übertrifft. Hochrechnungen haben gezeigt, daß sogar im Januar, im Monat der höchsten Verluste, Gewinne durch die Sonnenstrahlung und die innere Abwärme erzielt werden können.

Hinsichtlich der Kühllasten sind Licht- und Wärmegewinne unterschiedlich zu betrachten. Während eine maximale Ausnutzung der Tagesbelichtung anzustreben ist, muß gleichzeitig eine Reduktion des Wärmeeinfalls stattfinden.

Damit sind die an eine Fassade gestellten Anforderungen teilweise entgegengesetzter Art und bedingen die Entwicklung anpassungsfähiger Glashüllen.

Diese Anforderungen können auf unterschiedliche Weise erfüllt werden:

– beim Einfachglas durch die Zusammensetzung der Glasmasse und/oder durch die Veränderung der Eigenschaften ihrer Oberfläche;

– bei einem mehrschichtigen Aufbau, wie bei Verbund-, Isolier- und Mehrfachisoliergläsern, durch die Addition einzelner Funktionsschichten;

– beim Aufbau einer Fassade durch die Kombination mit zusätzlichen Sonnen- und Wärmeschutzmaßnahmen.

In der Regel unterscheidet man zwischen passiven, nicht steuerbaren Maßnahmen und aktiven, steuerbaren Maßnahmen. Erstere weisen feste Eigenschaften auf (z. B. Beschichtungen) und ermöglichen somit keine Anpassung an die wechselnden Jahres- und Wetterverhältnisse.

Aktiv steuerbare Maßnahmen arbeiten mit beweglichen Beschattungssystemen, sowohl mit tra-

A glass skin determines the levels of light and heat both entering or leaving a building. Heat losses, critical for the building's heat load, are becoming less and less significant in office buildings because on the one hand the heat loss transmission coefficient is continually being reduced through advances in glass technology and on the other hand the heat generated by the room's occupants, lighting and equipment is often greater than the heat loss. Simulations have shown that even in January, the month with the highest heat losses, solar radiation and waste heat from within the building can produce net heat gains.

In terms of cooling loads, light and heat gains have to be considered separately. While maximum exploitation of daylight is desirable, at the same time a reduction must be achieved in solar heat gain.

The technical requirements of a façade are thus in part conflicting and determine the development of adaptable glass skins.

The requirements can be met in a number of ways:

– in the case of single-glazing, through the composition of the base glass and/or through changing the surface properties;

– in the case of multi-layered constructions, such as laminated glass, insulating glass and multiple glazed units, through the addition of various interlayers to achieve specific performances or properties;

– in façade constructions, through combining glazing with additional solar and heat insulation measures.

Generally a distinction is made between passive, non-controllable measures and active, controllable measures. The first group is characterised by fixed properties (e. g. surface coatings) and as such do not allow for adaptation to changing seasons and weather conditions.

Actively controllable measures work with ad-

ditionellen Produkten, wie Lamellen oder Gitterstoffstoren, als auch mit moderneren, wie integrierten Rollosystemen mit IR-reflektierenden Folien usw. Sie können manuell von den Benutzern oder automatisch von einer zentralen Gebäudeleittechnik (GLT; engl. central building management systems, BMS) geregelt werden. Noch nicht ganz ausgereift sind aktiv steuerbare Systeme, die auf der Basis von physikalischen und chemischen Eigenschaftsveränderungen im mikroskopischen und molekularen Maßstab funktionieren.

justable shading systems, both with traditional products, such as louvres or screening blinds, as well as more modern products such as integrated roller blind systems with infrared-reflecting surfaces, etc. These can be operated manually by the users or automatically by a central building management system (BMS). Still undergoing technical improvement are actively controllable systems which operate on the basis of changes in physical and chemical properties at the microscopic or molecular level.

Glasmasse

Sand ist der wichtigste Rohstoff für die Glasherstellung; er enthält stets kleine Verunreinigungen, meistens Eisenoxide, die Verfärbungen bewirken. Der leichte Grünstich einer Glasscheibe ist auf einen Gehalt unter 0.1 % an Eisenoxid zurückzuführen. Der Gesamttransmissionsgrad variiert nach Glasdicke. Typische Kennwerte einer 4 mm dicken Scheibe sind τ 0.90 und g 0.87 (Planilux®).

Base Glass

Sand is the most important raw material in the manufacture of glass; it always contains a small amount of impurities, mostly iron oxide, which produce colour tints. The faint green tint in a pane of glass is due to a 0.1 % content of iron oxide. Total transmittance varies according to the thickness of the glass. Typical values of a 4 mm thick pane of glass are τ 0.90 and g 0.87 (Planilux®).

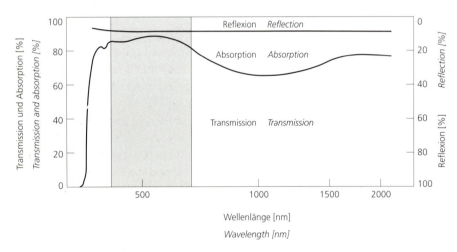

Spektrale Transmission eines üblichen Floatglases.
Spectral transmission properties of clear float glass.

Weißes Glas

Wegen der Nachfrage für die Herstellung von Solarkollektoren sind seit einiger Zeit reinere, eisenärmere Glasscheiben, das sogenannte «weiße Glas», auf dem Markt erhältlich. Die notwendige Reinheit der Zusammensetzung wird durch eine zusätzliche chemische Reinigung des Grundstoffs erreicht. Im Vergleich zu gewöhnlichem Glas verschieben sich die Kennwerte einer 4 mm dicken Scheibe auf τ 0.92 und g 0.90 (Planilux extra®).

Clear-White Glass

Increased demand from the manufacturers of solar collectors has led to the greater market availability of "clear-white glass" or architectural clear glass, i.e. purer panes of glass with less iron content. The required pure mix is achieved by additional chemical cleaning of the base materials. In contrast to ordinary glass panes transmittance values for a 4 mm thick pane of architectural clear glass are τ 0.92 and g 0.90 (Planilux® extra).

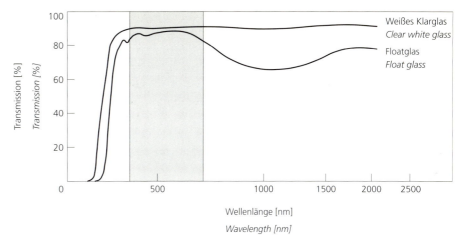

Spektrale Durchlässigkeit eines üblichen Floatglases, verglichen mit derjenigen eines weißen Glases.
Comparison of spectral transmission properties between standard float glass and clear white glass.

Gefärbtes Glas

Der Zusatz von Metalloxiden in der Glasmasse führt zu einer stärkeren Einfärbung, die eine höhere Absorption und somit eine Aufheizung bewirkt. Da die Wärmeabgabe nach innen nur ein Drittel beträgt, erfolgt eine Reduktion des Strahlungsdurchgangs. Nachteilig wirkt sich die zum Teil starke Aufheizung der absorbierenden Gläser aus, die im Innenraum oft als unangenehm empfunden wird. Eingefärbte Scheiben werden häufig beim Fahrzeugbau verwendet, weil hier der Fahrtwind eine wirksame Kühlung gewährleistet.

Die Farbpalette der eingefärbten Gläser wird stark durch das angewandte Herstellungsverfahren eingeschränkt. Da eine Floatglas-Anlage auf die Produktion von großen Mengen ausgerichtet ist, sind die Farben heute auf Grün, Rosa, Blau, Bronze und Grau reduziert.

Body Tinted Glass

The addition of metal oxides to the base glass leads to a stronger tint which produces a higher ratio of absorption and a resulting increase in the temperature of the glass. As heat transmission to the inside of the building is only one third, there is a reduction in solar energy transmission. A disadvantage of this absorbing glass is the often noticeable increase in temperature of the glass itself which is perceived to be unpleasant. Body tinted panes are often used in car manufacture because here the airstream when the vehicle is in motion serves to produce a cooling effect. The range of tints available is considerably restricted by the manufacturing process used. As float glass manufacturing installations are designed for the manufacture of large quantities, the only colour tints available at present are green, pink, blue, bronze and grey.

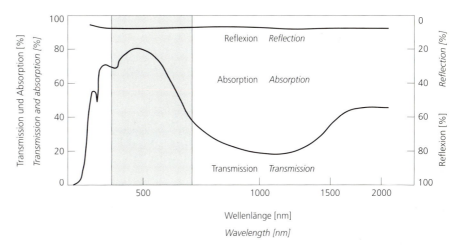

Spektrale Transmission eines grün eingefärbten Glases.
Spectral transmission properies of green body tinted glass.

Die grünen Gläser finden die größte Verbreitung. Sie sind für das nahe Infrarot nur wenig durchlässig, weil das Eisenoxid den Strahlungsbereich mit Wellenlängen von 700 bis 2500 nm besonders absorbiert.

Grau getönte Gläser, durch den Zusatz von Nickeloxid, und bronzefarbene Gläser, durch den Zusatz von Selen, werden zur Dämpfung der Helligkeit eingesetzt.

Heute sind aus ökologischen Gründen Fassaden aus Einfachglas für beheizte Gebäude wegen des Wärmeverlustes nicht mehr vertretbar. Sie werden aber für Überdachungen oder für unbeheizte Räume wie Ausstellungsgebäude, Wintergärten und Pufferzonen verwendet.

Die im Juli 1994 eingeweihte Waterloo International Station, Londoner Endstation der Ärmelkanal-Linie, liefert ein eindrückliches Beispiel einer einfachverglasten Halle. Die Tragstruktur des Daches wurde von Nicholas Grimshaw und Partner mit dem Ingenieur Antony Hunt von YRM Antony Hunt Associates entwickelt. Die flache Drei-Gelenk-Konstruktion besteht aus gebogenen Dreigurtträgern mit einem seitwärts verschobe-

Green-tinted glass is the most widely used. It only transmits low levels of the near infrared range because the iron oxide in the glass is a particularly good absorber of radiation in wavelengths from 700 to 2500 nm.

Grey-tinted glass, achieved by adding nickel oxide, and bronze-tinted glass, produced by adding selenium, are used to reduce glare. Today, for ecological reasons, façades made of single glazing are no longer acceptable for use on heated buildings. However, they are still used for canopies or for unheated rooms such as exhibition halls, winter gardens and buffer zones.

An impressive example of a single-glazed hall is the London terminus of the Channel Tunnel rail link – the new Waterloo International Station, officially opened in July 1994. The support structure of the roof was developed by Nicholas Grimshaw & Partners in association with the structural engineer Anthony Hunt of YRM Anthony Hunt Associates. Essentially it is a flattened 3-pin arch construction consisting of curved trusses with the center pin displaced to one side. The roof spans decrease from 50 m to

Die asymmetrische Gestalt des Daches wird durch die Verglasung im Bereich des kürzeren Bogenabschnitts hervorgehoben.
«Waterloo International Station», London, 1994, Nicholas Grimshaw und Partner.
The asymmetrical design of the roof is underlined by the curved glass wall marking the shorter section of the arch.
Waterloo International Station, London, 1994, Nicholas Grimshaw and Partners.

Die Drei-Gelenk-Konstruktion besteht aus gebogenen Dreigurtträgern mit seitwärts verschobenem Mittelgelenk; der kürzere Dreigurtträger mit außenliegendem Zuggurt; Detail der Glasbefestigung und der Neopren-Dichtung.
«Waterloo International Station», London, 1994, Nicholas Grimshaw und Partner.

The 3-pin arch construction consists of curved trusses with the centre pin displaced to one side; the shorter truss with the tension rods on the outside; detail of the glass fixing and neoprene joint.
Waterloo International Station, London, 1994, Nicholas Grimshaw and Partners.

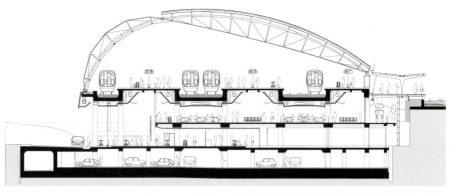

nen Mittelgelenk und Spannweiten von 35 m bis 50 m. Die asymmetrische Struktur ist von der zu einem früheren Zeitpunkt geplanten außenliegenden Geleiseführung und von einer städtebaulichen Einschränkung in der Bauhöhe maßgebend geprägt worden. Ihre Gestalt ist durch die Verglasung im Bereich des kürzeren Bogenabschnitts besonders hervorgehoben. Diese Glaswand weist einen komplexen Aufbau auf, der auf die wechselnden Spannweiten der Bogenträger und den unregelmäßigen Verlauf der Geleise zurückzuführen ist.

Da ein übliches System Tausende verschieden geformter und unterschiedlich großer Scheiben erfordert hätte, wurde eine schuppenartige Konstruktion mit lockeren Befestigungen entwickelt. Die 10 mm dicken vorgespannten Glasscheiben sind auf der Längsseite mit Aluminiumprofilen versehen, die durch Stiftverbindungen das Einhängen an die tragenden Pfosten sichern und die Halterungsnut für eine ziehharmonikaartige Neopren-Dichtung liefern. Die Überlappung in Quer-

35 m. The asymmetric structure is a response to the predetermined line of the tracks, and to specific local building regulations restricting height. The design is underlined on the curved glass wall marking the shorter section of the arch. Here the complexity is increased due to the varying span widths of the arched girders and the irregular line of the tracks.

A conventional system would have entailed using thousands of differently shaped and sized panes of glass and so, to avoid this, an imbricated structure was developed with flexible fixing points. The longer sides of the 10 mm thick toughened glass panes are mounted in aluminium profiles which are attached via pin connections to the support posts; these profiles also provide the mounting groove for the concertina-like neoprene seal. Overlapping junctions in a horizontal direction are enabled by further aluminium profiles with a sealing lip. In addition to allowing a high degree of standardisation this system also permits independent movement of all

richtung ist ebenfalls durch ein Aluminiumprofil mit einem lippenförmigen Dichtungsstreifen gewährleistet. Außer einem Höchstmaß an Standardisierung sichert das entwickelte System eine unabhängige Beweglichkeit aller Glasplatten, was infolge auftretender Windlasten, thermischer Ausdehnungen der Stahlkonstruktion und Torsionen der Plattform durch die einfahrenden Züge notwendig ist.

Die drei 1991 errichteten Aufzugstürme des Museums für Moderne Kunst «Reina Sofia» in Madrid sind mit einem klaren Floatglas umhüllt. Die Lösung entspricht der Vorgabe der Architekten J. L. Iñiguez und A. Vázquez an die Glasberater Ian Ritchie Architects, ein leichtes und sehr transparentes Volumen als Kontrapunkt zu der bestehenden massiven Fassade zu schaffen. Als Alternative zu klarem Glas stand auch eingefärbtes Glas zur Diskussion, aber die Computersimulationen der zu erwartenden Erwärmung infolge Absorption und sekundärer Wärmeabgabe zeigten, daß diese Lösung mehr Nachteile als Vorteile gebracht hätte.
Die Glashülle besteht aus vorgespannten, 12 mm dicken und 2.96 x 1.83 m großen Scheiben. Sie sind einzeln an der außenliegenden vorgespannten Edelstahlkonstruktion aufgehängt. Die punktförmige Hauptbefestigung erfolgt mit einer modifizierten Version des 905 Planar®-Systems am Kopf einer besonders gestalteten Konsole («Delphin»), die wegen der knappen Bauzeit mittels Laserschneidetechnik anstatt des Guß-

glass panes, an aspect which is essential under the conditions produced by wind loads, thermal expansion of the steel construction and torsions in the platform slab by trains entering and leaving.

The three lift towers built in 1991 at the "Reina Sofia" Museum of Modern Art in Madrid are enclosed in clear float glass. The design, produced by the glass advisors Ian Ritchie Architects in accordance with guidelines laid down by the architects, J. L. Iñiguez and A. Vázquez, represents the latter's wish for a light, very transparent volume as a counterpoint to the solid appearance of the existing façades. As an alternative to clear glass, tinted glass was considered, but computer modelling of the expected heating effect showed that absorption and reradiation would have resulted in more disadvantages than advantages.
The glass skin consists of large toughened panes, 12 mm thick and 2.96 x 1.83 in size. They are suspended individually from the external system of prestressed stainless steel rods. Using a modified version of the 905 Planar® system, the panes are bolted to the head of a specially designed bracket, the "Dolphin", which, because of time pressure, was produced by laser-cutting and not by casting. At the four corners are further fixing points which transmit horizontal wind loads via stainless steel spacers to the concrete support structure on the interior. A 12 mm wide joint separates each pane of glass for the purposes of

Die Aufzugstürme sind mit einer Hülle aus klarem Floatglas versehen; Edelstahlteile für die Glasbefestigung: oben die tragende Konsole für die Aufhängung einer Scheibe, «Delphin», unten der Abstandhalter für die horizontalen Windlasten.
Museum für Moderne Kunst «Reina Sofia», Madrid, 1991, Ian Ritchie Architects.
The lift towers are enclosed in a clear float glass skin; stainless steel elements for the fixings: above the glass support bracket, the "Dolphin", and below the spacer transmitting the horizontal wind loads.
Reina Sofia Museum of Modern Art, Madrid, 1991, Ian Ritchie Architects.

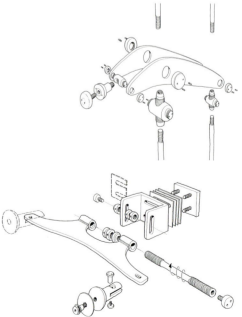

verfahrens gefertigt wurde. In den vier Ecken befinden sich weitere Befestigungspunkte, welche die horizontalen Windlasten über Abstandhalter aus Edelstahl auf die innenliegende Tragkonstruktion aus Stahlbeton übertragen. Eine 12 mm breite Fuge gewährleistet die Autonomie jeder Glasscheibe hinsichtlich thermischer Ausdehnung, Windlasten und Bruch.

Die Hierarchie des Gestaltungskonzeptes spiegelt sich in der Materialwahl: Beton für die Tragstruktur, Edelstahl für die Aufhängekonstruktion und Glas für den Raumabschluß.

Eine konkave Glaswand bildet den Raumabschluß des 1992 fertiggestellten Verwaltungs- und Druckereigebäudes der «Western Morning News» in Plymouth, England. Die von Nicholas Grimshaw und Partner entworfene Fassade paßt sich der umliegenden hügeligen Landschaft an und weckt mit ihrem schiffartigen Aussehen Assoziationen an die Seefahrtstradition der Stadt. Gleichzeitig übernimmt sie die Funktion eines riesigen Werbeschilds. Da die Fassaden-Neigung die Spiegelungen reduziert und die Transparenz des Gebäudes steigert, genießen die Passanten auf der Straße auch tagsüber eine eindrückliche Sicht auf die laufenden Druckmaschinen. Die Glashülle ist an den außenliegenden, leicht gebogenen Masten, den «Stoßzähnen», punktförmig aufgehängt. Ihre Geometrie wurde folgendermaßen festgelegt: Im Bereich des «Hecks» liegt der Glaseinteilung ein orthogonaler Raster mit einer Maschenweite von 2 x 2 m zugrunde.

thermal expansion, wind loads and breakage. The hierarchy of the design concept can be seen in the choice of materials: concrete for the frame, stainless steel for the glazing support structure, and glass for the building skin.

A concave glass wall encompasses the administration building and printing works of the Western Morning News in Plymouth, England. The shape of this façade, designed by Nicholas Grimshaw & Partners, echoes the surrounding hilly landscape, and at the same time its nautical shape hints at the town's seafaring tradition. It functions, too, as an enormous advertisement for the company. As the angle of the façade has the effect of reducing reflections, it is easy to see into the building and, especially during the day, passers-by are afforded an impressive view of the printing machines in operation. The glass skin is suspended at intervals from the lightly curved masts – the building's "tusks" – positioned on the building's exterior. The geometry was defined as follows: near to the "stern" the glazing follows a 2 x 2 m orthogonal grid; near the "prow" are two segments of a circle, 70 m radius in plan and 21.5 m in section, as in a double-curved toroid. This enabled one or two simplifications in the manufacturing and erection stages, as each glass pane is identical to the ones on either side of it, and the radius of curvature can be changed into a sequence of polygons. The 12 mm thick and 2 x 2 m large, toughened glass panes are bolted at the corners to cross-shaped fixing junctions.

Die konkave Glasfassade reduziert die Spiegelung und steigert damit die Transparenz.
«Western Morning News», Plymouth, England, 1992, Nicholas Grimshaw und Partner.
The concave glass façade reduces reflection and increases the transparency of the building skin. Western Morning News, Plymouth, England, 1992, Nicholas Grimshaw and Partners.

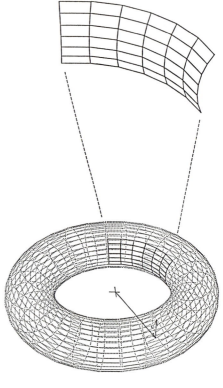

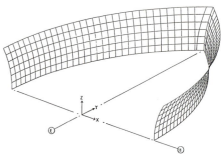

Im Bereich des «Bugs» sind zwei Kreissegmente, mit einem Radius von 70 m im Grundriß und von 21.5 m im Schnitt, maßgebend, was einem Ausschnitt einer doppelgekrümmten Translationsfläche eines Torus entspricht. Das führt zu einigen Vereinfachungen hinsichtlich der Herstellung und der Montage der Fassade, da jede Glasscheibe identisch mit ihren horizontal angrenzenden Nachbarn ist und der Krümmungsradius in einen polygonalen Verlauf umgewandelt werden kann.

Die 12 mm dicken und etwa 2 x 2 m großen vorgespannten Glasscheiben sind bei den Ecken an kreuzförmige Befestigungsknoten geschraubt. Da sie an der Spitze der «Stoßzähne» mit Zugstan-

As they are attached to the top of the "tusks" via steel tie bars, vertical forces are directed upwards, while horizontal forces are transmitted to the masts via lateral cantilevers made of spheroidal graphite cast iron. The separation of support members to transfer vertical and horizontal loads is strongly reminiscent of the façade of the Financial Times printing works, built by Nicholas Grimshaw & Partners in 1988 in the London Docklands. The same distribution of forces is translated here into a distinct organic form.

The rehearsal and concert hall of the Philharmonic Chamber Orchestra of the Netherlands is

Die Glashülle ist an den leicht nach außen gebogenen Masten, den «Stoßzähnen», abgehängt. Im Bereich des «Bugs» wurde die Einteilung der Scheiben gemäß der Geometrie eines Torus' festgelegt.
«Western Morning News», Plymouth, England, 1992, Nicholas Grimshaw und Partner.
The glass skin is suspended from the slightly curved masts, the "tusks". The geometry of the glass panes near the "prow" was defined by a double-curved toroid.
Western Morning News, Plymouth, England, 1992, Nicholas Grimshaw and Partners.

gen aus Edelstahl aufgehängt sind, werden die vertikalen Kräfte nach oben abgeleitet, während die horizontalen Kräfte über seitliche Ausleger aus Kugelstahlgraphit auf die Masten übertragen werden. Die Trennung in Tragglieder zur Abtragung der vertikalen und horizontalen Lasten erinnert stark an die Fassade der «Financial Times»-Druckerei, die Nicholas Grimshaw und Partner 1988 in den Londoner Docklands errichtet haben. Der gleiche Kräfteverlauf ist hier nun in eine ausgeprägt organische Form umgesetzt.

Der Probe- und Konzertsaal des Niederländischen Philharmonischen Kammerorchesters ist in einem vollverglasten Baukörper in der ehemaligen Amsterdamer Börse von Hendrik P. Berlage untergebracht. Der Entwurf der Architekten Pieter Zaanen & Associates, 1990, löst das akustische Problem der Nachbarschaft zweier Konzertsäle sehr elegant, ohne den Charakter des historischen Gebäudes durch schalldämmende Paneele an den Wänden zu verändern. Die Struktur besteht aus sechs innenliegenden kreuzförmigen Stahlstützen, mit Kreuzverbänden abgespannt, welche ein Raumfachwerk tragen. Während die gekurvte Glaswand, der «Cellobauch», an einer außenliegenden Konstruktion mit Rohrprofilen befestigt ist, hängen die drei geraden Glaswände von der Dachkonstruktion herunter. Die oberen Glasscheiben werden am Dachrand von zwei punktförmigen Schraubverbindungen gehalten. Sie tragen das Gewicht der weiteren

both housed within one fully glazed structure inside the former Amsterdam Stock Exchange designed by Hendrik P. Berlage. The design, drawn up in 1990 by the architects Pieter Zaanen & Associates, elegantly solves the acoustic problems created by the juxtaposition of two concert halls without the need to alter the historic character of the building by adding sound insulating panels to the walls. The structure consists of six, internally placed, cruciform steel columns, guyed with cross bracing, which support a space frame. While the "cello-shaped" curved glass wall is attached to an external tubular steel support structure, the three vertical glass walls are suspended from the top of the space frame. Each of the upper glass panes are attached via two bolted fixings. They carry the weight of the further four sheets below them, all attached to each other, like a coat of chain mail, by cross-shaped Quatro® joints (Octatube Space Structures Inc.). The toughened glass panels are grey-tinted, 8 mm thick and 180 x 180 cm in size; joints are 8–10 mm wide and stabilised with a vertical, tensile structure. An interesting effect is produced by different lighting situations: when the hall is not in use, the glass skin reflects the surrounding pale brick walls and the glass cube appears as a solid body. Yet as soon as the interior lighting is on, it appears light and transparent. The reverse is experienced from inside the cube – when the outside lights are put out, one is only aware of the space inside the glass cube.

Der vollverglaste Baukörper löst ein akustisches Problem, ohne den Charakter des historischen Gebäudes zu verändern (links); die hängenden Glaswände sind durch eine gespannte Konstruktion stabilisiert (rechts).
Probe- und Konzertsaal in der Amsterdamer Börse, 1990, Pieter Zaanen & Associates.
The fully glazed structure solves an acoustic problem without altering the character of the historic building (left); the suspended glazing is stabilized by a vertical tensile structure (right).
Rehearsal and Concert Hall in the Amsterdam Stock Exchange, 1990, Pieter Zaanen & Associates.

vier darunterliegenden Platten, die durch die kreuzförmigen Quatro®-Knoten (Octatube Space Structures Inc.) wie ein Kettenhemd miteinander verbunden sind. Die Verglasung besteht aus grau getönten, 8 mm dicken und 180 x 180 cm großen vorgespannten Glasscheiben mit einer Fugenbreite von 8–10 mm und wird durch eine vertikalgestellte, gespannte Konstruktion stabilisiert.

Sehr interessant ist die Wechselwirkung, die sich je nach Beleuchtungssituation einstellt: Wenn der Saal nicht benutzt wird und die Glashülle die umliegenden hellen Backsteinwände spiegelt, wirkt der Glaskubus als fester Baukörper. Er wirkt dagegen leicht und transparent, sobald die Innenbeleuchtung eingeschaltet wird. Eine umgekehrte Situation erlebt man von innen, wenn das Licht außerhalb gelöscht wird und plötzlich nur der Raum innerhalb des Glaskubus wahrnehmbar ist.

Photosensitives Glas

Eine besondere Entwicklung im Bereich der Einfärbung der Glasmasse stellen photosensitive Gläser dar, wie Louverre®, das die Corning Glass, New York unter Mitwirkung des Glasspezialisten James Carpenter 1983 auf den Markt gebracht hat. Dieses winkelabhängige durchsichtige Glas besitzt sowohl die Eigenschaft der Transparenz als auch die Sonnenschutzwirkung kleiner Jalousien. Die 1 mm dicken Lamellenstreifen haben untereinander einen Abstand von 3 mm. Ihre Winkeleinstellung wird bei der Herstellung bestimmt. Dazu wird die Glasplatte zuerst mit einer gelochten Vorlage abgedeckt und mit UV-Licht im ausgewählten Winkel bestrahlt, danach in einem Ofen erwärmt. Dadurch entsteht eine lamellenförmige Struktur im Glas, die eine Lichttransmission von 0.16–0.30 und eine Gesamtdurchlässigkeit von 0.35–0.44 aufweist.

Der Architekt Norman Foster wollte die Fassade der «Hongkong und Shanghai Bank» mit Louverre® ausstatten. In letzter Minute entschloß sich die Bauherrschaft – wahrscheinlich aus Kostengründen – leider anders.

Phototropes Glas

Die Eigenschaften von gefärbten Gläsern sind nicht veränderbar. Dagegen stellen die phototropen Gläser ein selbstregelndes System dar, da die Lichtdurchlässigkeit sich automatisch durch die Bestrahlung mit ultraviolettem oder kurzwelligem sichtbaren Licht vermindert. Die Photo-

Muster des photosensitiven Glases Louverre® von Corning Glass werden in den Fassadenprototyp eingesetzt.
«Hongkong and Shanghai Bank», Hongkong, 1979–86, Sir Norman Foster und Partner.
Prototypes of Louverre® photosensitive glass by Corning Glass are installed in the façade mock-up. Hongkong and Shanghai Bank, Hong Kong, 1979–86, Sir Norman Foster and Partners.

Photosensitive Glass

Photosensitive glass is a special development in tinting base glass. One example is Louverre®, introduced onto the market in 1983 by Corning Glass, New York, in collaboration with the glass specialist James Carpenter. This louvred clear glass combines in a single pane the qualities of transparence and the solar shading effect of narrow slatted blinds. The 1 mm thick louvre strips are spaced at 3 mm and their angle of tilt is defined at the manufacturing stage. The process consists of placing a template of horizontal slots over the glass sheet, then exposing the sheet to UV collimated light at the selected angle; the glass is then heated in a leer. This creates a louvre-shaped structure within the glass giving overall values for light transmittance of 0.16–0.30 and a total solar heat transmittance of 0.35–0.44.

The architect Sir Norman Foster wanted to use Louverre® to clad the façade of the Hongkong and Shanghai Bank. Sadly the client decided against it at the last minute – probably for reasons of cost.

Photochromic Glass

The properties of body tinted glass are unchangeable, whereas photochromic glass is self-adjusting, in that the light transmission decreases automatically in response to exposure to ultraviolet or short-wave visible light. The photo-

Spektrale Transmission des phototropen Glases von
Corning Glass.
*Spectral transmission properties of a Corning Glass
photochromic glass pane.*

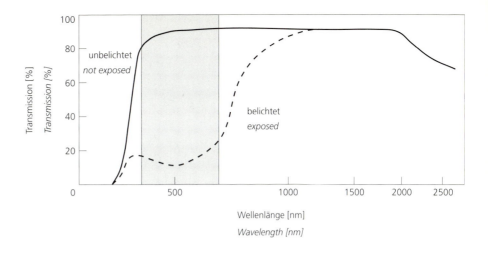

tropie basiert auf einer reversiblen Transformation eingelagerter silberhalogenidhaltiger Ausscheidungen. Braune oder graue phototrope Gläser werden für die Herstellung von Brillen verwendet. Sie weisen einen breiten Transmissionsbereich auf, der zum Beispiel bei den Photosolar® Superbrown-Gläsern nach 15 Minuten Belichtung von 0.91 auf 0.25 reduziert wird. Vorteile sind die lange Lebensdauer und die Beständigkeit gegen chemische Angriffe, Nachteile sind die automatische Abdunkelung sowohl im Sommer als auch im Winter und die damit verbundene Aufheizung der Scheibe.

Für eine Anwendung im Bauwesen sind die Produktionsmöglichkeiten von phototropem Glas heute bezüglich Menge und Dimensionen noch ungenügend. Um die Preise niedrig zu halten, hat Corning Glass Prototypen mit einer Dicke von 1 mm und eine Fläche von 1 m² zum Auflaminieren entwickelt.

Beschichtungen

Die Eigenschaften des Glases bezüglich Sonnen- und Wärmeschutz hängen von der Strahlungsdurchlässigkeit ab. Sie können durch dünne Schichten aus Edelmetallen und/oder Metalloxiden wesentlich verändert werden. Solche Beschichtungen haben einen Einfluß sowohl auf den Strahlungsbereich als auch auf dessen Intensität.

Reflektierende und selektive Beschichtungen
Ein guter Sonnenschutz wird durch die Verwendung von reflektierenden Beschichtungen erzielt. Eine erhöhte Reflexion führt zu einer Verminderung der Transmission und damit zu einer Reduktion der Gesamtdurchlässigkeit. Zur Zeit sind bei einer Tageslichttransmission τ von 0.10 bis

chromic process is based on a reversible transformation taking place in the in-built silver halide crystals. Brown or grey phototropic glass is used in the manufacture of spectacles. It has a wide transmission range, as used in, for example, Photosolar® Superbrown spectacles which after 15 minutes exposure reduce from 0.91 to 0.25. The advantages are that the glass is very durable and resistant to chemicals; disadvantages, however, are the automatic darkening both in summer and in winter, and the associated heating up of the glass itself.

For use in building the production of this type of glass is at present still rather limited in terms of quantity and size range. In an attempt to keep prices down, Corning Glass have developed 1 m² prototypes of 1 mm thickness, which can be used as glass laminates.

Surface Coatings

The properties of glass in terms of solar control and reduced emissivity depend on its level of radiation transmission. This can be changed considerably by the addition of thin layers of precious metals and/or metal oxides. Such coatings affect both the radiation range transmitted and also its intensity.

Reflective and Selective Coatings
Effective solar control can be achieved by the use of reflective coatings. Increased reflection properties lead to a reduction in the level of transmission, and consequently also to a reduction in the total transmission. At present total energy transmission values g of 0.20 to 0.70, with a daylight transmittance τ of 0.10 to 0.60, are typical for insulated glazing used in our latitudes. Not only solar shading but also light and heat gains are

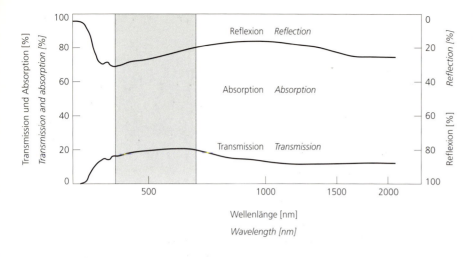

0.60 Gesamtenergie-Transmissionsgrade g von 0.20 bis 0.70 für Isolierverglasungen üblich in unseren gemäßigten Breiten, da nicht nur der Sonnenschutz maßgebend ist, sondern auch Licht- und Wärmegewinne zu berücksichtigen sind.

Reflektierende Beschichtungen können sowohl auf klares als auch auf gefärbtes Glas aufgetragen werden (Parsol®). Da letzteres per se eine höhere Absorption aufweist, werden tiefere g-Werte erzielt.

Ein besserer Wärmeschutz wird durch niedrigemissive Beschichtungen, die sogenannten «low-E coatings», erreicht. Sie können die Emissivität der Glasoberfläche von $\varepsilon \approx 0.85$ bis $\varepsilon \approx 0.05$ und damit die Abstrahlung im Infrarotbereich bis auf 20 % reduzieren, ohne die Lichtdurchlässigkeit unter 0.70 zu senken. Die heute auf dem Markt angebotenen Gläser bewegen sich im Bereich zwischen $\varepsilon \approx 0.05$ und $\varepsilon \approx 0.15$. Sie sind bei den Isoliergläsern besonders wichtig, da die Wärmeabstrahlung bis zu zwei Dritteln des Wärmeverlustes ausmacht. Solche Beschichtungen werden als selektiv bezeichnet, weil sie im sichtbaren Strahlungsbereich weitgehend transmittierend, im infraroten Bereich hingegen stark reflektierend sind.

Zur Zeit werden Low-E-Beschichtungen für die Verglasung von Motorfahrzeugen (GM, Ford, Saint-Gobain) intensiv erforscht. Ziel ist, die sonst in den Innenraum eines Fahrzeuges einfallende Wärmestrahlung schon an den Windschutzscheiben reflektieren zu können.

Die Entwicklung von hoch-lichtdurchlässigen und gleichzeitig stark IR-reflektierenden Beschichtungen entspricht auch den Anforderungen, die heute an die Glasarchitektur gestellt werden: Bei vollverglasten Gebäudehüllen soll

factors to be considered in these temperate zones.

Reflective coatings can be applied to both clear glass and tinted glass (Parsol®). As the latter has higher absorption properties to start with, lower g-factors are achieved. Better thermal insulation is achieved by low emissivity, or low-E coatings. They can reduce the emissivity of the surface of the glass from ε 0.85 to ε 0.05, thus reducing infrared radiation to 20%, without bringing the light transmittance down below 0.70. Glass currently available on the market is generally in the area between ε 0.05 and ε 0.15. This glass is particularly important for insulating glass as heat radiation can account for up to two thirds of the heat loss. Such coatings are referred to as selective because they transmit most of the visible light, but have a high level of reflectance in the infrared range.

At present intense research is being carried out on low-E coatings for use in motor vehicles (GM, Ford, Saint-Gobain). The aim here is, at the level of the windscreen, to reflect the heat radiation normally entering the car interior.

The development of surface coatings which transmit a maximum of light and at the same time have high levels of infrared reflectivity is in tune with current demands placed on glass architecture: fully glazed building skins should ensure both maximum natural lighting and minimum heat loss.

Solar control and reduced emissivity glass is generally used in laminated glass insulating units or multiple glazing units.

Manufacturing Process. The surface coatings are applied either on-line, at the end of the float

eine maximale natürliche Belichtung bei minimalem Wärmeverlust gewährleistet werden. Sonnenschutz- und Wärmeschutzgläser werden meistens in mehrschichtigen Konstruktionen, wie Verbund- und Isoliergläsern, verwendet.

Herstellungsverfahren. Die Beschichtungen werden entweder on-line, d. h. unmittelbar nach der Glasherstellung in der Floatanlage, oder off-line, also in einem späteren Arbeitsvorgang, aufgetragen.

On-line werden die Beschichtungen des Typs Hard-coating durch einen Pyrolyseprozeß aufgebracht. Das Ausgangsmaterial wird auf das etwa 600 °C warme Floatglasband flüssig oder in Pulverform aufgetragen und eingebrannt. Damit bildet sich auf einer Seite der Glasscheibe eine harte Schicht mit einer Dicke von 100-400 nm, welche gegen Abnutzung und chemische Einwirkungen beständig ist. Glasscheiben mit Hard-coating können als Einfachverglasung eingesetzt werden.

Für den Sonnenschutz werden reflektierende Metalloxidschichten, vorwiegend aus Titan, Chrom, Nickel und Eisen, verwendet, die auch absorbierende Funktionen übernehmen können. Typische Kennwerte einer Antelio®-Glasscheibe sind g 0.40–0.69 und τ 0.21–0.63. Als Wärmeschutzschicht wird fluordotiertes Zinnoxid mit einer Siliziumoxid-Unterschicht verwendet.

Off-line werden die Glasscheiben durch das Tauch- oder das Vakuumverfahren beschichtet. Diese Herstellungsweisen führen meistens, aber nicht immer, zu weicheren Schichten, den sogenannten Soft-coatings. Ihr Vorteil liegt in einer größeren Flexibilität bei der Einstellung der

glass manufacturing process, or off-line, at a later point.

Hard coatings are applied on-line by pyrolysis. The base material used for the coating is poured, in liquid or powder form, onto the layer of float glass heated to 600 °C and then fired. As a result of this a chemically resistant and durable hard layer, 100–400 nm thick, is formed on one side of the glass sheet. Glass panes with hard coatings can be used in single-glazing.

For solar shading layers of reflecting metal oxides are used, mainly titanium, chrome, nickel and iron, which also possess absorbing properties. Typical values for an Antelio® glass pane are g 0.40–0.69 and τ 0.21–0.63. A layer of fluorine doped zinc oxide on a base of silicon oxide is used to reduce the radiative heat loss.

Off-line coatings are applied to glass panes by dipping them into chemical solutions or under conditions of vacuum. These methods generally, but not always, lead to softer layers, known as soft coatings. Their advantage lies in a greater flexibility in the control of light transmittance and total solar heat transmittance, by specifiying composition and thickness of the layers.

In the dipping process, glass is immersed into chemical solutions, slowly extracted and then fired. The coatings, on both sides, are generally of titanium oxide and, in the near infrared range, they are more active through reflection than absorption.

In the vacuum process the coatings are applied to one side either by cathode sputtering or by evaporation in a multi-chamber high-vacuum facility. Soft coatings consist of 6 to 9 individual

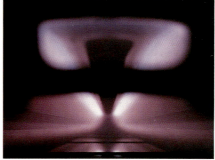

Off-line-Beschichtung in einer Hochvakuum-Anlage und Kathoden-Zerstäubung in der Prozeßkammer bei Glas Trösch, Bützberg, Schweiz.
Off-line coating in a high-vacuum facility and cathode sputtering in a chamber unit at Glas Trösch, Bützberg, Switzerland.

Licht- und Gesamtdurchlässigkeit durch die Wahl von Schichtenaufbau und -dicke.

Beim Tauchverfahren werden die Scheiben in bestimmte Lösungen eingetaucht, langsam herausgezogen und anschließend gebrannt. Die beidseitigen Beschichtungen bestehen meistens aus Titanoxid und sind im Infrarot-Bereich hauptsächlich durch Reflexion und weniger durch Absorption aktiv.

Beim Vakuumverfahren werden die Schichten durch Kathoden-Zerstäubung (Sputtern) oder durch Verdampfung in einer Mehrkammern-Hochvakuum-Anlage einseitig auf die Glasscheiben aufgebracht. Soft-coatings bestehen aus 6 bis 9 Einzelschichten, wobei heute die Anlagen oft für 12–15 Schichten ausgerüstet sind. Solche Schichten können in beliebigen Dicken (6–12 nm) mit sehr hoher Gleichmäßigkeit aufgetragen werden, was insbesondere für eine gute Transparenz erforderlich ist. Die Soft-coatings sind weich und gegen aggressive Luftverschmutzung und mechanische Beanspruchung empfindlich, weshalb sie durch einen Schutzbelag oder durch den Einbau in Isoliergläser geschützt werden. Dennoch sind einige Produkte mit wetter- und abnutzungsbeständigen Beschichtungen erhältlich, zum Beispiel das Sonnenschutzglas Cool-Lite®, welches Einstellungen von τ 0.04–0.52 und g 0.08–0.46 ermöglicht.

Für den Wärmeschutz werden Low-E-Beschichtungen aus leitfähigen Metallschichten auf der Basis von Gold, Silber, Kupfer und Aluminium verwendet. In den letzten Jahren hat sich als Basis Silber durchgesetzt, weil es eine optimale Farbneutralität bei höchster Lichttransmission bietet (Planitherm®). Die Funktionsweise der Low-E-Beschichtungen basiert auf einem Interferenzvorgang, welcher durch Metall- und Metalloxidschichten und deren Reihenfolge und Dicke hervorgerufen wird. Da der mehrschichtige Aufbau einer Low-E-Beschichtung auch die optischen Eigenschaften bezüglich Reflexion und Absorption verändern kann, werden oft die Funktionen von Sonnenschutz und Wärmeschutz kombiniert (Planisol®). Solche Soft-coatings ermöglichen somit die gleichzeitige Steuerung der Emissivität, der Reflexion, der Absorption und der Transmission, und sie können sogar die Farbe sowohl bei der Transmission als auch bei der Reflexion bestimmen.

Die Low-E-Beschichtungen bilden nur eine mögliche Variante der selektiven Beschichtungen.

layers, but many manufacturers have the capability of producing 12 to 15 layers. The layers can be applied in a range of thicknesses (6–12 nm) at a high degree of uniformity, which is essential for good transparence. As soft coatings are susceptible to aggressive air pollution and mechanical stress, they have an additional protective layer or are built into insulated glazing units. However some weather and stress-resistant soft coatings are available on the market, for example Cool-Lite®, a solar glass which can be manufactured with values of τ 0.04–0.52 and G 0.08–0.46.

To reduce radiative heat loss, low-E coatings of conductive metal layers basing on gold, silver, copper and aluminium are used. In recent years silver has become popular as a base because it offers optimum colour neutrality as well as high light transmittance (Planitherm®).

Low-E coatings work by a process of interference, brought about by the succession and various thicknesses of the layers of metals and metal oxides. As the several layers of a low-E coating can also alter the optical properties with respect to reflection and absorption, the functions of solar control and reduced radiative heat loss are often combined (Planisol®).

Such soft coatings thus enable the control of emissivity, reflection, absorption and transmission, and can even determine the colour for both transmission and reflection. The low-E coatings are just one possibility of a number of different coatings. At present other products are also being manufactured which are based on this process of interference, e.g. cold mirror, anti-reflection and dichroic coatings.

Cold Mirror Coatings. The effect of cold mirror coatings is the opposite of that of low-E coatings,

Spektrale Reflexion eines low-E beschichteten Glases, verglichen mit einem unbehandelten Floatglas.
Spectral reflectance properties of low-E coated glass, compared to untreated float glass.

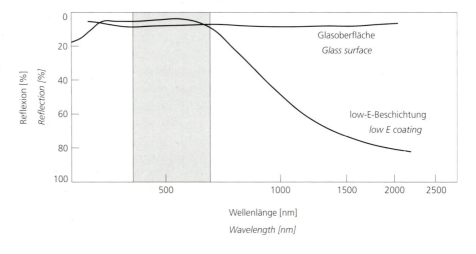

Die vertikalen Glasschwerter sind mit horizontalen dichroitischen Glasscheiben ausgesteift.
«Sweeny Chapel» im «Christian Theological Seminary», Indianapolis, USA, 1985–87, James Carpenter / E. L. Barnes.
The vertical blades of glass are braced by horizontal bands of dichroic glass.
Sweeny Chapel in the Christian Theological Seminary, Indianapolis, USA, 1985–87, James Carpenter / E.L. Barnes.

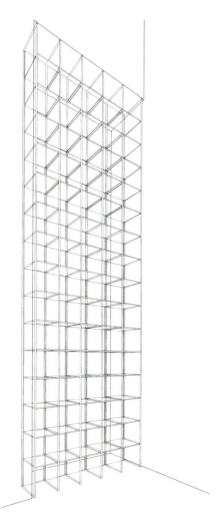

Zur Zeit werden auch andere Produkte hergestellt, die auf Interferenzvorgängen basieren, z.B. kaltlichtspiegelnde, entspiegelnde oder dichroitische Beschichtungen.

Kaltlichtspiegelnde Beschichtungen weisen praktisch eine umgekehrte Wirkung der Low-E-Beschichtungen auf, weil sie die sichtbaren Wellenlängen reflektieren, während der IR-Bereich durchgelassen wird. Solche Beschichtungen werden bei den Reflektoren der dichroitischen Lampen verwendet.

Entspiegelnde Beschichtungen reduzieren die Reflexion eines normalen Glases von 0.09 auf 0.02–0.03 und steigern damit die Lichttransmission. Ihre Anwendung ist nicht nur für das Ausstellen von Gegenständen hinter Glas, sondern auch bei Mehrfach-Isolierverglasungen von Vorteil, da sie die natürliche Reflexion an den zahlreichen Glasoberflächen verringern.

Dichroitische Beschichtungen werden normalerweise für Spezialfilter in der Meß- und Labortechnik eingesetzt. Durch Interferenzvorgänge zerlegen sie das Licht in die Spektralfarben, die je nach Einfallswinkel durchgelassen oder reflektiert werden. Damit ergeben sich unterschiedliche Farben in Reflexion und Transmission. Bei der Herstellung im Tauchverfahren oder durch Kathoden-Zerstäubung werden 10 bis 40 Schichten auf 1 x 1 m große Scheiben aufgetragen. Der Vorgang wird mehrmals wiederholt, bis die optische Spezifikation erreicht ist.

Dichroitische Gläser wurden von Glasberater James Carpenter mehrmals für Kunst am Bau eingesetzt. 1985–87 hat er zwei Fenster für die «Sweeny Chapel» im «Christian Theological Seminary» in Indianapolis, Indiana/USA (Architekt: E.L. Barnes), realisiert. Sie zeigen, wie ein einfacher, weißer, rechteckiger Raum durch ein Spiel von Licht und Farbe vollständig verändert werden kann. Das größere Fenster, 9.35 m hoch und 3.06 m breit, ist durch aussteifende Glasschwerter in fünf Felder unterteilt und mit waagerecht liegenden Scheiben ausgefacht. Da in der Vertikalen normales Floatglas und in der Horizontalen dichroitische Gläser verwendet wurden, zeichnet sich ein farbiges Lichtspiel der transmittierten und reflektierten Strahlen entlang der Wand ab. Interessant ist, wie sich der Licht-

because they reflect visible light wavelengths, while admitting the infrared range. Such coatings are used in the reflectors of dichroic lamps.

Anti-reflection Coatings reduce the reflection of normal glass from 0.09 to 0.02–0.03 and thus increase light transmission. The use of this type of glass is not just restricted to use in displaying objects behind glass, but is also advantageous in multiple glazed units where it brings about a reduction of the reflection from the various glass surfaces.

Dichroic Coatings are normally used for special filters in measuring and laboratory instruments. The interference effect of these coatings divides the light into spectral colours, such that, depending on angle of incidence, one range of wavelengths is transmitted and the remainder reflected. This gives rise to different colours in reflection and transmission. 10 to 40 layers of dichroic coatings can be applied to 1 x 1 m panes of glass by means of a vacuum deposition process. The process is repeated until the optical specification is reached.

Dichroic glass was used for several art works for buildings by the glass consultant James Carpenter. Between 1985 and 1987 he created two windows for the Sweeny Chapel in the Christian Theological Seminary in Indianapolis, Indiana (Architect: E.L. Barnes). They show how a simple, square, white room can be completely transformed by the play of light and colour. The largest window, 9.35 m high and 3.06 m wide, is divided into five sections by vertical clear glass blades, which are stabilized with horizontal stiffeners of dichroic glass. As the vertical glass sections are of ordinary float glass, but the horizontal ones are dichroic glass, light falls through these glass strips in a coloured interplay of transmitted and reflected rays along the wall. Interesting changes takes place according to the time of day or year, due to the changing position of the sun and angle of incidence of the sun's rays.
One design which did not get past the drawing board stage was intended for the entrance area of the Chiswick Park office building in London, 1989–91, designed by Sir Norman Foster. For this project James Carpenter designed the "dichroic glass spine", a 21.5 m high tensile structure which was to be suspended in front of

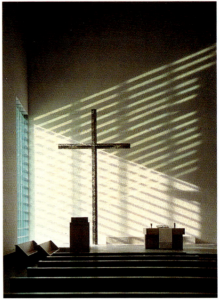

Farbe-Effekt je nach Tages- und Jahreszeit verändert, weil der Winkel der einfallenden Sonnenstrahlen mit dem Sonnenstand immer wieder wechselt.

Auf dem Papier geblieben ist der Entwurf für die Gestaltung des Eingangsbereiches des Bürogebäudes Chiswick Park, London, 1989–91, von Sir Norman Foster und Partner. James Carpenter entwarf dafür die «Dichroic Glass Spine», eine 21.5 m hohe gespannte Struktur, die vor der Schrägverglasung des Atriums schweben sollte. Die filigranartige Konstruktion aus Edelstahl-Zugstangen wäre mit dichroitischen Gläsern ausgefacht worden. Durch die rhombusförmigen, rot reflektierenden und blau transmittierenden und aufgrund der Geometrie in verschiedene Neigungswinkel gestellten Scheiben hätte man ein abgestuftes farbiges Lichtspiel im Atrium erleben können (siehe Abbildung Seite 20).

the inclined glazing of the atrium. The filigree construction of stainless steel rods would have been filled in with panels of dichroic glass. This arrangement of various angled, red-reflecting and blue-transmitting, rhombus-shaped panes would have produced a graduated play of coloured light in the atrium (see illustration p. 20).

Ceramic-Enamel Coatings
Frit-coated glass has a 100–150 nm thick ceramic-enamel layer which is both weather resistant and durable. The hard layer is produced by applying an enamel frit, composed of finely ground-glass powder with various additives and colour pigments, onto a sheet of glass, and firing at approx. 650 °C, the temperature at which glass softens sufficiently to fuse the frit to the glass surface. The glass is then cooled in air to toughen it, a process which would in any case be necessary because the coloured layers increase the absorp-

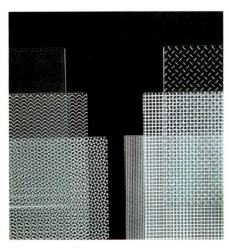

Gläser mit Emaille-Mustern.
Glass panes with fritted patterns.

Emailbeschichtung

Ein emailliertes Glas weist eine 100–150 nm dicke keramische Beschichtung auf, die abnutzungs- und witterungsbeständig ist. Die harte Schicht entsteht, wenn eine Emailfritte, bestehend aus feingemahlenem Glas mit Zusatzmitteln und Farbpigmenten, auf die bereits fertiggestellte Glasscheibe aufgetragen wird und nochmals bei ca. 650 °C, etwa der Erweichungstemperatur des Glases, eingebrannt und mit der Scheibe unlösbar verschmolzen wird. Anschließend werden die emaillierten Scheiben mit Luft gekühlt, um eine Vorspannung zu bewirken. Diese Behandlung wäre ohnehin erforderlich, weil die Farbschichten die Absorption des Glases steigern und damit zu einer erhöhten thermischen Beanspruchung führen. Für die Emailschichten steht eine große Anzahl von opaken bis transparenten Farben zur Verfügung. Ganzflächige opake Scheiben werden in blinden Brüstungs- und Deckenbereichen als hinterlüftete Verkleidung eingesetzt (Emalit®, Litex®). In den letzten Jahren sind vermehrt emaillierte Glasscheiben mit Punkt-, Linien- und Strichmustern mit gleichmäßigem oder verlaufendem Bedruckungsgrad zur Anwendung gekommen. Die Muster werden entweder durch Walzendruck oder durch Siebdruck aufgetragen. Solche emaillierten Scheiben können für Glasbrüstungen eingesetzt werden, wie bei der «Queen's Stand» in Epsom, 1988–92, von Richard Horden Associates.

Die Verwendung von emaillierten Glasscheiben führt zu interessanten Tag- und Nacht-Effekten, wie beim Glasdach auf dem Quai de Londres entlang der Meuse in Verdun, Frankreich. Die Spezialisten für Glaskonstruktionen Rice-Francis-Ritchie, RFR, haben 1988 eine leichte, filigrane

tion of the glass and lead to increased thermal stress. A wide range of ceramic-enamel coatings are available, from opaque to transparent colours. Opaque glass is used as ventilated cladding in spandrels and parapets (Emalit®, Litex®). In recent years more fritted glass panes are becoming available which have various patterns and extents of dots, lines or meshes. The patterns are either applied in a rolling process or by screen printing. Such fritted glass can be used for glass balustrades such as used for the Queen's Stand in Epsom, 1988–92, by Richard Horden Associates.

The use of fritted glass panels can produce interesting effects by day and night, as for example the glass roof at the Quai de Londres along the Meuse river in Verdun, France. Rice-Francis-Ritchie, RFR, specialists in glass construction, designed 1988 a filigree glass and steel construction which has a different appearance by day and by night. During the day the white dashed frit pattern on the glass roof makes it appear like a cloud floating between the masts, but at night it becomes a light-scattering surface when lit by indirect light.

The support structure of the glass roof consists of slightly inclined masts, 5 m apart; every third span being stabilised by a tubular steel support. Two Vierendeel girders form the roof construction. They are fixed by means of a pin-joint connection to the masts and supported in their inclined position via tie rods attached to the head and foot of the masts. The 1.3 x 1.5 m large glass panels are suspended under the roof construction at intervals via swivel bolted fixings (RFR patent) and spring spacers.

Under strong wind conditions, the 160 m long

Glasbrüstung mit weiß gestreiftem Emailmuster.
«Queen's Stand», Epsom, England, 1988–92,
Richard Horden Associates.
Glass balustrade with fritted white-striped pattern.
Queen's Stand, Epsom, England, 1988–92, Richard Horden Associates.

Stahl- und Glaskonstruktion entworfen, die bei Tag und bei Nacht unterschiedliche Erscheinungsformen zeigt. Tagsüber scheint das mit einem weißen gestrichelten Emailmuster versehene Glasdach wie eine Wolke zwischen den Masten zu schweben. In der Nacht wandelt es sich dagegen in eine lichtstreuende Fläche, wenn es von indirekter Beleuchtung erhellt wird. Die Tragstruktur des Glasdaches besteht aus leicht schräggestellten Masten im Abstand von 5 m, und jedes dritte Feld ist durch ein Stahlrohr stabilisiert. Zwei Vierendeel-Träger bilden die Dachkonstruktion. Sie sind gelenkig an den Masten befestigt und in ihrer leicht geneigten Lage mit Zugstangen von Mastenkopf und -fuß abgespannt. Die 1.3 x 1.5 m großen Glasscheiben sind mit dem punktförmigen Befestigungssystem mit Kugelgelenk RFR und mit Stahlfedern von unten an der Dachkonstruktion aufgehängt. Die 160 m lange Stahlstruktur erfährt bei starken Windstößen unregelmäßig verteilte Bewegungen, die zum Bruch der vorgespannten Glasscheiben führen könnten. Darum sind die gelenkigen Verschraubungsköpfe mit Stahlfedern versehen, welche ständig die Planität der vier Befestigungspunkte sicherstellen.

Die Verkleidung der Fußgängerverbindung im Flughafen München II, 1991–92 erbaut, stellt ein weiteres Beispiel der Verwendung von emaillierten Glasscheiben dar. Die 600 m langen Durchgänge bieten eine witterungsgeschützte Verbindung zwischen dem Terminal West, dem Hotel und Kongreßzentrum Kempinski und den Parkhäusern. Die Vorstellung einer «kontrollierten» Transparenz wurde von den amerikanischen Architekten Murphy & Jahn durch das Wechselspiel von Blechpaneelen, Lochblechen und Verglasungen mit unterschiedlichen Bedruckungsmustern umgesetzt. Die emaillierten Glasscheiben schaffen am Tag eine sichtbare Raumbegrenzung zwischen Innen- und Außenraum, die auch nachtsüber besteht, wenn sie durch die indirekte Beleuchtung erhellt wird.

Abgesehen von der erzielten ästhetischen Wirkung übernimmt eine Emailbeschichtung auch die Funktion eines Sonnenschutzes, weil durch die Auswahl des Bedruckungsgrades sowohl der Gesamtdurchlaßfaktor als auch die Lichtdurchlässigkeit beeinflußt werden können. Beispielsweise führt ein 20%iger Deckungsgrad bei einem normalen 6 mm dicken Floatglas zu einem g von

steel structure is subject to irregularly distributed movements, and this could lead to breakage in the toughened glass panes; to prevent this, the swivel bolted fixings and spring spacers were used to ensure the constant alignment four fixing points.

The cladding in the passenger corridors at Munich II airport, built 1991–92, is a further example of the use of fritted glass. The 600 m long corridor provides protection against the weather for passengers walking between Terminal West, the Kempinski Hotel and Congress Center and the car parks. The American architects Murphy & Jahn interpreted the idea of "controlled" transparency in an interplay of sheet metal panels, perforated panels and variously patterned glazing. By day and by night (when lit by indirect light) the fritted glass panes visibly separate internal and external space.
In addition to the desired aesthetic effect, the ceramic-enamel coating also has a solar shading function, in that the extent of the patterning can determine the total solar heat transmittance as well as light transmittance. For example, a 20 % cover on standard 6 mm float glass can give a g-factor of 0.74 and a τ-factor of 0.70; a 60 % cover gives g 0.52 and τ 0.49.

Angular Selective Coatings
Angular selective coatings control the solar and visible transmission according to the selected directions. A promising new development is the creation of a microscopic metallic slatted structure directly on the glass surface, using a process of magnetic deposition. This structure has mini-

Dank dem weiß gestrichelten Emailmuster scheint das Glasdach zwischen der filigranen Stahlstruktur zu schweben.
«Quai de Londres», Verdun, Frankreich, 1988, Rice-Francis-Ritchie, RFR.
The fritted white dashed pattern gives the impression of the glass roof floating in the filigree steel structure.
Quai de Londres, Verdun, France, 1988, Rice-Francis-Ritchie, RFR.

Emailbeschichtungen mit unterschiedlichen
Mustern schaffen eine «kontrollierte» Transparenz.
Verbindungsgänge im Flughafen München II,
1991–92, Murphy & Jahn.
Fritted glass panes with various patterns create a
"controlled" transparency.
Passenger corridors at Munich II airport, 1991–92,
Murphy & Jahn.

0.74 und einem τ von 0.70, ein 60%iger Dek-
kungsgrad zu einem g von 0.52 und einem τ von
0.49.

Winkelabhängige selektive Beschichtungen
Eine Variante stellen winkelabhängige selektive
Beschichtungen dar, welche die Sonnen- und
Lichtstrahlen nur bei bestimmten Einfallswinkeln
durchlassen. Erfolgversprechend sind Entwicklungen, die die Erzeugung einer lamellenförmi-
gen metallischen Mikrostruktur direkt auf der
Glasoberfläche durch magnetischen Nieder-
schlag vorsehen. Da der Durchblick nach außen
meistens einen anderen Winkel als der Strah-
lungseinfall aufweist, hindert die mikroskopische
Struktur die Sicht nach außen kaum. Durch die
Wahl der Schichtendicken, der Zwischenabstän-
de und der Neigungswinkel kann die Sonnenschutzwirkung beliebig eingestellt werden.

Einen weiteren Schritt in der Beschichtungstech-
nologie stellt die Entwicklung von veränderbaren
Maßnahmen mit thermotropen oder -chromen
Materialien dar sowie mit elektrochromen oder
Flüssigkristall-Schichten. Obwohl zurzeit die Entwicklung von Schichten zum Auflaminieren noch
viele Probleme stellt, hat der Gedanke großes
Zukunftspotential. Mike Davies meint, daß eine
ausgereifte industrielle Herstellung von solchen
Beschichtungen enorme ökonomische Konse-
quenzen im Bauwesen haben wird. Sie würde die
Rückkehr zur schlichten Bearbeitungstechnolo-
gie der Einfachverglasung bedeuten und so zu
einer Verminderung der Vergla-sungskosten führen, da die zweite Glasscheibe, der Randverbund
und die Versiegelung überflüssig würden.

mal effect on the ability to see through the glass
from inside the building, as the angle at which
radiation strikes the glass is different from the
angle at which we look out. By regulating the
thicknesses of the strips, the spacing between
them, and their angle of tilt, the level of solar
control required can be determined.

A further step in coatings technology is the development of controllable devices involving thermotropic or thermochromic materials and electrochromic or liquid crystal layers.
Although at present the development of coatings
which can be laminated onto the glass is still
unsatisfactory, the idea has great potential for the
future. Mike Davies believes that the developed
industrial manufacture of such coatings will have
enormous economic consequences in building.
It would mean the return to the simple manufacturing processes used for single glass pane and
as such would lead to a reduction in glazing
costs, as the second glass pane, the edge bond
and sealing would be superfluous.

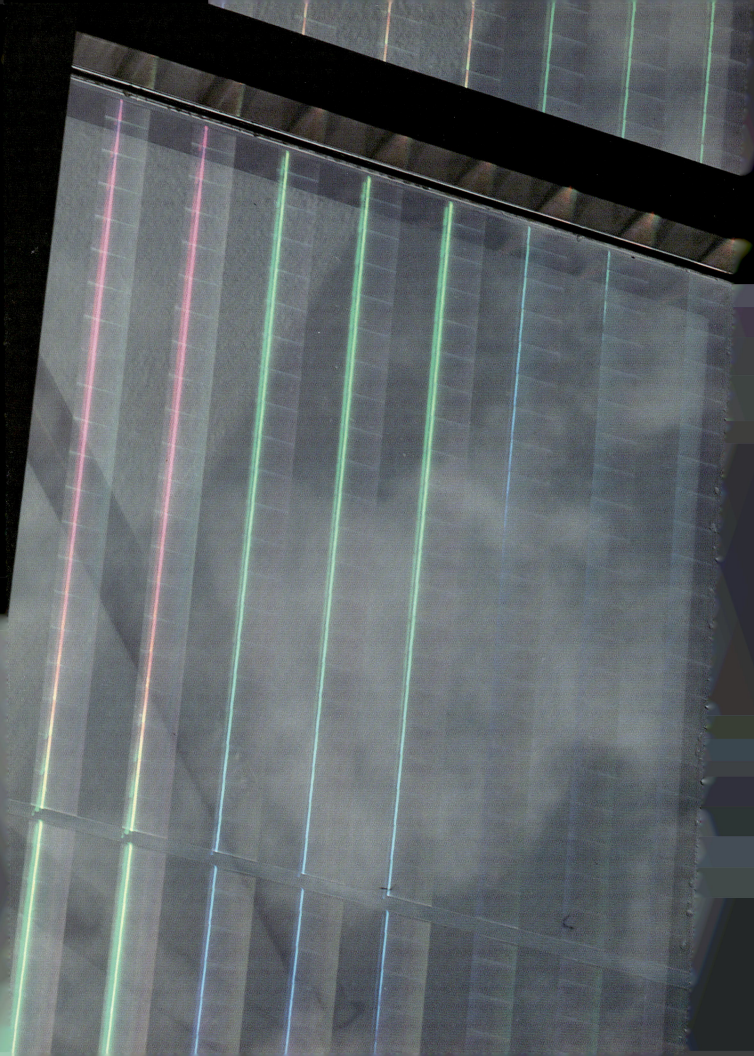

Das Verbundglas   Laminated Glass

Ein mehrschichtiger Aufbau ermöglicht die weitgehend unbeschränkte Kombination von Glasscheiben mit oder ohne Beschichtungen und die Schaffung von unterschiedlich breiten Scheibenzwischenräumen mit verschiedenen Möglichkeiten für die Integration von Wärme- und Sonnenschutzmaßnahmen.

Verbundgläser bestehen aus zwei oder mehreren Scheiben, die durch eine zäh-elastische Kunststoffolie, z. B. aus Polyvinyl-Butyral (PVB), verbunden sind. Sie werden hauptsächlich als Sicherheitsgläser verwendet, weil die PVB-Folie bei einem Bruch das Ablösen der Splitter verhindert. Die Sicherheit bei Durchbruch, Beschuß und Explosion läßt sich durch unterschiedliche Glas- und Foliendicken optimieren.

Als Zwischenschicht können verschiedene Arten von Folien eingelegt werden: durchsichtige, gefärbte und gemusterte; wärmedämmende, UV-absorbierende und reflektierende Folien; Folien mit Drahteinlagen für Sicherheits-, Alarm- oder Heizzwecke. Einen Sonderfall stellt der Gießharzverbund dar, welcher für dickere Einlagen, z. B. bei Photovoltaik-Modulen und Schallschutzgläsern, verwendet wird. Verbundgläser werden praktisch immer bei Schräg- und Dachverglasungen verwendet, um das Verletzungsrisiko bei Personen auf ein Minimum zu reduzieren.

The use of bonded panes of glass enables an almost limitless combination of glass panes with or without coatings; spacings between the panes can be of various widths, and various measures for solar and thermal protection can be integrated in the cavities between the panes.

Laminated glass consists of two or more panes of glass which are bonded together with a plastic material, e.g. polyvinyl butyral (PVB). This type of glass is generally used as safety glass because the PVB layer prevents the glass splinters from scattering in case of breakage. By combining different types and thicknesses of glass and bonding materials, specific performances can be achieved in terms of increased resistance to breakage, bullets or explosions.

A number of different materials can be used as an interlayer: transparent, coloured or patterned film; thermally insulating, ultraviolet-absorbing or reflecting film; or wired interlayers to meet safety, security or heating requirements. A special type of laminated glass is bonding with resin, which is used for thicker interlayers, such as those incorporating photovoltaic modules, or for acoustic glass. Laminated glass is almost always used for glass roofing and sloping glazing, so as to reduce the risk of injury from flying glass in case of breakage.

Holographisch-optische Elemente zerlegen hier das Licht in einen abstrakten Regenbogen, sie könnten aber auch Schriftzüge oder Logos erzeugen und somit als Informationsträger dienen.
Reihenhäuser an der IGA '93, Stuttgart,
HHS Planer + Architekten.
Holographic structures here diffract the light into an abstract rainbow, but they can also be used to form wording and logos and thus serve as information carriers.
Terrace housing at the IGA '93, Stuttgart,
HHS Planners + Architects.

Ein neueres Beispiel dafür ist etwa die Überdachung des Bahnhofs und der Postautostation in Chur, 1985–92 von den Architekten Brosi und Obrist und Partner unter Mitwirkung von Peter Rice entworfen. Das große, gewölbte Glasdach bietet den Benutzern der öffentlichen Verkehrsmittel Schutz vor der Witterung und stellt gleichzeitig eine architektonisch gelungene Nahtstelle zwischen Alt- und Neustadt dar.

Das 50 m weit gespannte Dachtragwerk wird über den Geleisen und der Postautoplattform von Doppelstützen getragen. Es besteht aus 12 Paaren von Stahlrohrbögen, die an beiden

A recent example of this is the roof of the railway and bus station in Chur (Switzerland), 1985–92, designed by the architects Brosi and Obrist and Partners, together with the glass specialists Rice-Francis-Ritchie. The large curved glass roof gives passengers protection from the weather, and at the same time it forms an architectural link between the old part of the town and the new. Supported on paired tubular columns, the roof structure spans 50 m across the tracks and the platforms. The roof consists of 12 pairs of tubular steel arcs, bearing at both ends on the paired columns by means of an articulated connection.

Verbundgläser aus vorgespannten Floatscheiben
wurden bei diesem weitgespannten Tonnengewölbe
eingesetzt.
Überdachung des Bahnhofs und der Postautostation,
Chur, Schweiz, 1985–92, Brosi, Obrist und Partner.
*Laminated glass of toughened float panes was used
for this wide-span barrel vault.*
*Roofing of the railway and bus station, Chur,
Switzerland, 1985–92, Brosi, Obrist and Partners.*

Seiten gelenkig aufgelagert sind. Zum Scheitel
der Tonne hin laufen sie, gleichsam wie «Zitro-
nenschnitze», auseinander. Bei der Dachhaut
wurden Verbundgläser mit dem Achsmaß 2.02 x
0.95 m aus zwei 8 mm dicken vorgespannten
Floatglas-Scheiben verwendet. Die vom Scheitel
bis zur Wasserrinne verlaufende Fuge ist mit
einem Neoprenprofil und Aluminium-Preßleisten
gedichtet, während in der Querrichtung eine
Silikonfuge die Wasserdichtheit sicherstellt.

Verbundgläser mit weißen Scheiben wurden
1988 für die Glaspyramide des Louvre in Paris
verwendet. Diese signalisiert den neuen Haupteingang des Museums und überdacht das unter
dem Bodenniveau liegende Informationszentrum
für die Besucher. Da sie in der Mitte der Cour
Napoléon steht, umgeben von historischen Fassaden, haben die Architekten I. M. Pei und Partner ein abstraktes, kristallines Volumen vorgeschlagen, das den Kontrast mit der alten Bausubstanz auf ein spannungsvolles Minimum reduzieren sollte. Die Vorstellung der Architekten, die
Pyramide als möglichst unsichtbaren und imma-
teriellen Baukörper erscheinen zu lassen, hat sowohl die Bauingenieure als auch die Glashersteller vor große Herausforderungen gestellt. Die
Tragstruktur sollte so leicht wie möglich sein
und die Verglasung ein Maximum an Transparenz bei einem Minimum an Verspiegelung gewährleisten.
Insbesondere die Transparenz stellte herstel-
lungstechnische Probleme. Es mußten aus

Towards the apex of the roof the arcs diverge,
defining the outer rim of a "lemon slice". The
laminated glass units used in the roof skin each
consist of two 8 mm thick, toughened float glass
panes, 2.02 x 0.95 m in size. The panel-to-panel
junctions running from the apex to the gutter are
sealed with neoprene profiles and aluminium
compression caps while the horizontal butted
joints are silicon-sealed.

Laminated glass with clear white panes were
used for the glass pyramid built in 1988 at the
Louvre in Paris. The pyramid marks the new
main entrance to the museum and acts as the
roof over the visitors' information centre which
is situated underground directly below this point.
As the entrance is located in the middle of the
Cour Napoléon, surrounded by historic façades,
the architects, I.M. Pei and Partners, proposed
an abstract crystalline volume which would provide an exciting, but not intrusive contrast to the
existing buildings. The architects' idea of making
the pyramid appear as invisible and immaterial
as possible was a great challenge to both construction engineers and glass manufacturers
alike. The support structure was to appear as
light as possible, and the glazing should reduce
reflection to a minimum while guaranteeing
maximum transparence.
The transparence presented the greatest difficul-
ties for the manufacturers. Safety considerations
dictated the use of laminated glass, but as a result
of the 45° angle of the sides, the pyramid would

Verbundgläser aus «weißen» Scheiben wurden eingesetzt, um den Kontrast mit der historischen Bausubstanz auf ein spannungsvolles Minimum zu reduzieren; Detail der unterspannten Konstruktion mit Druckstäben und Zugstangen aus Edelstahl.
Glaspyramide des Louvre, Paris, 1988,
I. M. Pei und Partner.
Laminated glasses of clear white panes have been selected to reduce the contrast with the historic building to an exciting minimum; detail of the tensile structure with compression struts and tension rods in stainless steel.
Glass pyramid at the Louvre, Paris, 1988,
I. M. Pei and Partners.

Sicherheitsgründen Verbundscheiben verwendet werden. Als Folge davon hätten aber die beiden um 45° geneigten Seitenflächen der Pyramide bei horizontalem Durchblick durch eine Gesamtdicke der Verglasung von 60 mm einen starken Grünstich aufgewiesen, so daß die Architekten extra-weißes Glas verlangten. Da aber damals die industrielle Fertigung für solche Dimensionen noch nicht ausgereift war, mußten die Scheiben handwerklich gegossen, geschliffen und poliert werden.

Eine weitere Aufgabe bestand darin, die perfekte Ebenheit der gesamten Seitenfläche und die Planität der einzelnen Scheiben zu gewährleisten, um ein Minimum an Deformationen in der Reflexion zu erzielen.

Die konstruktive Antwort auf all diese Anforderungen ist eine räumlich unterspannte Tragstruktur mit Edelstahldruckstäben von 50 mm und -zugstangen von 10–15 mm Durchmesser. Die filigranartige Konstruktion trägt die Profile der sekundären Konstruktion, wo die 3 x 1.9 m großen rhombusförmigen Verglasungselemente befestigt werden. Letztere sind Verbundgläser mit zwei 10 mm dicken extra-weißen Scheiben, die durch Silikon-Verklebung mit einem Aluminiumrahmen verbunden sind für die Befestigung auf der sekundären Konstruktion. Die nur 2 mm breiten Fugen sind mit einem silberfarbenen Silikon-Spezialkitt ausgefüllt.

Ein ganz aktuelles Beispiel für die Verwendung von weißen Verbundgläsern ist die im Bau be-

have appeared distinctly green when viewed horizontally through a total thickness of 60 mm. For this reason the architects specified the use of extra-clear white glass. At the time the pyramid was built, however, industrial manufacturing processes were not capable of producing this specification to such a size, and the panes had to be poured, ground and polished by hand. A further objective was to produce as perfect a plane as possible on the sides, which meant a corresponding uniformity in the individual panes, with the aim of minimizing reflection distortions. The structural answer to all these requirements was a tensile structure supporting the glass from underneath with 50 mm diameter stainless steel compression struts and 10–15 mm diameter tension rods. This filigree construction carries the profiles of the secondary construction to which are attached the 3 x 1.9 m sized rhombus-shaped glazing units. The units are composed of 10 mm thick, clear white glass which is silicon bonded to an aluminium frame for attachment to the secondary construction. The narrow, 2 mm joints are finished with a special silver-coloured silicon seal.

A very recent example of the use of laminated clear white glass is the glass hall being built by von Gerkan Marg and Partners in collaboration with Ian Ritchie Architects as a part of the new exhibition buildings at Leipzig Fair, 1994–95. The hall is both entrance to and covered link between the different exhibition halls. Under this roof are also the ticket desks, cloakrooms and

findliche Glashalle als Teilobjekt der «Neuen Messe Leipzig», 1994–95, von Gerkan Marg und Partner mit Ian Ritchie Architects. Sie bildet einen überdachten und geschützten Raum, der als Eingang und Verbindungsachse der Messehallen dient. In diesem Raum sind unter anderem auch Kassen, Garderoben und Cafés untergebracht.

Die 240 m lange, 80 m breite und 28 m hohe Glashalle weist außenliegend eine filigrane Stahlkonstruktion und innenliegend eine hochtransparente Glashaut auf. Die Tragstruktur besteht aus einem gewölbten Gitternetz aus Stahlrohrprofilen mit einem quadratischen Modul von 3.12 m und darüber Fachwerkbögen im Abstand von 25 m, welche die Aussteifung der Konstruktion gewährleisten. Die Verglasung ist 50 cm unter dem Gitternetz an vier gelenkigen Punkthaltern aufgehängt und besteht aus 3.12 x 1.54 m großen, ca. 20 mm dicken Verbundscheiben aus vorgespanntem weißem Glas. Die 20 mm breiten Fugen zwischen den Scheiben sind mit einem Kunststoffprofil verschlossen. Im Scheitelbereich

cafés. The glazed hall is 240 m long, 80 m wide and 28 m high; it has a filigree steel construction on the outside and a highly transparent glass skin below this. The load-bearing structure consists of an arched tubular steel grid, based on a 3.12 m square module, and over this grid, at 25 m spacing, are trussed arches which brace the whole structure. Each glass panel is suspended 50 cm below the steel grid from four articulated fixing points. The laminated glass panels are 3.12 x 1.54 m in size, approx. 20 mm thick and of toughened architectural clear white glass. The 20 mm wide joints between the panes are sealed with a silicone profile. Near the apex of the domed roof the glass has a 75 % white frit to shade the central area.

Functional Layers

A promising new development are functional layers, which can be used to achieve specific performances in terms of light transmittance and thermal insulation; these layers consist either of films which are angle-selective or light-bending, or

Die Transparenz der gewölbten Glashalle wird durch den Einsatz von Verbundscheiben aus «weissem» Glas gesteigert; Modellaufnahmen von innen (oben) und außen (unten).
Glashalle «Neue Messe Leipzig», Leipzig, 1994–95, von Gerkan Marg und Partner mit Ian Ritchie Architects.
The transparency of the barrel-vaulted glass hall is enhanced by the use of laminated panes of clear white glass; model photos of the interior (top) and of the outside (bottom).
The glass hall of the new Leipzig Fair buildings, Leipzig, 1994–95, by von Gerkan Marg and Partners in collaboration with Ian Ritchie Architects.

sind die Gläser mit einer 75%igen weißen Email-beschichtung zur Verschattung des zentralen Bereichs versehen.

Funktionsschichten

Vielversprechend ist zur Zeit die Entwicklung von Funktionsschichten, die für Licht- und Wärmeschutz eingesetzt werden können: winkelabhängig-selektive oder lichtumlenkende Schichten sowie aktiv veränderbare Schichten, die mit thermotropen oder thermochromen Substanzen sowie mit Flüssigkristallen oder elektrochromen Materialien funktionieren.

Winkelabhängig-selektive Schichten

Winkelabhängig-selektive Schichten sind licht-durchlässige Folien, welche die Lichtstrahlen nur bei einem bestimmten Winkeleinfall zerstreuen und damit undurchsichtig werden. Im Prinzip

layers which have actively variable transmission characteristics, based on thermotropic and thermochromic materials, or liquid crystals or electrochromic materials.

Angle-Selective Films

Angle-selective layers are light-transmitting films which only scatter incident light from a particular angle and thus become non-transparent. In principle they are composed of a microscopic louvred grid structure created on a 0.28 mm thick polymer film by a process of photopolymerisation, mostly by ultraviolet light. During the exposure at the manufacturing stage, a particular angle can be set, or only part of the film exposed. The range available at present consists of three different fixed angle settings (maximum pane size of 2.40 x 1.80 m), for use where visual screening is required (Angle 21®).

2000 mm Distanz   *2000 mm distance*

1000 mm Distanz   *1000 mm distance*

300 mm Distanz   *300 mm distance*

C-Typ   *A-Typ*   *B-Typ*

Winkelabhängig-selektive Schichten weisen eine mikroskopische Struktur wie ein Lamellenraster auf, welche die Lichtstrahlen bei einem bestimmten Winkeleinfall zerstreut und die Durchsicht verhindert. *Angle-selective films are composed of a microscopic louvred grid structure which is light-scattering from a particular angle and thus become non-transparent .*

bestehen sie aus einer mikroskopischen Lamellenstruktur, die in einer 0.28 mm dicken Polymerfolie durch Photopolymerisation, meistens UV-Bestrahlung, hervorgerufen wird. Beim Belichtungsvorgang während der Herstellung können verschiedene Winkel eingestellt oder Teilbelichtungen ausgeführt werden. Auf dem Markt sind Produkte mit drei Winkeleinstellungen (in der maximalen Größe von 2.40 x 1.80 m) erhältlich, die beim Sichtschutz zum Einsatz kommen (Angle 21®).

Schichten mit holographisch-optischen Elementen

Eine weitere Maßnahme zur Kontrolle der einfallenden Sonnenstrahlung bieten holographisch-optische Elemente (HOE). Durch den physikalischen Effekt der Beugung ermöglichen sie verschiedene Varianten der Lichtlenkung, vergleichbar derjenigen von Spiegeln, Linsen, Prismen und anderen optischen Elementen. Die HOE sind Aufzeichnungen von Interferenzmustern, die durch Laserlicht auf einem hochauflösenden photographischen Film erzeugt werden, welcher dann in ein Verbundglas eingebettet wird. Das Beugungsgitter bewirkt die Lichtumlenkung, welche nur für den eingestellten Einfallswinkel erfolgt, was bedeutet, daß die Hologramme dem Lichteinfall nachgeführt werden müssen. Aus herstellungstechnischen Gründen werden derzeit die einzelnen kleinformatigen 8 x 8 cm großen Hologramme zuerst im Taktverfahren auf einen 1 x 2 m großen Film belichtet, welcher danach entwickelt wird. Der Einsatz von HOE in der Fassade wurde bisher durch die unzureichende UV-Stabilität vermindert. Durch ein neues Produktionsverfahren scheint dieses Problem nun gelöst. Hinsichtlich einer vollautomatischen Serienproduktion sind einige Fortschritte zu verzeichnen, insbesondere was die Herstellung von großformatigen Masterhologrammen anbelangt.

Sofern die lichtempfindliche Schicht nicht direkt auf Glas aufgebracht wurde, ist das Endprodukt eine Folie, die zum Schutz vor Feuchtigkeit und Verschmutzung zwischen zwei Glasscheiben eingebettet werden muß.

In der Architektur können holographisch-optische Elemente für Lichtumlenkung, Verschattung und Ausblendung sowie für Displayholographie eingesetzt werden.

Ein Beugungsgitter mit parallelen Linien mit gleichen Abständen lenkt das Sonnenlicht an die

Holographic Diffractive Films

A further method of controlling solar radiation is presented by holographic diffractive structures (HDS). Various possibilities for light deflection result from the physical effect of diffraction, similar to the effects created by mirrors, lenses, prisms and other optical elements. The HDS are three-dimensional recordings of laser light patterns created on high-resolution photographic film which is then laminated between two panes of glass. The diffraction grating deflects light only from a predetermined angle of incidence, which means that the holograms are electronically controlled to track the sun, or changing angle of light across the sky. Current manufac-

Verschiedene Arten von holographisch-optischen Elementen (HOE).
Different kinds of holographic diffractive structures (HDS).

Art *Kind*	Aufsicht *Top view*	Vertikalschnitt *Vertical section*	Horizontalschnitt *Horizontal section*
Gitter (parallele Linien mit gleichen Abständen) *Grating (equidistant parallel lines)*			
		Umlenkung und Dispersion in einer Richtung *Changing the direction of light and dispersion without focusing*	
Zylinder-zonenplatte (parallele Linien mit unterschiedlichen Abständen) *Cylindrical zone plate (parallel lines with different distances)*			
		Umlenkung und Fokussierung in Brennlinien, die aufgrund der Dispersion für die einzelnen Spektralfarben an verschiedenen Orten liegen. *Changing the direction of light and focusing in focal lines, separate for each wave length*	
Seitenband-zonenplatte (konzentrische Ellipsen mit unterschiedlichen Abständen) *Off-axis zone plate (concentrical elliptical lines with different distances)*			
		Umlenkung und Fokussierung in Brennpunkten, die aufgrund der Dispersion für die einzelnen Spektralfarben an verschiedenen Orten liegen. *Changing the direction of light and focusing in focal points, separate for each wave length*	
	Infrarot *Infrared*	Rot *Red*	Blau *Blue*

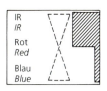

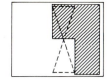

| IR |
| IR |
| Rot |
| Red |
| Blau |
| Blue |

100% Transmission
100% transmission

IR-Ausblendung
IR-cutting out

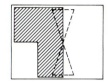

100% Ausblendung
100% cutting out

50% Ausblendung
50% cutting out

Eine Seitenbandzonenplatte fokussiert die einzelnen Spektralfarben auf unterschiedliche Brennpunkte, so daß der Strahlungsdurchgang mit einer beweglichen Blende nach Spektralbereichen geregelt werden kann.

An off-axis zone plate concentrates the individual spectral colours on different focal points; this makes it possible to use a moveable stop to regulate transmission of the various spectral wavelengths.

Kombination von passiven und aktiven Maßnahmen zur Nutzung der Sonnenstrahlung.
Reihenhäuser an der IGA '93, Stuttgart,
HHS Planer + Architekten.

Combination of passive and active measures to exploit solar radiation.
Terrace housing at the IGA '93, Stuttgart,
HHS Planners + Architects.

Decke wie ein Spiegel und steigert die Tageslicht-beleuchtung in der Raumtiefe.

Eine Struktur mit parallelen Linien mit unterschiedlichen Abständen, die Zylinderzonenplatte, fokussiert dagegen das Licht auf eine Brennlinie wie eine Linse, was den Wirkungsgrad von Streifen mit Photovoltaikzellen für die Gewinnung von Solarenergie steigern kann.

Eine Auslegung mit konzentrischen Ellipsen mit unterschiedlichen Abständen, die sogenannte Seitenbandzonenplatte, zerlegt das einfallende Licht in einzelne Spektralfarben und fokussiert sie auf Brennpunkte, welche an verschiedenen Orten liegen. Damit besteht die Möglichkeit, eine bewegliche Blende einzusetzen, um den Strahlungsdurchgang nach Spektralbereichen zu regeln und sogar eine totale Ausblendung unerwünschter Wellenlängen, z. B. IR-Strahlung, zu bewirken.

Displayhologramme sind von den Kreditkarten her bekannt. Sie können auch eine Fassade in einen Informationsträger verwandeln, da sie Schriften oder Signete durch Reflexion des Lichteinfalles visualisieren können.

Eine erste Anwendung von HOE-Schichten zeigen die experimentellen Reihenhäuser an der Internationalen Gartenbauausstellung in Stuttgart 1993 (IGA '93) des Architekturbüros HHS Planer + Architekten in Zusammenarbeit mit dem Institut für Licht- und Bautechnik der Fachhochschule Köln (ILB).

Das Grundkonzept des Entwurfs kombiniert aktive und passive Maßnahmen: die Nutzung der Sonnenstrahlung für die Tagesbeleuchtung und für die Erzeugung von Wärmeenergie und elektrischem Strom einerseits sowie ihre Regelung durch ein geeignetes Sonnenschutzsystem, welches das ganze Jahr über eine optimale Anpassung an die Wetter- und Lichtverhältnisse erpassung an die Wetter- und Lichtverhältnisse er-

ture is limited to a process of scanning exposure of small, 8 x 8 cm format holograms, aligned next to each other across a 1 x 2 m large sheet of film which is then developed. A former problem concernced with the stability of the film on exposure to ultraviolet light has now been solved by a new manufacturing process.

Some progress has been made in moving towards fully-automated series production, particularly in the manufacture of large-format master holograms. When the light-sensitive layer is not applied directly to the glass, then the final product is a film which has to be laminated between two sheets of glass for protection against damp and dirt.

In architecture holographic diffractive structures can be used for light direction, shading and visual screening, as well as for display holography.

A diffraction grating with equally spaced parallel lines redirects the sunlight onto the ceiling like a mirror and increases daylight levels further back in the room.

On the other hand a structure with parallel lines and varying spacing, known as a cylindrical zone plate, concentrates light on focal lines, in the same way as a lens; this effect can be used to increase the performance of strips with photovoltaic cells for exploiting solar energy.

An arrangement of concentrical elliptical lines with varying spacing, known as the off-axis zone plate, divides incident light into the individual spectral colours and concentrates them on focal points at different places. This makes it possible to use a movable stop to regulate the transmission of the various spectral wawelengths; thus a particular wawelength, such as infrared, can be blocked out totally.

Display holograms are already known from their use on credit cards. They can also transform a façade into an information carrier, in that they

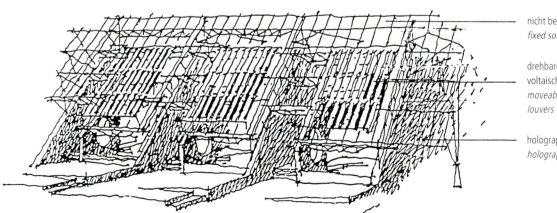

nicht bewegliche Solarzellen
fixed solar cells

drehbare holographisch-photovoltaische Glaslamellen
moveable holographic-photovoltaic louvers

holographische Displays
holographic displays

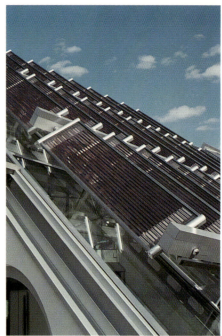

möglicht andererseits. Zu diesem Zweck sind drehbare Lamellen mit holographisch-optischen Elementen entwickelt worden, die dem Sonnenazimut computergesteuert nachgefahren werden und die nach Süden geneigte Verglasung der Wintergärten beschatten. Die einfallende direkte Sonnenstrahlung wird von konzentrierenden Hologrammen, die im außenliegenden Verbundglas der Lamellen eingebettet sind, auf einer 11 mm dahinterliegenden, mit Siebdruckstreifen versehenen Glasscheibe gebündelt und dort reflektiert. Da die undurchlässigen Streifen nur 50 % der Fläche belegen, kann das diffuse Tageslicht ungehindert durchkommen und die Wohnräume belichten. Um die konzentrierte direkte Strahlung aktiv zu nutzen, wurden die Siebdruckstreifen im mittleren Haus mit Solarzellen belegt. Elektrischer Strom wird auch im oberen Teil des Glasdachs durch 0.9 x 2.7 m große Photovoltaik-Module gewonnen, die mit 10 x 10 cm messenden polykristallinen Silizium-Solarzellen ausgestattet sind. Sie bieten zugleich einen Sonnenschutz: Da zwischen den einzelnen Modulen nur 35 % der Strahlung durchkommt, wird bei der steilen sommerlichen Sonnenstrahlung eine Verschattung der Wohnräume erzielt.
Außerhalb der gedeckten Wintergärten sind weitere Verbundgläser mit holographischen Schichten in die Schrägverglasung eingesetzt. Hier zerlegen die HOE das Licht in einen abstrakten Regenbogen. Durch die Möglichkeit, die aufgebrachten Strukturen mit Schriftzügen oder Logos

can present lettering or symbols by reflecting the incident light.

One of the first examples of HDS layers in building is in the experimental terrace housing at the International Garden Show in Stuttgart in 1993 by the architects HHS Planer + Architekten in collaboration with the Institute for Light and Building Technology of the Polytechnic of Cologne. The basic design idea combines passive and active methods in a system with a two-fold purpose: firstly to provide a solar protection system which is effective throughout the whole year and adaptable to light and weather conditions; and secondly to exploit solar energy for daylighting in the building and for heat energy and electricity. To achieve this aim, movable louvres were designed with integrated holographic diffractive structures which shade the south-facing glazing in the winter gardens. In addition these structures are computer-controlled to track the azimuth of the sun. Direct sunlight falling on the glass is concentrated in focal lines by cylindrical holograms laminated in the exterior glass of the louvres, and directed onto a pane of glass placed 11 mm behind; this glass is patterned with fritted strips from which the direct sunlight is then reflected. As the non-transmitting strips cover only 50 % of the surface area, diffuse daylight can pass through to illuminate the interior.
To make use of the concentrated direct light, the fritted strips in the middle house were fitted with

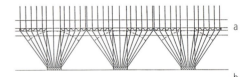

Direkte Sonnenstrahlung
Direct sunlight

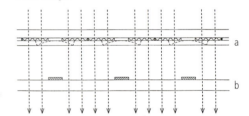

Diffuse Sonnenstrahlung
Diffuse sunlight

Die nach Süden geneigte Verglasung der Wintergärten (links) und die drehbaren Lamellen mit holographisch-photovoltaischen Schichten (rechts); Schnitt durch die Lamellen: Verbundglas mit fokussierenden Hologrammen (a) und Scheibe mit Solarzellen (b).
Reihenhäuser an der IGA '93, Stuttgart, HHS Planer + Architekten.
The south-facing angled glazing of the winter gardens (left) and the tracking louvres with holographic-photovoltaic layers (right); section through the louvres: laminated glass with concentrating holograms (a) and glass with photovoltaic strips (b).
Terrace housing at the IGA '93, Stuttgart, HHS Planners + Architects.

zu versehen, kann die Fassade zu einem Kommunikationsträger für die Betrachter werden.

Schichten mit Photovoltaik-Modulen

Innerhalb des Kapitels Verbundgläser stellen Photovoltaik-Module (PV) ein Sonderthema dar. Sie ermöglichen die aktive Nutzung der Sonnenstrahlung durch Umwandlung in elektrischen Strom; daneben können sie eine passive Sonnenschutzmaßnahme darstellen.

Die bekanntesten PV-Produkte sind Silizium-Solarzellen, wobei zwischen mono- und poly-(multi-)kristallinen sowie amorphen, also nichtkristallinen Solarzellen unterschieden wird. Die monokristallinen Solarzellen sind opak, blau oder dunkelgrau bis schwarz und weisen einen hohen Wirkungsgrad (14–16 %) auf. Sie sind teuer, weil sie in einem aufwendigen Verfahren aus Silizium-Kristall hergestellt werden müssen. Die polykristallinen Solarzellen sind meistens blau und opak. Sie sind günstiger, weil sie aus gegossenen Silizium-Blöcken gewonnen werden, weisen aber einen etwas niedrigeren Wirkungsgrad (11–13 %) auf.

Kristalline Solarzellen werden als 0.4 mm dicke Scheiben mit den Maßen von 10 x 10 cm bis 15 x 15 cm hergestellt. Danach werden sie zu Modulen zusammengebaut und in den Zwischenraum des Verbundglases mit Gießharz eingebettet. Je nach Aufbau sind durchsichtige, transluzide und undurchsichtige Module verfügbar. Bei transparenten und transluziden Modulen kann die Lichttransmission je nach Wahl der Abstände zueinander zwischen 4 % und 30 % eingestellt werden.

Polykristalline Silizium-Zellen sind für die Sanierung der Glasfassade des Verwaltungsgebäudes Stawag, Stadtwerke Aachen, 1991, vom Architekten Georg Feinhals verwendet worden. Um die Werbewirkung mit licht- und wärmetechnischen Anforderungen in Einklang zu bringen, wurden spezielle lichtstreuende und isolierende Glaselemente entwickelt. Im außenliegenden Verbundglas sind die PV-Zellen mit einem Abstand von 5 mm miteinander vergossen (Optisol®-Fassade). Innenliegend wurde ein Verbundglas mit einer milchigen Zwischenschicht verwendet. Die Verglasung läßt ca. 0.08 des einfallenden Lichts durchkommen und beleuchtet den Innenraum gleichmäßig.

Wegen ihrer potentiell geringeren Kosten erwecken amorphe Solarzellen derzeit großes Interesse. Dank der Dünnschichttechnologie erfor-

photovoltaics. On the upper part of the glass roof, too, photovoltaic modules convert solar energy into electricity; here the modules are 0.9 x 2.7 m in size and fitted with 10 x 10 cm polycrystalline silicon solar cells. The modules also offer a degree of shading from the steeply angled radiation in the summer, because only 35 % of the radiation penetrates the spaces between the modules through to the living areas below. Beside the covered winter gardens are further laminated glass areas with holographic layers incorporated in the sloping sections. Here the HDS break the light up into an abstract rainbow. The possibility of altering fixed structures by adding wording or logos can transform a façade into an information carrier displaying messages or advertising to those passing by outside.

Layers with Photovoltaic Modules

Within this chapter on laminated glass, photovoltaic modules (PVs) are a special topic. They enable the active use of solar radiation by turning it into electrical energy; in addition they can also represent a form of passive solar protection. The most well known PV products are silicon solar cells, available in three types: monocrystalline, poly- or multicrystalline, and amorphous, i.e. non-crystalline solar cells.

The monocrystalline solar cells are opaque, blue or dark grey to black, and they have a high efficiency (14–16 %). They are expensive because they are made from silicon crystals in a complicated manufacturing process.

The polycrystalline solar cells are mostly blue or opaque. These are cheaper because they are made from poured silicon blocks, but they have a lower efficiency (11–13 %).

Crystalline solar cells are produced as 0.4 mm thick discs in sizes from 10 x 10 cm to 15 x 15 cm. These discs are then put together to form modules and embedded with resin in the cavity in a laminated glass unit. According to composition, the result can be either a transparent, translucent or non-transparent module. Light transmission through transparent and translucent modules can be set from 4 % to 30 % according to the choice of spacing.

Polycrystalline silicon cells were used in 1991 in Aachen by the architect Georg Feinhals for the renovation of the glass façade of the Stawag administration building. Special light-scattering and insulating glass elements were developed in order to meet both the needs in terms of lighting

Verschiedene Photovoltaik-Module: oben eine monokristalline Solarzelle, in der Mitte polykristalline Solarzellen, unten eine semitransparente amorphe Solarzelle.

Different photovoltaic modules: a monocrystalline solar cell (top), two polycrystalline solar cells (middle), and a semi-transparent amorphous solar cell (bottom).

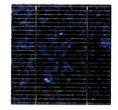

dert ihre Herstellung weniger Material und niedrigere Temperaturen. Damit können die Schichten auf verschiedene Träger wie Glas, Stahl- oder Kunststoffolien aufgetragen werden. Leider ist der Wirkungsgrad mit 5–7 % noch recht tief. Vollflächige amorphe Siliziumzellen sind meistens rotbraun oder rötlich durchscheinend.

Auf dem Markt sind auch semitransparente amorphe Solarzellen erhältlich. Dafür werden Teilflächen der auf Glas aufgebrachten dünnen Schichten mittels Lasertrenntechniken abgetragen, so daß transparente Stege zwischen den aktiven Flächen resultieren, welche bis 12 % des Lichtes durchlassen und einen Blick wie durch eine halbgeschlossene Jalousie gewähren (Asi-Glas®).

Als Alternative zu den amorphen Silizium-Solarzellen wecken auch andere Materialien vermehrt Interesse, wie CdTe und CuInSe₂ die sich mittels bewährten Dünnfilm- und Tauchverfahren herstellen lassen. Für kleine Flächen sind im Labor bis 16 % Wirkungsgrad erreicht worden. Produktionswerte liegen aber heute noch bei 8 %.

Durch die Kombination von mehreren Dünnfilm-Solarzellen mit unterschiedlicher Spektralcharakteristik läßt sich die Nutzung der einfallenden Strahlung optimieren. Sogenannte «Tandemzellen» haben im Labor bis 12 % Wirkungsgrad erreicht; eine weitere Steigerung scheint möglich. Vielversprechender sieht es mit «Tripelzellen» mit einer dreifachen Schichtabfolge aus. Hier scheinen 10 % Wirkungsgrad auch für größere Produktionsmengen realistisch.

Obwohl die PV-Zellen wirtschaftlich gesehen noch nicht mit anderen Stromerzeugungsarten konkurrieren können, sorgen wachsendes Umweltbewußtsein, unterstützende Vorschriften sowie Finanzierungshilfe durch öffentliche Kreditgelder schon jetzt für ihre Verbreitung.

Temperaturabhängige Schichten

Es handelt sich dabei um Schichten, die bei Temperaturwechsel den Strahlungsdurchgang durch reversible physikalische Veränderungen automatisch steuern können.

Thermotrope Schichten

Thermotrope Schichten wirken über den gesamten Sprektralbereich und gehen bei steigender Temperatur vom klaren und lichtdurchlässigen zum opaken und lichtstreuenden Zustand über. Das Grundmaterial besteht aus zwei Komponen-

and insulation, as well as the desire to maintain and exploit the corporate image as projected through the façade. In the exterior laminated glass the PV cells have a gap of 5 mm between them. (Optisol® Façade). On the inside a laminated glass with an opaque interlayer was used. The glazing lets through approx. 0.08 of the incident light and provides an even illumination of the interior space.

Amorphous solar cells are attracting great interest at present, because of their potentially lower costs. Thanks to thin-film technology they can be manufactured using less material and at lower temperatures. The films can be applied to various carriers such as glass, plastics or steelfoils. Unfortunately the efficiency is still relatively low, values of 5–7 % are typical. Large area of amorphous silicon cells are mostly red-brownish, or, when transparent, slightly reddish.

Also available are semi-transparent amorphous solar cells. They are produced by removing partial areas of the thin film by means of a laser separation process, in order to create narrow transparent strips between the opaque surfaces, which allow up to 12 % of the incident light to pass through. The impression gained is that of looking through a half-open louvre blind (Asi-Glass®).

As alternatives to amorphous silicon solar cells other materials are attracting increasing interest – materials such as CaTe and CuInSe₂. These cells can be built using established thin film technologies or even by a dipping process. In smaller areas up to 16 % efficiency has been reached under laboratory conditions. Production values, however, do not exceed 8 % so far.

Optimised exploitation of solar energy can be achieved by combining several thin film layers with different spectral responses. So-called tandem cells have reached up to 12 % efficiency under laboratory conditions, slightly higher values seem possible. Further possibilities are offered by triple cells which consist of a succession of three thin film layers. Efficiencies of 10 % in production quantities are becoming realistic. Although PV cells cannot yet compete economically with other ways of generating energy, they are gaining ground due to a generally increasing concern for the environment, supportive regulations and financial help from public funding.

Temperature-Dependent Layers

Temperature-dependent layers can automatically

ten mit unterschiedlichem Brechungsindex, zum Beispiel aus Wasser und einem Kunststoff (Hydrogel) oder aus zwei verschiedenen Kunststoffen (Polymerblend). Bei niedrigen Temperaturen ist die Mischung homogen und weist eine hohe Transmission auf. Bei höheren Temperaturen ändern die Polymere ihre Konfiguration – von gestreckten Ketten hin zu zusammengeklumpten Kügelchen, die eine Lichtstreuung verursachen. Die Veränderung vom transmittierenden zum streuenden Zustand ist reversibel. Typische Werte im sichtbaren Bereich bewegen sich zwischen 0.80–0.90 und 0.10–0.50 und die Gesamttransmissionen zwischen 0.80–0.90 und 0.05–0.40.

In den vergangenen Jahren sind zwei Produkte entwickelt worden: Cloud Gel® und TALD®. Cloud Gel® von Suntek Co. ist ein Hydrogel, das mit einer Schichtdicke von beispielsweise 1 mm zwischen zwei Glasscheiben bei Temperaturvariation eine Reduktion der solaren Transmission von 0.82 auf 0.05 aufweist, die zwischen 25 °C und 30 °C sehr stark und bis 50 °C gleichmäßig abnimmt.

TALD® (*t*emperatur-*a*bhängige *L*icht*d*urchlässigkeit) ist ebenfalls ein Hydrogel. Eine Schicht mit einer Dicke von 1 mm, eingebettet zwischen zwei Glasscheiben, weist solare Transmissionswerte zwischen 0.47 und 0.84 auf. Die Eintrübungstemperatur kann durch die Zusammenstellung der Mischung beliebig zwischen 5 °C und 60 °C eingestellt werden.

Das Hauptproblem der Hydrogele liegt in ihrem Wasseranteil, welcher eine gute Dichtigkeit und Maßnahmen bei Erreichung des Gefrierpunkts verlangt.

Thermotrope Schichten aus Kunststoff (Polymerblend) umgehen diese Probleme. Die Eintrübung

control light transmission by reversible physical changes which are activated by a change in temperature.

Thermotropic Layers

Thermotropic layers operate mainly over the entire solar spectrum, changing state with increasing temperature from clear and light-transmitting to opaque and light-scattering. The basic material consists of two components with differing refractive indices, for example water and a polymer (hydrogel) or two different polymers (polymer blend). At lower temperatures the mixture is homogeneous and has a high transmission factor. At higher temperatures, however, the configuration of the polymers alters – from stretched chains to clumps which scatter light. This change from a transmitting to a scattering state is reversible. Typical visible transmission values lie between 0.80–0.90 and 0.10–0.50 and solar energy transmission values lie between 0.80–0.90 and 0.05–0.40.

In recent years two products have been developped: CloudGel® and TALD®.

CloudGel®, by Suntek Co., is a hydrogel which, as a 1 mm thick layer sandwiched between two glass panes and subjected to temperature changes, displays a reduction in solar energy transmission from 0.82 to 0.05; between 25 °C and 30 °C the drop is most marked, and a more even transition takes place up to 50 °C.

TALD® is also a hydrogel. A 1 mm thick layer of TALD® sandwiched between two panes of glass has solar energy transmission values of between 0.47 and 0.84. The temperature at which clouding occurs can be predetermined by controlling the chemical composition at the manufacturing stage – the range lies between 5 °C and 60 °C.

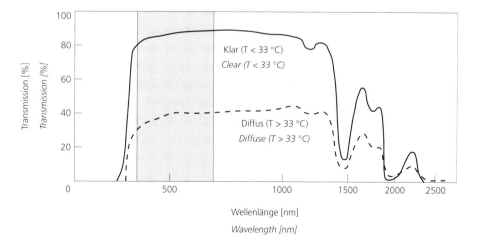

Spektrale Transmission einer 1 mm dicken thermotropen Schicht von TALD®.

Spectral transmission of a 1 mm thick thermotropic layer of TALD®.

ist gleichmäßiger abgestuft, und der Moment ihres Beginns zwischen 30 °C und 100 °C kann durch das Verhältnis bei der Mischung eingestellt werden.

Thermochrome Schichten

Beim Erwärmen verändern thermochrome Schichten die Strahlungstransmission hauptsächlich im nahen IR-Bereich, so daß sie im metallischen Zustand als niedrig-emissive Schichten eingesetzt werden können, um die langwellige Sonnenstrahlung oder die Wärmeverluste durch Emissivität zu dämmen. Dafür eignen sich Übergangsoxide, zum Beispiel Vanadiumoxid (VO_2). Unterhalb einer bestimmten Temperatur ist das Material halbleitend oder dielektrisch mit geringer Absorption im IR-Bereich, darüber tritt das metallische, IR-reflektierende Verhalten ein. Einige Forschungen laufen in diese Richtung, und Experimente mit dünnen Vanadiumoxid-Schichten sind bereits durchgeführt worden.

Elektrooptische Schichten

Im Hinblick auf eine «intelligente Glasfassade» scheinen Entwicklungen von Schichten mit Flüssigkristallen oder mit elektrochromen Materialien die meisten Aussichten auf Erfolg zu haben. Sie ermöglichen eine aktive Steuerung der Strahlungsdurchlässigkeit durch das Anlegen einer elektrischen Spannung und können über eine zentrale Gebäudeleittechnik (GLT) oder über integrierte Mikrochips die Glashülle an die veränderlichen Licht- und Wetterverhältnisse anpassen.

Schichten mit Flüssigkristallen

Schichten mit Flüssigkristallen (liquid crystals, LC) sind von Uhren und PC-Displays her bekannt. Diese LC-Systeme arbeiten nach dem Prinzip, daß sich die kettenförmigen Moleküle der Flüssigkristalle elektrisch ausrichten lassen und damit der Durchgang von polarisiertem Licht gesteuert werden kann. Im normalen, spannungslosen Zustand sind die Moleküle zufällig gerichtet, so daß sie das einfallende Licht zerstreuen. Beim Anlegen einer Spannung richten sie sich entlang der Linien des elektrischen Feldes aus. Das System wird dann lichtdurchlässig und bleibt es, solange das Spannungsfeld aufrechterhalten wird. Daß sie ohne Stromzufuhr undurchsichtig sind, ist denn auch der große Nachteil von LC-Schichten.

Das Einstellen von verschiedenen Stufen erfolgt

The main problem of hydrogels is their water content which requires a good seal and special measures when temperatures reach the freezing point.

Thermotropic layers made of polymers (polymer blends) avoid this problem. The clouding in such layers changes more gradually with temperature, and the point at which it starts to occur can be set in the range from 30 °C to 100 °C, again by controlling the composition at the manufacturing stage.

Thermochromic Layers

On being heated, thermochromic layers undergo a change in their transmission properties, mainly in the near infrared range; this makes them suitable for use in their metallic state as low-emissivity coatings to reduce long-wave solar radiation or heat loss by emission. Particularly suited here are transition metal oxides, such as vanadium dioxide (VO_2). Below a certain temperature the material assumes a semiconductor or dielectric state with low absorption in the infrared range; as the temperature increases, it proceeds to a metallic state causing infrared reflectivity. Research is being carried out in this direction at present, and experiments using thin-film vanadium dioxide have already been performed.

Electro-Optic Layers

With respect to an "intelligent glass façade", developments in the field of liquid crystal layers or layers of electrochromic material seem to hold the most promise. By applying a voltage, the light and/or solar transmission of these layers can be actively controlled in accordance with the prevailing light or weather conditions, either via a central building management system (BMS) or via microchips integrated into the glass skin.

Liquid Crystal Layers

We are already familiar with liquid crystal layers (or LCs) in watches and PC screens. These LC systems work on the principle that liquid crystal molecule chains can be influenced electrically to permit the transmission of polarized light. Without an applied voltage, the molecules are randomly oriented and the incident light is scattered. When a voltage is applied, the molecules align themselves along the lines of the electrical field; in this state the system is then able to transmit light, as long as the electrical field is maintained. The main disadvantage, however, of LC

durch aufwendige und daher teure Steuerungssysteme, welche den Lichtdurchgang dimmen.

Für die Verwendung als Verglasung bereiten insbesondere die großen Flächen und die Aufwärmung der Scheibe Probleme, was Funktionsstörungen hervorrufen kann. Darum kommen Systeme mit Flüssigkristallen zur Zeit vor allem im Innenbereich zur Anwendung. In Kombination mit Sonnenschutzgläsern besteht aber die Möglichkeit, sie auch im Fassadenbau zu verwenden. Künftig sollte die Stabilität der Moleküle bei UV-Strahlung verbessert werden.

Eine weitere Möglichkeit sind die sogenannten «Guest-Host»-Typen. Hier sind dichroitische Farbmoleküle mit den Flüssigkristallen gemischt, um eine stärkere Absorption zu bewirken. Im cholesterinischen Zustand sind die Moleküle in parallelen Ebenen geschichtet, wobei die Flüssigkristalle aber eine unterschiedliche Ausrichtung aufweisen. Vorteil der «Guest-Host»-Systeme ist eine Funktionstüchtigkeit bis 100 °C. Sie wurden für Brillengläser und Autorückspiegel entwickelt. Prototypen von Rückspiegeln haben eine Reflexion von 0.12 und 0.48 im sichtbaren Bereich erreicht.

Die aussichtsreichste Lösung stellt die Mikroverkapselung («polymer dispersed liquid cristal», PDLC; «nematic curvilinear aligned phase», NCAP) dar. Bei der Mikroverkapselung (PDLC/NCAP) sind die kettenförmigen Moleküle in Kügelchen von 1–10 · 10³ nm Durchmesser eingeschlossen und in einer Kunststoffschicht zwischen zwei elektrisch leitfähigen ITO-beschichteten Kunststofffilmen eingebettet.

Unter elektrischer Spannung werden die Moleküle ausgerichtet, und die Folie wirkt fast transparent. Die verbleibende leichte Eintrübung ist auf die restliche Reflexion der Kügelchen zurückzuführen und bildet einen Nachteil der Mikroverkapselung. Ohne elektrisches Feld wird das Licht gestreut, und das System erscheint milchigtrüb beziehungsweise opak. Unbefriedigend ist auch die geringe Beständigkeit gegenüber der UV-Strahlung.

layers is the fact that they are non-transparent when no voltage is applied across them.

The setting of various levels is achieved by complicated – and therefore also expensive – control systems to adjust light transmission.

For use in glazing, problems occur when large surfaces of glass are used and as a consequence of the temperature increase in the glass itself, which can lead to malfunctioning of the light control. For this reason liquid crystal systems are primarily used for inside aplications at present. However, in combination with solar control glazings there is also a possibility of using them in façades. Development work is going on to improve the ultraviolet stability of the molecules.

A further possibility is presented by the so-called "guest-host types". Here dichroic dye molecules mixed with liquid crystals are used with the aim of achieving higher absorption. In the cholesteric-nematic structure the direction of the long axis of the molecule is slightly displaced with the liquid crystals displaying a different alignment. The advantage of the "guest-host" systems is their functionality up to 100 °C. They were developed for use in spectacles and rear view mirrors for cars. Prototypes for rear view mirrors have achieved reflectances of 0.12 to 0.48 in the visible range.

The most promising solution is presented by micro-encapsulation ("polymer dispersed liquid crystal", PDLC; and "nematic curvilinear aligned phase", NCAP). This material (PDLC/NCAP) contains encapsulated chains of molecules as balls of 1–10 · 10³ nm radius within a polymer matrix sandwiched between two electrodes, which are usually ITO-coated polyester films.

When subject to an electrical charge, the molecules chains straighten and the film appears almost transparent. Any remaining slight clouding is due to the reflection from the balls and as such is one of the disadvantages of micro-encapsulation. When no electrical charge is present, light is scattered and the system appears milky white

Mikroverkapselte Flüssigkristalle: im spannungslosen Zustand sind die Moleküle zufällig gerichtet, so daß sie das Licht zerstreuen; beim Anlegen einer Spannung richten sie sich entlang der Linien des elektrischen Feldes aus, und das System wird lichtdurchlässig.

Beispiel einer Glastrennwand mit Flüssigkristallen im opaken und im durchsichtigen Zustand: Priva-Lite®.

Micro-encapsulated liquid crystals: without an applied voltage the molecules are randomly oriented and the system scatters light. When a voltage is applied, the molecules align themselves with the electrical field and the system transmits light.

Example of a glass partition with liquid crystals in opaque and transparent states: Priva-Lite®.

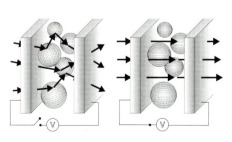

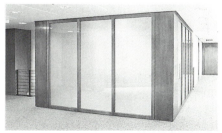

Prototypen mit einer Lichttransmission von 0.48 bis 0.76 sind schon hergestellt worden. Im Handel sind Produkte wie Priva-Lite®, das eine Lichtdurchlässigkeit von 0.70 im opaken und 0.73 im durchsichtigen Zustand aufweist. Die Folien sind ca. 0.3 mm stark und maximal 1 x 2.80 m groß. Je nach Einbau im Verbundglas sind verschiedene Gesamtdicken und neutrale, bronzefarbene, graue und grüne Farbtöne erhältlich. Zur Zeit können Priva-Lite®-Folien bei Temperaturen von −40 °C bis +40 °C einwandfrei eingesetzt werden, was zwar den problemlosen Einbau in Innenräumen, jedoch die Verwendung im Fassadenbau nur in Kombination mit zusätzlichen Sonnenschutzmaßnahmen gestattet. Bei höheren Temperaturen bilden sich Flecken mit unterschiedlicher Opazität, und ab +100 °C sind die Folien vollständig transparent.

Elektrochrome Schichten
Elektrochrome Schichten nutzen die Eigenschaft einiger Materialien, Ionen aufzunehmen oder abzugeben und damit ihre Transmission im sichtbaren und unsichtbaren Strahlungsbereich zu ändern. Im Prinzip funktionieren sie wie ein Akkumulator: ein Ionenspeicher, ein Ionenleiter und ein elektrochromes Material sind zwischen zwei Trägermaterialien – Glas oder Kunststoff – mit transparenten Elektroden gestellt. Die chemische Reaktion findet statt, wenn bei Anlegen einer elektrischen Spannung Ionen hin- und herverschoben werden. Da die Schichten einige Zeit aufgeladen bleiben, ist die Stromzufuhr nur während des Ionenaustauschs notwendig. Dieser Aufbau läßt sich aber verschiedentlich variieren. Zum Beispiel können gewisse Elektrolyten auch als Ionenspeicher wirken. Oder es können zwei elektrochrome Materialien, das eine gefärbt im reduzierten Zustand und das andere im oxidierten Zustand, kombiniert werden, was zu einer verstärkten Wirkung beitragen kann. Oder es können mehrere Schichten verwendet werden, da der Effekt additiv ist. Wolframoxid (WO_3) ist die elektrochrome Substanz, mit der am häufigsten experimentiert wird, weil sie im sichtbaren Bereich die größte Intensitätsvariation zwischen transparent und dunkelblau aufweist. Es können aber auch bronzefarbene (NiO) oder schwarze (IrO_2) Tönungen, oder sogar Farbwechsel – wie Rot zu Blau (CoO_x) und Gelb zu Grün (Rh_2O_3) – erzielt werden. Die Schichten können mit der Dünnschichttechnologie, durch Sputtern oder Aufdämpfen,

or opaque. One further problem is the low stability against ultraviolet radiation.
Prototypes with light transmission factors from 0.48 to 0.76 have already been produced. Available on the market are products such as Priva-Lite®, which has a light transmission factor of 0.70 in the opaque state, and 0.73 in the transparent state. The film is approx. 0.3 mm thick and a maximum of 1 x 2.80 m in size. Depending on the particular laminated glass construction different overall thicknesses can be obtained, and a range of colour tints in neutral, bronze, grey and green.
At present Priva-Lite® films can be used without problems in the temperature range from −40 °C to +40 °C, which makes them perfectly adequate for interior use, but restricts their use in façades to combinations with other solar shading devices. At higher temperatures patches of differing opacities develop, and above 100 °C the films are completely transparent.

Electrochromic Layers
Electrochromic layers exploit the ability of some materials to accept or shed ions, thus influencing the transmission properties in the visible and invisible radiation range. In principle they function in the same way as an accumulator: an ion storage layer, an ion conductor and an electrochromic material are placed between two substrates – glass or plastic – with transparent conductors. The chemical reaction takes place when the ions are shuttled forwards and backwards through the application of a voltage. As the layers remain charged for some time, the voltage need only be applied during the ion exchange process.
This system can be varied somewhat. For example certain electrolytes can act as an ion storage layer. Or two electrochromic materials can be combined to increase the desired light regulating effect; one of them is coloured in the reduced state and the other in the oxidized state, which increases the desired effect. Or several layers can be used to create an additive effect.
Tungsten oxide (WO_3) is a chromogenic material which is subject to most testing at present, because it has the greatest variation of intensity in the visible range between transparent and dark blue. However, other colours can also be produced, from bronze (NiO) or black (IrO_2) to changing colours, such as red to blue (CoO_x) and yellow to green (Rh_2O_3).
The layers can be applied either by thin film tech-

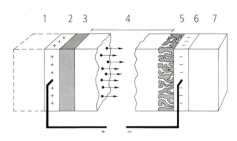

Aufbau von elektrochromen Schichten: 1 Glasscheibe; 2 transparente Elektrode; 3 Ionenspeicher; 4 Ionenleiter; 5 elektrochromes Material; 6 transparente Elektrode; 7 Glasscheibe. – Die chemische Reaktion findet statt, wenn beim Anlegen einer elektrischen Spannung Ionen hin- und herverschoben werden.
Basic design of electrochromic layers: 1 glass; 2 transparent conductor; 3 ion storage film; 4 ion conductor (electrolyte); 5 electrochromic film; 6 transparent conductor; 7 glass. – The chemical reaction takes place when the ions are shuttled forwards and backwards through the application of electrical field.

Prototyp einer Verbundscheibe mit elektrochromen Schichten aus Wolframoxid im klaren und im verdunkelten Zustand (Dornier Aerospace).
Prototype of a laminated glass with electrochromic layers of tungsten oxide in clear and coloured states (Dornier Aerospace).

sowie mit chemischen Verfahren hergestellt werden.

Elektrochrome Systeme, die, über Abstufungen, zwischen einem transparenten und einem absorbierenden Zustand eingestellt werden können, eignen sich als Sonnen- und Blendschutz hervorragend sowohl für Gebäudeverglasungen als auch für die Scheiben von Flugzeugen, Straßen- und Bahnfahrzeugen. Daß daran ein großes Interesse besteht, zeigt die hohe Anzahl an Patentgesuchen, die in den letzten Jahren in Japan und den USA eingereicht wurden.

Zur Zeit wird die Entwicklung von elektrochromen Gläsern für die Anwendung bei Automobilen und Flugzeugen intensiv betrieben. Die Beanspruchung durch hohe Temperaturen von 90 °C bis 120 °C und die kleinen Dimensionen der Scheiben wirken sich in diesem Bereich – anders als bei einer Anwendung im Bauwesen – wegen der relativen Kurzlebigkeit der Objekte weniger nachteilig aus.

Auf dem Markt befinden sich bereits aktiv steuerbare Autorückspiegel von Donnelly und Gentex, aber auch Prototypen von Glasschiebedächern für Autos (Nissan Motors, Donnelly, Daimler-Benz-Dornier).

Für die Verwendung im Bauwesen sind Verbundgläser mit elektrochromen Schichten als Prototypen mit maximal 0.5 m² Fläche produziert worden. Probleme bereiten die hohen Kosten für die transparenten Elektroden und deren relativ geringe Leitfähigkeit, die die Schaltgeschwindigkeit der elektrochromen Elemente mit zunehmender Fläche stark herabsetzt.

Als Idealwerte für solche Verglasungen definiert Dr. Carl Lampert, Lawrence Berkeley Laboratory, California, eine Steuerung der Transmission wie folgt: im nahen infraroten Bereich zwischen 0.10 und 0.70; im sichtbaren Bereich zwischen 0.10 und 0.20 im farbigen, abgedunkelten Zustand, und 0.60–0.80 im klaren, transparenten Zustand; eine Schaltgeschwindigkeit von 1 bis 50 Sekunden bei einer Schaltspannung von 1–5 V sowie ein «Gedächtnis» von 1 bis 24 Stunden. Beim Museum «Seto Bridge», Kojima, Japan, 1988, wurden von der Asahi Glass versuchsweise 196 elektrochrome Scheiben von 40 x 40 cm installiert. Sie ermöglichen die Betrachtung des Unterwasserpanoramas, während sich ihre Farbe im Takt der Musik von Hell- zu Dunkelblau verändert. Weitere 45 x 40 cm große Prototypen sind 1988 für die Verglasung im Haus Daiwa, Mita-City, Japan, eingesetzt worden.

nology, as sputtering or chemical vapour deposition, or by sol-gel technology.

Electrochromic systems which can be switched back and forth between transparent and absorbing states, are an ideal device of protection against sun and glare both in buildings as well as for glazing in aircraft, road vehicles or trains. The great interest in this area is witnessed by the large number of patent applications which have been registered in Japan and the USA in recent years.

At present intense research is being carried out in the development of electrochromic glass for use in cars and airplanes. In contrast to use in building, the stress from high temperatures from 90 °C to 120 °C and the small dimensions of the panes are not so critical, because of the relative short operational lifespan. Already available on the market, produced by Donnelly and Gentex, are actively controllable rear view mirrors for cars; prototypes for glass sunroofs for cars (Nissan Motors, Donnelly, Daimler-Benz-Dornier) have also been developed.

For use in buildings, so far the only developments in laminated glass with electrochromic layers are limited to prototypes with a maximum size of 0.5 m². Problems arise due to the high costs of the transparent conductors and the drop in the electrical field with increasing surface area, which greatly reduces the switching speed of the electrochromic elements.

According to Dr Carl Lampert, of the Lawrence Berkeley Laboratory in California, the ideal ranges for control of transmission in glazing are as follows: between 0.10 and 0.70 in the near infrared range; in the visible range between 0.10 and 0.20 in the coloured, darkened state and 0.60–0.80 in the clear, transparent state; a switching speed of 1 to 50 seconds at a switching voltage of 1–5 V and a "memory" of 1 to 24 hours.

In 1988 at the Seto Bridge Museum in Kojima, Japan, Asahi Glass installed as an experiment 196 electrochromic panes, 40 x 40 cm in size. They allow the visitor to view the underwater panorama, while, in time to the music, the colours change from pale to dark blue. More prototypes, in a size of 45 x 40 cm have been installed as part of the glazing in Daiwa House, built in 1988 in Mita-City, Japan.

Installation mit 196 elektrochromen Scheiben von 40 x 40 cm, die ihre Farbe im Takt der Musik von Hell- zu Dunkelblau verändern.
Museum «Seto Bridge», Kojima, Japan, 1988, Asahi.
Installation with 196 electrochromic panes 40 x 40 cm in size; the panes change colour from pale to dark blue in time to the music.
Seto Bridge Museum, Kojima, Japan, 1988, Asahi.

Das Isolierglas   Insulating Glass

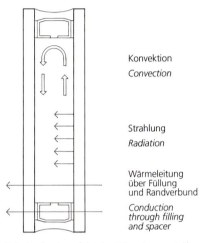

Konvektion
Convection

Strahlung
Radiation

Wärmeleitung
über Füllung
und Randverbund
*Conduction
through filling
and spacer*

Beim Isolierglas erfolgt der Wärmetransport über vier Wege: Konvektion, Strahlungsaustausch zwischen den Glasoberflächen und Wärmeleitung über die Füllung oder über den Randverbund.
The heat transport through an insulating glass unit takes place in four different ways: convection, radiation exchange between the glass surfaces and conduction through the filling or the edge seal.

Linke Seite: Isoliergläser mit emaillierten Scheiben können als Sonnenschutzmaßnahme dienen, da Musterdesign und Bedruckungsgrad genau nach den Anforderungen festgelegt werden können.
Gebäude «B3», heute British Petroleum, Stockley Park, London, 1989, Sir Norman Foster und Partner.
Left page: Insulating glass with fritted panes can be used for solar shading, because pattern design and extent of cover can be set exactly to the required specifications.
"B3" building, today British Petroleum, Stockley Park, London, 1989, Sir Norman Foster and Partners.

Die Wärmeverluste einer einfachen Verglasung können mit dem Einsatz von Isoliergläsern mindestens halbiert werden.

Ein Isolierglas ist eine Verbundkonstruktion aus zwei oder mehreren Glasscheiben, die am äußeren Rand durch ein oder mehrere Abstandprofile schubfest und gasdicht verbunden sind. Damit entsteht ein Scheibenzwischenraum von 8–20 mm Tiefe, der mit einer Füllung aus trockener Luft oder Edelgas als Wärmepuffer wirkt.

Der Wärmetransport von der Warmseite zur Kaltseite erfolgt über vier Wege: durch Strahlungsaustausch zwischen den gegenüberliegenden Glasoberflächen, durch Konvektion im Scheibenzwischenraum, durch Wärmeleitung über die Füllung oder über den Randverbund.

Die Wärmeleitung über den üblichen Abstandhalter läßt sich nur begrenzt beeinflussen, weil dort Druck-, Zug- und Schubkräfte aufgenommen werden müssen. Eine Reduktion der Wärmeverluste kann durch die Veränderung der anderen drei Parameter erzielt werden.

Die Abstrahlung der Glasoberfläche kann mit einer niedrig-emissiven (Low-E) Beschichtung von etwa 0.85 bis auf 0.10 oder sogar darunter gesenkt werden. Während ein normales Isolierglas mit unbeschichteter Oberfläche und einem 12 mm breiten, mit Luft gefüllten Zwischenraum einen k-Wert von 3 W/m^{2}K aufweist, führt die Low-E Beschichtung zu einem k-Wert unter 2 W/m^{2}K.

Füllungen mit Gas

Die Wärmeleitfähigkeit einer Füllung mit trockener Luft ist niedrig. Durch Edelgase wie Argon, Krypton oder Xenon können die Werte aber noch weiter gesenkt werden, weil sie eine niedrigere Wärmeleitung und eine geringere Konvektionsneigung aufweisen. Bei der Wahl sind ökonomische Überlegungen ausschlaggebend. Das Argon kann kostengünstig aus der Luft gewonnen werden, weil es 1 % der Luftanteile ausmacht; dage-

Heat losses associated with standard single glazing can be reduced by at least 50 % by using insulating glass units.

Insulating glass consists in two or more panes separated along the edges by one or more spacers, which seal the cavity and are shear resistant. The resulting 8–20 cm cavity between the panes acts as a thermal buffer and can be filled with dehydrated air or inert gas.

Heat transport from the warm side to the cold side takes place in four different ways: by convection in the cavity, by radiation exchange between the opposite glass surfaces, and by conduction through the filling and the edge seal.

Conduction levels through the standard spacers can only be slightly reduced, because here compression, tension and shear forces have to be taken up. A reduction in heat losses can be achieved by altering the other three parameters.

The radiative heat losses from the surface of the glass can be reduced from approximately 0.85 to 0.10 or even lower by the application of a low-emissivity (low E) coating. While normal insulating glass with an uncoated surface and 12 mm cavity filled with air has a U-value of 3 W/m^{2}K, a low-E coating can produce a U-value of below 2 W/m^{2}K.

Gas Fillings

The thermal conductivity of a filling with dehydrated air is low. By using inert gases such as argon, krypton or xenon the values can be further reduced, because these gases have lower thermal conductivity and convection properties than normal air. The choice of which gas to use depends on economic factors. Argon is cheap to obtain, because it makes up 1 % of normal air; krypton on the other hand makes up only 0.0001 % and xenon 0.000009 %, and therefore are correspondingly more expensive. The U-values of a double pane insulating glass with a low-E coating and a 15 mm cavity filled with argon are

gen sind Krypton zu 0.0001 % und Xenon gar nur zu 0.000009 % in der Luft enthalten und daher wesentlich teurer. Die k-Werte eines Zweifach-Isolierglases mit einer Low-E Beschichtung, einem 15 mm breiten Zwischenraum und einer Füllung mit Argon liegen bei 1.3 W/m²K, mit Krypton bei 1.1 W/m²K.

Zurzeit sind die Amortisationskosten von Krypton und ähnlichen Gasen noch sehr hoch, aber eine größere Nachfrage könnte eine Preissenkung mit sich bringen.

Eine Senkung des k-Werts unter 1 W/m²K kann durch das Anbringen einer dritten Scheibe, durch das Einspannen mehrerer low-E-beschichteter Folien oder durch Evakuierung des Scheibenzwischenraumes erfolgen.

Ein Dreifach-Isolierglas wird mit zwei low-E-beschichteten Scheiben und unterschiedlichen Gasfüllungen hergestellt: mit Argon wird ein k-Wert von 0.9 W/m²K im Silverstar Super® (g = 0.47, τ = 0.68), mit Krypton ein k-Wert von 0.7 W/m²K im Klimatop® (g = 0.45, τ = 0.66) und ein k-Wert von 0.5 W/m²K im Silverstar 2000® (g = 0.37, τ = 0.57) erreicht.

Eine andere Möglichkeit besteht im Einspannen von Folien mit Low-E Beschichtungen. Damit wird das Gewicht und die Dicke der dritten Glasscheibe vermieden. Das HIT® mit zwei low-E-beschichteten Folien in einem Zwischenraum von 60 mm erreicht einen k-Wert von 0.6 W/m²K (z. B. g = 0.40 und τ = 0.55), und das Superglass®, ebenfalls mit zwei low-E-beschichteten Folien, aber mit einem schmaleren Zwischenraum von 17 mm bis 33 mm, weist einen k-Wert von 0.7 W/m²K (g = 0.34, τ = 0.62) auf.

Die Variante der Evakuierung des Scheibenzwischenraumes schaltet den Kostenfaktor der Edelgase aus, läßt aber andere Probleme auftreten. Der Randverbund eines Vakuumglases muß eine sehr hohe Dichtigkeit garantieren und die unterschiedlichen thermischen Ausdehnungen der beiden Glasscheiben schubfest aufnehmen. Dafür scheint ein Glasverbund (Glaslote) sehr geeignet, aber dieser erhöht die Wärmeleitung und damit die Verluste im Randbereich. Wegen des Vakuums sind Abstandhalter im Zwischenraum notwendig. Ihre Dimensionierung und die Entfernung voneinander müssen hinsichtlich punktueller Spannungen auf der Glasoberfläche, Wärmeleitung bei den Kontaktstellen und klarer Durchsicht optimiert werden. Am US Solar Energy Research Institute (SERI, Golden,Colorado, USA) sind Prototypen mit sehr kleinen Glas-

about 1.3 W/m²K; a krypton filling gives a U-value of 1.1 W/m²K.

The amortization costs of krypton and similar gases are at present still very high, but increased demand could lead to a drop in price.

The U-value can be lowered below 1 W/m²K by introducing a third pane of glass or through the use of several low-E coatings or by evacuating the air space.

Triple-pane insulated glazing is composed of two low-E coated panes and various gas fillings: argon produces a U-value of 0.9 W/m²K in Silverstar Super® glass (g = 0.47, τ = 0.68); krypton achieves a U-value of 0.7 W/m²K in Klimatop® (g = 0.45, τ = 0.66) and of 0.5 W/m²K in Silverstar 2000® glass (g = 0.37, τ = 0.57).

A further possibility is presented by inserting various suspended low-E coated films between the insulating glass panes; this saves the weight and thickness of a third pane of glass. HIT® glass with two low-E coated films in a 60 mm cavity achieves a U-value of 0.6 W/m²K (e.g. g = 0.40 and τ = 0.55), and Superglass®, also with two low-E coated films, but with a smaller cavity of 17 mm to 33 mm, achieves a U-value of 0.7 W/m²K (g = 0.34, τ = 0.62).

The option of creating a vacuum in the cavity avoids the costs involved with using inert gases, but gives rise to other problems. The edge seal of vacuum glass must be extremely tight and able to withstand the stress from thermal expansion and shear forces between the glass panes. A glass edge seal (soldered glass) would seem to be suitable for such situations, but is associated with higher heat losses in the edge zone through conduction. Vacuum cavities also require spacers, or pillars, in the cavity itself. Their spacing and dimensions must be carefully balanced to fit in with the stress pattern across the surface of the glass, conduction at the contact points and the need for unobstructed visibility. At the US Solar Energy Research Institute (SERI, Golden, Colorado, USA) prototypes have been developed using very

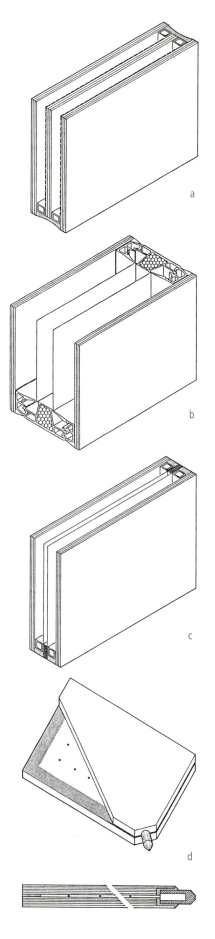

Verschiedene Typen von Isoliergläsern:
Dreifach-Isolierglas: a) Silverstar® 2000; Isoliergläser mit Folien: b) HIT® und c) Superglass®; d) Vakuumgläser mit Abstandhalter und Randverbund aus einer Glaslote.

Different types of insulating glass units:
Triple glazing: a) Silverstar® 2000; Insulating glass with films: b) HIT® and c) Superglass®; d) Vacuum glazing with spacer and soldered glass edge seal.

kugeln von 0.5 mm Durchmesser im Abstand von 50 mm untersucht worden. Aufgrund der Ergebnisse könnte ein Vakuumglas, bestehend aus zwei Scheiben mit einer Low-E Beschichtung, einen k-Wert von 0.6 W/m²K erreichen, doch wird die Entwicklung bis zur industriellen Reife noch einige Jahre in Anspruch nehmen.

Bei den Isoliergläsern finden alle bis jetzt beschriebenen Glasscheiben ihren Einsatz. Das Niederländische Architekturinstitut (NAI) in Rotterdam, vom Architekten Jo Coenen 1988–93 erbaut, kann als typisches Beispiel für die neuen Ganzglasfassaden mit Wärme- und Sonnenschutzfunktion angesehen werden.
Die Anlage befindet sich zwischen der stark befahrenen Rochussenstraat und dem Museumspark. Entlang der Straße erstreckt sich das Archivgebäude, welches die Besucher zum Eingang des Hauptgebäudes lenkt. Der viergeschossige, vollverglaste Baukörper wirkt wie in die monumentale Pergola eingehängt. Er beherbergt die Bibliothek und die Verwaltung, darunter liegen das Foyer und die Cafeteria. Seitlich ist die große Aula mit Galerien für Ausstellungen angeschlossen. Die Glasfassade ist eine Pfosten-Riegel-Konstruktion mit einem Achsabstand von 3.12 m und einer regelmäßigen Unterteilung von 1.12 m in der Höhe. Die Isoliergläser bestehen aus einem innenliegenden Verbundglas (4 + 4 mm) mit einer low-E Beschichtung, einem Zwischenraum von 16 mm mit Gasfüllung, und einer außenliegenden 8 mm dicken Scheibe.

small glass balls of 0.5 mm diameter, spaced at 50 mm. Tests indicate that these prototypes, used with a vacuum cavity between two panes of glass with a low-E coating, could achieve a U-value of 0.6 W/m²K, but several years work lie ahead before this type of glass can go into industrial production.

All the various types of glass so far described can be used in insulating glass units. A typical example of the new all-glass façades which provide thermal protection and solar shading is the Netherlands Architectural Institute (NAI) designed and built by the architect Jo Coenen between 1988 and 1993.
The building complex is located between the busy Rochussenstraat and the Museum Park. Following the line of the road is the archives building which leads the visitors to the entrance of the main building, a four-storey, fully glazed structure which appears to be suspended in a monumental pergola. Inside are the library and the administration areas with a foyer and cafeteria below. At the side there is access to the main auditorium with exhibition galleries. The glass façade is a mullion and transom frame construction with horizontal spacing of 3.12 m and a regular 1.12 m vertical spacing. The insulating glazing consists of an interior laminated glass unit (4 + 4 mm) with a low-E coating, a 16 mm cavity filled with gas, and an external 8 mm thick pane. The units are attached to the façade structure by means of an encircling EPDM gasket fixing system.

Klare Isoliergläser steigern die Transparenz und die Leichtigkeit eines Gebäudes.
Niederländisches Architekturinstitut, Rotterdam, 1988–93, Jo Coenen.
Clear insulating glass enhances the transparency and the lightness of a building.
Netherlands Architectural Institute, Rotterdam, 1988–93, Jo Coenen.

Sie sind mit einem umlaufenden Kunststoffprofil (EPDM) an der Fassadenkonstruktion befestigt.

Ein weiteres Beispiel einer vollverglasten Hülle ist der neue Flughafen von London, «Stansted», 1991 von Sir Norman Foster und Partner fertiggestellt. Ziel des Entwurfskonzepts war ein transparenter Terminal, welcher eine einfache Orientierung der Passagiere durch Sichtverbindung zu den Flugzeugen ermöglicht. Die eingeschossige Abfertigungshalle befindet sich zwischen dem geschlossenen Sockelgeschoß, das alle Serviceeinrichtungen beherbergt, und der filigranartigen Dachkonstruktion mit Gitterwerkkuppeln und Lichtöffnungen. Sie ist an allen vier Seiten durch eine 11.5 m hohe Glasfassade in Pfosten-Riegel-Bauweise abgeschlossen. Die Unterkonstruktion ist in Felder mit einem Achsabstand von 3.60 m und einer Höhe von 1.83 m unterteilt, auf welchen die Glaselemente durch Anpreßleisten von außen befestigt sind. Da die Glasfassade bei der Vorfahrt und der Flugpiste mit einem breiten Vordach weitgehend vor den Sonnenstrahlen geschützt ist, wurden hier nur transparente Isoliergläser eingesetzt. Dagegen sind die seitlichen, der Sonne ausgesetzten Ost- und Westfassaden im oberen Teil mit transluzenten Isoliergläsern ausgestattet. Um den wärmetechnischen Anforderungen zu genügen, wurden die Isoliergläser Climaplus® N verwendet. Der Aufbau der 3.6 x 1.83 m großen Glaselemente besteht aus einer außenliegenden vorgespannten, 8 mm dicken Scheibe, einem 16 mm breiten Zwischenraum

A further example of a fully glazed skin is the new London airport, Stansted, designed and built in 1991 by the architects Sir Norman Foster and Partners. The aim of the design was a transparent terminal which would facilitate passenger orientation by enabling visual contact with the aeroplanes.

The one-storey departures and arrivals hall is topped by a filigree roof construction with grid domes and light openings; below the hall is an enclosed basement containing all the services. The hall is enclosed on all four sides by an 11.5 m high framed façade in glass. The subframe grid is divided into rectangular sections, spaced 3.60 m horizontally and 1.83 m vertically. The glazing units are attached to this frame from the outside by means of a pressure caps system. As the glass façades facing the apron and at the passenger approach side are protected from the sun by a wide canopy, only standard transparent insulating glass was used here.

However, the east and west façades, both subject to strong solar radiation, have translucent insulating glass in the upper parts. The type of glass used to meet the thermal insulation requirements was Climaplus® N. The 3.6 x 1.83 m glazing units consist of an exterior, 8 mm thick pane of toughened glass, a 16 mm wide cavity filled with inert gas and an interior, 6 mm thick pane of toughened glass with a low-E coating.

The junction between roof edge and façade shows an interesting detail: as the movements between roof and façade can be as much as 20 cm

Transparente und transluzente Isoliergläser wurden miteinander kombiniert, um Durchsicht und Blendschutz sicherzustellen (links); für die Verbindung von Dach und Glasfassade wurde ein spezielles, scherenförmiges Verbindungsteil entwickelt.
Flughafen «Stansted», London, 1981–91, Sir Norman Foster und Partner.

Transparent and translucent insulating glass are combined to achieve transparence and protection from glare. A special, scissors-like connector was developed for the junction of roof and glass façade.
Stansted Airport, London, 1981–91, Sir Norman Foster and Partners.

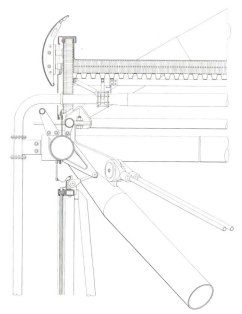

mit Edelgasfüllung und einer innenliegenden vorgespannten, 6 mm dicken low-E-beschichteten Scheibe.

Interessant ist das Anschlußdetail zwischen Dachrand und Fassade. Da die Bewegungen zwischen Dach und Fassade in den drei Richtungen bis zu 20 cm ausmachen, wurde ein Verbindungselement entwickelt, welches nur die horizontalen und nicht die vertikalen Lasten überträgt. Die verbleibende horizontale Fuge ist durch einen transparenten, 12 mm dicken Glasstreifen und eine Kunststoffmembrane luftdicht abgeschlossen.

Einen interessanten Lösungsansatz bietet die Verwendung von Sonnenschutzgläsern mit verschiedenen Reflexionseinstellungen im selben Objekt. Die Verglasung der ersten U-Bahn-Station in Genua, vom Renzo Piano Building Workshop 1990 erbaut, besteht aus Gläsern mit unterschiedlich blauen Reflexionsgrad. Sie sind hinsichtlich ihrer Lage in bezug auf die Neigungswinkel und die entsprechende Sonneneinstrahlung gewählt, wobei die Unterschiede von bloßem Auge kaum feststellbar sind. Die Verglasung besteht aus Isoliergläsern von etwa 60 x 240 cm Größe. Außenliegend wurden blaue Reflexionsgläser mit einer Lichtdurchlässigkeit τ von 0.18, 0.27 und 0.36 (SolarSiv®) gewählt, innenliegend ein Verbundglas wegen der Bruchgefahr durch den erhöhten Luftdruck beim Einfahren der U-Bahn-Züge. Die Scheiben sind mit Silikon auf horizontallaufende Profile aus Aluminium verklebt und

in any of three directions, a scissors-like connection was developed which would transfer only the horizontal and not the vertical loads. The remaining horizontal gap is an airtight joint consisting of a transparent, 12 mm thick glass strip and a plastic membrane.

Seldom insulating glass with different reflective properties is used in the same building. An example is Renzo Piano's underground station in Genoa, built in 1990, uses insulating glass with varying blue reflection properties according to their position on the building's skin and their angle in relation to the sun. The differences are hardly perceptible to the human eye.

The glazing units are of insulating glass and approximately 60 x 240 cm in size. On the outer layer blue reflecting glass is used, with a light transmittance τ of 0.18, 0.27 and 0.36 (SolarSiv®). The inner layer is a laminated glass to meet the safety requirements in view of increased air pressure caused by incoming trains. The panes are silicon-bonded onto horizontal aluminium profiles, and secured with safety clamps to guard against loosening. The glazing support frame is fixed directly to the steel arch structure by means of cast aluminium elements. The whole structure of the underground station is basically a barrel vault composed of 36 two-pin curved steel girders divided into five sections which are cross-braced in a longitudinal direction.

Die Isoliergläser mit unterschiedlich blauen Reflexionsscheiben wurden in bezug auf die Neigungswinkel und die entsprechende Sonneneinstrahlung gewählt.
U-Bahn-Station, Genua, 1990,
Renzo Piano Building Workshop.
Insulating glass with varying blue reflection properties according to the position of the individual panes in relation to the sky.
Underground station, Genoa, Italy, 1990,
Renzo Piano Building Workshop.

mit Sicherungsklammern gegen das Ablösen versehen. Die Unterkonstruktion ist durch Gußteile
aus Aluminium direkt auf der Tragstruktur aus
gebogenen Stahlträgern befestigt. Im Prinzip bildet die Konstruktion ein Tonnengewölbe aus 36
zweigelenkigen Bogenträgern, die in fünf Abschnitte unterteilt und mit Kreuzverbänden in der
Längsrichtung ausgesteift sind.

Ungewöhnlich ist auch der Einsatz von geprägtem Gußglas. Das Glasdesign für den Hauptsitz
der Lloyd's Versicherungsgesellschaft in London,
von Richard Rogers Partnership 1986 fertiggestellt, hat eine fast zweijährige Entwicklungs-
arbeit beansprucht. Zunächst waren hohe Anforderungen an die lichttechnischen Eigenschaften
gestellt: Einerseits sollte eine gute Streuung des
Tageslichts erreicht werden, um den Innenraum
weitgehend auszuleuchten, andererseits eine diffuse Reflexion des Kunstlichts im Raum selbst, so
daß abends keine Vorhänge nötig sind. Auch die
Herstellung bereitete einige Probleme, so die
Einhaltung des strengen geometrischen Noppen-
musters, die Notwendigkeit der Vorspannung sowie die Realisierung einer geeigneten Oberfläche
für eine gute Haftung des Randverbundes. Bei
der Ausführung wurden beide Glasoberflächen
geprägt, die eine mit einem engen, kontinuierli-
chen Raster, die andere mit einem breiteren, linsenförmigen Design, das von der Abwicklung des
Walzendurchmessers und der Unterteilung der
Fassade bestimmt wurde.

Die Verwendung emailbeschichteter Gläser in
der Isolierverglasung stellt ein Sonderthema dar.
Seit längerer Zeit sind in der Fassadengestaltung
vollflächige, undurchsichtige Glasscheiben im
Brüstungs- und Deckenbereich bekannt. Dagegen ist der Einsatz von Scheiben mit bedruckten Mustern relativ neu. In der Automobilindu-
strie werden emailbeschichtete Scheiben sowohl
aus funktionellen als auch aus ästhetischen
Gründen verwendet. Die schwarzen, emaillierten
Randstreifen der Front- und Heckscheiben schützen die Klebefläche zwischen Glas und Karosserie
vor der negativen Auswirkung der UV-Strahlung.
Inzwischen sind solche Streifen aus dekorativen
Gründen immer breiter und mit verlaufendem
Bedruckungsgrad gestaltet worden.
Bei der Gestaltung von Glasfassaden ist eine ähn-
liche Entwicklung festzustellen. In den 70er
Jahren waren emaillierte Randstreifen beim rah-
menlosen «Structural glazing» notwendig, um

Rolled glass is a type of glass seldom used. The
patterned glass used by the Richard Rogers
Partnership for the headquarters of Lloyd's
Insurance in London in 1986 took almost two
years to develop. High technical optical specifications were required of the glass: on the one hand
it should achieve an optimum scattering of daylight, to bring light into the back of the offices,
and on the other it should be capable of diffusely
reflecting the artificial light in the interior, so as
to obviate the need for screening the windows
from the inside in the evening. Manufacturing
problems were encountered, e.g. in producing
an even geometric sparkle pattern, in toughening
the glass panes and in producing a suitable surface for a good seal at the edges. In fact both sides
of the glass were rolled, one side being pressed
with a narrow continuous grid pattern, the other
with a wider lens-shaped design determined by
the diametre of the metal roller and the division
of the façade.

The use of fritted glass in insulated glazing units
is a special topic. Large expanses of non-transparent glass panels have long been used for parapets and spandrels in façade design, but the use
of patterned glass is relatively new. In the auto-
mobile industry fritted glass panes are used for
both functional and aesthetic reasons. The
black fritted edge strip on the front and rear
windscreens protects the seal between the glass
and the bodywork from the negative effects of
ultraviolet radiation. These strips have gradually become wider and more decorative,

Isoliergläser mit geprägtem Gußglas sind unge-
wöhnlich. Das in fast zweijähriger Arbeit entwickelte
«Lloyd's»-Design soll eine gute Streuung des Tages-
lichts und eine diffuse Reflexion der künstlichen
Beleuchtung im Innenraum erreichen.
Lloyd's Hauptsitz, London, 1978–86,
Richard Rogers Partnership.
*Insulating glass units with rolled glass are seldom
used: Developed over a two year period, this special
"Lloyd's" glass is reputed to both scatter daylight
well and to give diffuse reflection of the artificial
lighting inside.*
*Lloyd's Headquarters, London, 1978–86,
Richard Rogers Partnership.*

die Klebeflächen des Randverbundes gegen die UV-Strahlung zu schützen. Dann kam aus mehr ästhetischen als funktionellen Gründen die Idee auf, auch die restliche Fläche mit Mustern zu versehen. Das Musterdesign und der Bedruckungsgrad können auch als Sonnenschutzmaßnahme eingesetzt werden, weil der Durchlaßfaktor g genau nach den Anforderungen eingestellt werden kann. Dagegen hat eine Emailbeschichtung keine Auswirkung auf den k-Wert eines Isolierglases. Bedruckungsmuster können interessante Tiefenwirkungen erzielen, da sie aus großer Entfernung wie ein Schleier wirken, der sich, aus der Nähe betrachtet, auflöst. Der Vorhangeffekt kann sich aber als Nachteil herausstellen, besonders wenn emailbeschichtete Gläser im Durchsichtsbereich eingesetzt werden.

Emailbeschichtete Gläser wurden für die Fassade des 1989 fertiggestellten Bürogebäudes «B3», heute British Petroleum, Stockley Park, London, von Sir Norman Foster und Partner, verwendet.

sometimes printed with a decreasing pattern. In the design of glass façades a similar development can be observed. In the 1970s a fritted edge strip for use in "structural glazing" was necessary to protect the edge seal agains ultraviolet radiation. The idea was then developed, more for aesthetic reasons than functional ones, of extending the pattern to cover the whole of the glass surface. The pattern and the extent of cover can also be used for solar shading, because the total solar energy transmission coefficient, g-value, can be set exactly to the required specifications. On the other hand a fritted surface has no effect on the U-value of insulating glass. Fritted glass can achieve interesting veiling effects, because the further you are away from the glass, the more difficult it is to see through it. This "curtain" effect can be a disadvantage, particularly when fritted glass is used for glazing at view out level.

Fritted glazing was used by Sir Norman Foster and Partners in the façade of the B3 office build-

Isoliergläser mit Emaillerastern können eine Schleierwirkung hervorrufen. Im Durchsichtsbereich wurden Scheiben mit einem weißen Rand und punktförmigen Verlaufrastern eingesetzt.
Gebäude «B3», heute British Petroleum, Stockley Park, London, 1989, Sir Norman Foster und Partner.
Fritted glazing can achieve veiling effects. A fritted glass with a white edge and decreasing dot pattern was used for the window sections.
"B3" building, today British Petroleum, Stockley Park, London, 1989, Sir Norman Foster and Partners.

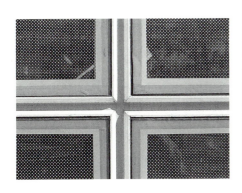

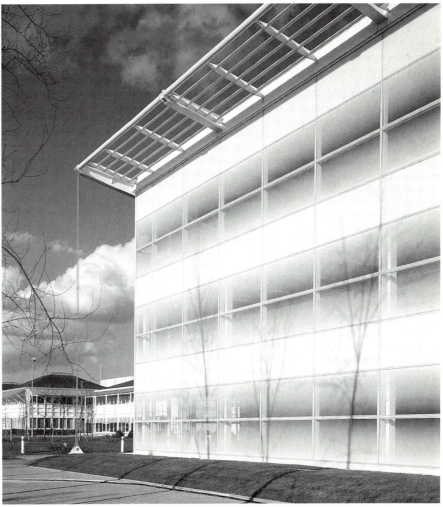

Im Bereich der Deckenkonstruktion sind vollflächig weiß emaillierte Scheiben eingesetzt worden, im Durchsichtsbereich der Büros ein Klarglas mit einem weißen Rand und punktförmigen Verlaufrastern mit einem Bedruckungsgrad von 5 % bis 95 %. Das Isolierglas besteht aus zwei vorgespannten, 6 mm dicken Scheiben mit einer Low-E Beschichtung; der k-Wert beträgt 1.6 W/m²K, der g-Wert 0.48 und der τ-Wert 0.60. Die Glaselemente wurden bei der Herstellung mit einem umlaufenden Rahmen versehen, welcher einerseits der Einhängung in die Pfosten-Riegel-Konstruktion dient, andererseits als mechanische Halterung der Glasscheibe. Die 15 mm breiten Fugen zwischen den Glaselementen sind mit grauem Silikon versiegelt.

Ebenfalls im Stockley Park steht das Bürogebäude «B8» von Ian Ritchie Architects, das nach dem Prinzip «Kern und Hülle» in 36 Wochen Bauzeit 1990 fertiggestellt wurde. Aus Zeitgründen ist die Glasfassade mit kleinen Änderungen aus dem standardisierten Planar®-System entwickelt worden. Die 1.385 x 3 m großen Isoliergläser sind in den vier Ecken mit der punktförmigen Befestigung Planar® 905 versehen und durch Edelstahlkonsolen an die tragenden Pfosten eingehängt. Ihr Aufbau besteht aus einer innenliegenden vorgespannten, 6 mm dicken Scheibe mit einer Low-E Beschichtung, einem Zwischenraum von 16 mm mit Argonfüllung und einer außenliegenden vorgespannten, 12 mm dicken Scheibe, die im Decken- und Brüstungsbereich eine

ing, now British Petroleum offices, at Stockley Park, completed in 1989. White fritted glass was used at the level of the floor slabs. For the transparent view out sections clear glass with a white edge and a decreasing dot pattern covering between 5 % and 95 % was used. The insulating glass consists of two panes of 6 mm toughened glass with a low-E coating; the U-value is 1.6 W/m²K, the g-value is 0.48 and the τ-value is 0.60. At the manufacturing stage the glass elements were fitted with an edge frame which would both hold the glass in position and serve as the fixing attachment to the façade sup-port frame. The 15 mm wide joints between the glazing units are sealed with a grey silicon seal.

Also in Stockley Park is the B8 office building by Ian Ritchie Architects which was built on the "shell and core" principle in a period of 36 weeks in 1990. For reasons of time the glass used for the façade was a modified version of the standardised Planar® system. The 1.385 x 3 m sized insulating glass units are fitted at four corners with Planar® 905 bolts and suspended in stainless steel pins bolted to the mullions. The inward-facing side of each unit is a 6 mm toughened pane with low-E coating, and on the outside is a 12 mm toughened pane; between these two panes is a 16 mm cavity filled with argon gas. On the outside at the level of the parapets and floor slabs, the glazing has a fritted stripe pattern with 70 % cover. The unusual thickness of the outer

Isoliergläser mit einem Streifenmuster wurden für ie Abgrenzung des Duchsichtsbereichs eingesetzt. Die ungewöhnlich dicke Außenscheibe verleiht der Fassade einen Grünstich. Die Scheiben sind durch Bolzen an den vier Ecken befestigt.

Gebäude «B8», Stockley Park, London, 1990, Ian Ritchie Architecs.

Insulating glazing with fritted stripe pattern was used to define the view out. The unusual thickness of the outer pane gives the façade a green tint. The glass units are fixed at four corners with bolts.

"B8" building, Stockley Park, London, 1990, Ian Ritchie Architects.

weiße Emailbeschichtung mit einem Streifenmuster und einem Bedruckungsgrad von 70 % aufweist. Die ungewöhnliche Dicke der Außenscheibe ist aus akustischen Gründen wegen des naheliegenden Heliports notwendig und verleiht der Fassade den typischen Grünstich der Glasmasse. Die 12 mm breiten Fugen sind mit schwarzem Silikon abgedichtet.

Die Schleierwirkung kann auch ein wesentliches Merkmal eines Gestaltungskonzeptes bilden, wie bei der Glasfassade des Verwaltungsgebäudes für «Cartier» in Fribourg, Schweiz, 1990, der Architekten Jean Nouvel, Emmanuel Cattani und Associés. Die Glaswand dient als Werbeträger der Firma und ist einfach und direkt mit dem Schriftzug «Cartier» versehen. Da die Lage in Sichtweite der Autobahn eine gewisse Dynamik mit sich bringt und eine banale Wiederholung monoton wäre, wurde der Kontrast Schrift zu Hintergrund, positiv zu negativ, allmählich umgekehrt und aufgelöst. Der Effekt entsteht durch die Kombination von Punktmustern mit zwei unterschiedlichen Bedruckungsgraden. Dafür wurde auf der innenliegenden Seite des Isolierglases eine silberfarbige Beschichtung kalt aufgetragen, welche den Unterschied zwischen bedruckten und unbedruckten Flächen durch die Spiegelung des umliegenden Panoramas zusätzlich steigert.

panes is necessary to give acoustic protection from a nearby heliport. This thickness also gives rise to the characteristic green tint of the glass façade. The 12 mm joints are sealed with black silicon.

The veiling effects which can be achieved on glass can be used as a major component of the design concept of a building, as, for example, the glass façade of the "Cartier" administration building in Fribourg, Switzerland, built by Jean Nouvel, Emmanuel Cattani and Associés in 1990.
The glass wall serves as an advertising carrier for the company with the wording "Cartier" appearing simply and directly on the façade itself. As the building's location within sight of the motorway lends a certain dynamism to the situation, the monotony which would result from simple repetition of the wording has been avoided through a gradually reversed contrast between wording and background across the length of the façade – from positive to negative.
He achieves this effect by using two dot patterns with varying coverage; on the inside of the insulating glass a silvery coating was cold applied, which further increases the difference between printed and unprinted sections by reflecting the surrounding panorama.

Mit Schriftzügen bedruckte Gläser können als Werbeträger dienen. Das Logo «Cartier» wird hier durch die Wechselwirkung zwischen Buchstaben und Hintergrund hervorgehoben.
«Cartier»-Gebäude, Fribourg, Schweiz, 1990, Jean Nouvel, Emmanuel Cattani und Associés.
Glazing printed with wording serves as an advertising carrier: the logo "Cartier" is emphasized through a gradually reversed contrast between lettering and background
Cartier building, Fribourg, Switzerland, 1990, Jean Nouvel, Emmanuel Cattani and Associates.

Füllungen mit wärmedämmenden Eigenschaften

Transparente Wärmedämmungen (TWD) sind weitere Maßnahmen zur Senkung der Wärmeverluste. Ihr Vorteil gegenüber den üblichen Wärmedämmungen ist ihre hohe Durchlässigkeit für die eintreffende Licht- und Wärmestrahlung, was die zusätzliche Nutzung der Sonnenenergie ermöglicht.

Da die transparenten Wärmedämmungen meistens lichtstreuend sind, wird die diffuse Transmission τ_{diff} maßgebend.

Zur Anwendung kommen transparente und transluzente Materialien wie Glas, Acrylglas (PMMA), Polycarbonat (PC) und Quarzschaum in verschiedener Schichtdicke und Strukturierung. Da sie einen Schutz vor Witterung und mechanischer Beschädigung benötigen, werden sie zwischen zwei Scheiben eingebaut.

Eine Aufteilung nach vier unterschiedlichen geometrischen Anordnungen der Struktur vereinfacht die Übersicht.

Eine erste Gruppe bilden mehrere, parallel zur Außenfläche hintereinander angeordnete Ebenen, die getrennte Luftschichten bilden. Dieses Anordnungsprinzip bringt höhere Reflexionsverluste mit sich, die zum Teil mit antireflektierenden Beschichtungen zu mildern sind. Es bietet aber dafür die Möglichkeit, mehrere Low-E Beschichtungen einzusetzen, welche die Wärmeverluste durch Abstrahlung reduzieren. Zu dieser Gruppe gehören Mehrfachverglasungen,

Fillings with Insulating Properties

Transparent insulation materials (TIM) are a further device used to reduce heat losses. The advantage of TIM over traditional insulation lies in their high transmission of incident light and near infrared radiation which leaves the possibility open for exploiting the solar energy.

As most transparent insulation materials scatter light, light transmission is given in terms of diffuse transmission, or τ_{diff}.

Various transparent and translucent materials can be used for transparent insulation, such as glass, acrylic glass (PMMA), polycarbonate (PC) and quartz foam, in varying thicknesses and structures. To protect them from the effects of weather and mechanical stress, these layers are sandwiched between two panes of glass.

A division into generic types of geometric media of the structure simplifies their classification. The first group consists of a build-up of several layers, arranged behind one another parallel to the glass surfaces and enclosing separate air spaces. This arrangement entails higher reflection losses, an effect which can be partly reduced by the use of anti-reflection coatings. However this type offers the possibility of using several low-E coatings to reduce heat loss through reradiation. Examples in this first category are glazing systems comprising multiple panes of glass, such as double or triple glazings, or plastic films. A second group are the structures arranged perpendicular to the exterior surface, such as louvres, honeycombs and capillaries, which divide

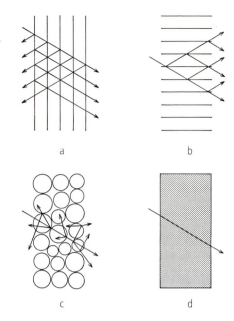

Transparente Wärmedämmungen können nach vier geometrischen Ordnungsprinzipien eingeteilt werden:
a) Strukturen parallel zur äußeren Glasebene;
b) Strukturen senkrecht zur äußeren Glasebene;
c) Kammerstrukturen; d) quasi-homogene Strukturen.
Transparent insulation materials can be classified into four geometric structure types: a) structures parallel to the exterior surface; b) structures perpendicular to the exterior surface; c) cavity structures; d) quasi-homogeneous structures.

Verschiedene transparente Wärmedämmungen:
TWD®-Wabenstrukturen, Oka-Lux®-Kapillarstrukuren und Basogel®-Aerogelkügelchen.
Different transparent insulation materials: TWD®-honeycomb structures, Oka-Lux® capillary structures and granular aerogel Basogel®.

Den Wabenstrukturen wurde eine mit einem farbigen Bandmuster bedruckte Außenscheibe vorgelagert. Technorama-Gebäude, Düsseldorf, 1990, Gottfried Böhm.

An outer pane printed with a coloured stripe pattern is placed in front of the honeycomb structures. Technorama building, Düsseldorf, 1990, Gottfried Böhm.

Isolierglas mit eingelegten Kapillarstrukuren: Oka-Lux®.

Insulating glass unit with integrated capillary structures: Oka-Lux®.

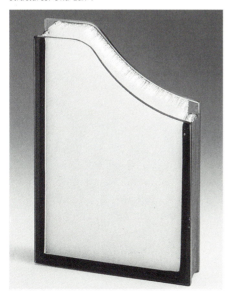

wie Zweifach- und Dreifachisoliergläser, sowie Mehrfachfoliensysteme.

Eine zweite Gruppe stellen senkrecht zur Außenfläche gerichtete Strukturen dar, wie Lamellen, Waben oder Kapillaren, die den Scheibenzwischenraum in kleine Luftzellen unterteilen. Diese Anordnung weist den Vorteil geringerer Reflexionverluste auf, da die einfallende Sonnenstrahlung durch Mehrfachreflexion an den parallelen Wänden weitergeleitet wird, was zusätzlich für die Tiefenausleuchtung von Räumen mit Tageslicht benutzt werden kann. Ein anderer Vorteil ist die weitgehende Ausschaltung der Konvektion, die durch das Verhältnis der Zellendurchmesser zur Tiefe bestimmt wird. Wabenstrukturen bestehen aus transparentem Polycarbonat (PC) mit UV-stabilisierenden Zusätzen. Sie werden als endlose Multistegplatte mit quadratischen Zellenquerschnitten von 4 mm Seitenlänge in einer Breite von 700 mm und einer Höhe von 15 mm extrudiert (AREL®, TWD® Kaiser). Danach werden sie in der gewünschten Länge mittels Heizdrahttechnik geschnitten und so die Seiten automatisch miteinander verschweißt. Eine Färbung des Kunststoffes ist möglich, was allerdings eine höhere Absorption bewirkt. Die Wabenstrukturen werden bei der üblichen Einbaudicke von 50 mm bis 100 mm lose in eine Doppelverglasung eingeschlossen. Der k-Wert einer 100 mm dicken Wabenstruktur (PC) liegt zwischen 0.80 und 0.90 W/m²K, der τ_{diff}-Wert bei 0.57 und der g_{diff}-Wert bei 0.64. Ein Beispiel für die Anwendung transparenter Wärmedämmung bietet das Technorama-Gebäude in Düsseldorf, von Architekt Gottfried Böhm 1990 in Zusammenarbeit mit dem Ingenieurbüro Kaiser Bautechnik erstellt. Hier wird eine mit einem farbigen Bandmuster bedruckte Außenscheibe dem regelmäßigen Lochbild der Wabenstruktur spielerisch vorgelagert, was der Fassade eine Tiefenwirkung verleiht. Kapillarstrukturen sind aus vielen Röhrchen aus Kunststoff oder Glas zusammengesetzt. Die Kunststoffröhrchen aus Acryl (PMMA) oder Polycarbonat (PC) haben einen Durchmesser von 1–4 mm, je nachdem, ob vorwiegend lichtstreuende Eigenschaften oder eine hohe Strahlungstransmission gefragt sind. Sie werden aufeinandergeschichtet und mittels Heizdrahttechnik in der benötigten Dicke geschnitten und damit automatisch am Rand zusammengeklebt. Eine 100 mm dicke Kapillarplatte aus Polycarbonatröhrchen von 3 mm Durchmesser erreicht einen k-Wert von

the cavity into small air cells. This type has the advantage of lower optical losses, as the incoming beam is reflected several times from the parallel surfaces and transmitted in a forward direction. This opens up the possibility of increasing levels of natural daylight at the back of deep rooms. A further advantage is that convection currents are suppressed, an effect resulting from the relationship between the diameter and the depth of the air spaces.

Honeycomb structures consist of transparent polycarbonate (PC) with ultraviolet-stabilising additives. They are extruded as continuous honeycomb structures, 700 mm wide and 15 mm high (AREL®, TWD®Kaiser); the rectangular honeycomb cells have 4 mm side lengths. These structures are then cut to the required length using resistance wire technology, and the sides are automatically welded together. The material can be colour-tinted, but this leads to higher absorption. Generally these honeycomb structures are used in thicknesses of between 50 mm and 100 mm, and they are sandwiched loosely in a double glazed unit. The U-value of a 100 mm thick honeycomb structure (PC) is between 0.80 and 0.90 W/m²K, the τ_{diff} value is approximately 0.57 and the g_{diff} is 0.64.

An example of the use of transparent insulation material is in the Technorama building in Düsseldorf, designed in 1990 by Gottfried Böhm, in collaboration with Kaiser Bautechnik. Here a playful effect is created by placing a pane of glass with a coloured stripe pattern in front of the regular cell spacing of the TIM honeycomb structure. This has the effect of adding depth to the façade.

Capillary structures are made up of many small plastic or glass tubes. The plastic tubes, of acrylic (PMMA) or polycarbonate (PC), have a diameter of 1–4 mm, depending on whether light-scattering properties or higher radiation transmission are desired. The tubes are built up in layers and cut to the desired thickness by means of resistance wire technology and automatically bonded together at the edges. A 100 mm thick capillary sheet made from acrylic tubes, 3 mm in diameter, will achieve a U-value of 0.89 W/m²K and a τ_{diff} of 0.69 (Oka-Lux®).

Capillary structures made of glass have great resistance to high temperatures and are more durable than plastic, but require an extremely careful choice of diameter and thickness, as glass has a seven times higher heat conductivity

0.89 W/m²K und einen τ_{diff} von 0.69 (Oka-Lux®). Kapillarstrukturen aus Glas weisen eine große Beständigkeit gegenüber hohen Temperaturen und eine längere Lebensdauer als Kunststoff auf, verlangen aber eine äußerst sorgfältige Optimierung bei der Wahl von Durchmesser und Wandstärke, da Glas eine siebenfach höhere Wärmeleitung als Kunststoff aufweist. Prototypen mit Röhrchen von 1–8 mm Durchmesser, einer Wandstärke von 0.1 mm und 100 mm Länge haben k-Werte von 1 W/m²K erzielt.

Ein drittes Prinzip stellen Kammerstrukturen dar, die aus der Kombination von parallelen und senkrechten Anordnungen resultieren. Dazu gehören Materialien mit Strukturen in der Größenordnung von einigen Millimetern, wie Acrylschaum. Obwohl sich damit Wärmeverluste durch Konvektion weitgehend ausschalten lassen, sind die Verluste durch Reflexion, wie bei den parallelen Strukturen, und durch die Wärmetransporte mittels Wärmeleitung maßgebend.

Der vierten Gruppe werden quasi-homogene Strukturen zugeordnet, wie Aerogele und Xerogele, die mikroskopische Kammerstrukturen aufweisen. Ein Aerogel ist ein hochporöses filigranes Skelett aus 2–5 % Silikat und 95–98 % Luftfüllung, das eine hohe Strahlungsdurchlässigkeit und Wärmedämmfähigkeit aufweist.

Beide Eigenschaften sind auf seine Struktur zurückzuführen. Da die Skelettpartikel kleinere Dimensionen als der größte Teil der sichtbaren Wellenlängen aufweisen, bewirken sie eine minimale Lichtstreuung, und das Auge nimmt das Aerogel als homogenes Material wahr. Hingegen ist die milchige oder leicht bläuliche Färbung auf die Absorption von kleinen Inhomogenitäten in der Struktur zurückzuführen. Hinsichtlich der Wärmedämmeigenschaften sind die Dimensionen der Luftzellen ausschlaggebend. Da sie weniger als 20 nm groß sind, werden die Luftmoleküle in ihrer Bewegung gehindert, was die Konvektion reduziert. Der Wärmetransport dagegen wird durch kontinuierliche Absorptions- und Emissionsprozesse im Material selbst stark gedämpft. Damit kann ein Isolierglas mit einer Füllung aus einer 20 mm dicken Aerogelplatte einen theoretischen k-Wert von 0.7 W/m²K und eine Strahlungstransmission von 0.69 τ_{diff} erreichen. Die Wärmedämmeigenschaften lassen sich durch Evakuierung des Zwischenraumes zusätzlich verbessern, und der k-Wert könnte mit einem Druck von 50–100 mbar bis auf 0.37 W/m²K gesenkt werden. Da die monolithische Füllung gleichzei-

than plastic. 100 mm thick prototypes with tubes of 1–8 mm diametre and of 0.1 mm wall thickness have achieved U-values of 1 W/m²K.

A third variety is the cavity type, which combines parallel and vertical structures. Here materials with bubble structures in the order of a few millimeters are used, such as acrylic foam. Although these largely suppress heat losses through convection, the losses through reflection, as with the parallel structures, and through heat conduction are a limiting factor.

The fourth group consists in the quasi-homogeneous structures, such as aerogels and xerogels which have microscopic cavity structures. An aerogel is a highly porous filigree structure of 2–5 % silicate and 95–98 % air interspace.

It has high radiation transmission and thermal insulation properties. Both properties are a result of its structure. Since most of the particles in the structure are smaller than the wavelengths of visible light, they are not strongly scattering, and the eye perceives the aerogel as a homogeneous material. The milky or slightly blue tinge, however, is due to the absorption of small non-uniformities in the structure. With regard to the thermal insulation properties the dimensions of the air microcells are critical. As they are smaller than 20 nm, the movement of the air molecules is restricted and convection is reduced. Heat transport on the other hand is strongly suppressed by the continuous absorption and reradiation processes in the material itself. Thus insulating glass with a filling of 20 mm thick aerogel can have a theoretical U-value of 0.7 W/m²K and a transmission of $\tau_{diff.} = 0.69$. The thermal insulation properties can be additionally increased by creating a vacuum in the cavity, and at a pressure of 50–100 mbar the U-value could be reduced to 0.37 W/m²K. As the monolithic filling also acts as a spacer between the two panes of glass, it simplifies the manufacturing process for vacuum insulating glass.

Development work is being carried out on these areas at present, with the aim of bringing onto the market a product with a U-value below 0.4 W/m²K, which would mean 0.5 W/m²K for a 1 x 1 m unit.

Apart from improvements in light transmission, transparence and thermal insulating properties there are further problems encountered with the aerogels. The edge seal should have low heat conductivity and remain completely tight, because aerogels are very susceptible to water pen-

tig als Abstandhalter für die beiden Scheiben dient, wird die Herstellung eines Vakuumisolierglases vereinfacht. Aufgrund solcher Voraussetzungen sind Forschungsarbeiten im Gange, um ein Produkt mit einem k-Wert unter 0.4 W/m²K, was 0.5 W/m²K für ein 1 x 1 m großes Element mit Randverbund bedeutet, zur Marktreife zu entwickeln.

Neben der Verbesserung bezüglich Lichtdurchlässigkeit, Transparenz und Wärmedämmeigenschaften sind aber bei den Aerogelen noch weitere Probleme zu lösen. Der Randverbund soll eine niedrige Wärmeleitfähigkeit aufweisen und vollständig dicht bleiben, weil Aerogele aufgrund der Kapillarkräfte hochgradig wasserempfindlich sind.

Zurzeit ist die Herstellung von Aerogelplatten auf eine Größe von bis zu 60 x 60 x 3 cm beschränkt, weil sie sehr aufwendig und damit teuer ist (Airglass AB, Schweden). Einerseits ist ein spezielles Trocknungsverfahren mit hohem Druck und hoher Temperatur notwendig, andererseits muß die Platte selbst planparallel und ohne Oberflächenfehler sein, um die optischen Qualitäten von Glas zu erreichen.

Eine kostengünstigere Alternative bietet die Herstellung von Aerogelkügelchen von 1–6 mm Durchmesser, die lose in den Scheibenzwischenraum eingefüllt werden. Das Granulat weist allerdings etwas schlechtere optische und thermische Eigenschaften auf. Die Reflexion wird wegen der vielen Kugeloberflächen erhöht, was die Transmission vermindert. Die Füllung wirkt zudem lichtstreuend und weniger durchsichtig. Wegen

etration due to their capillary structure. At present the manufacture of monolithic aerogels is limited to a panel size of 60 x 60 x 3 cm, because their production is very complicated and expensive (Airglass AB, Sweden). On the one hand a special high-pressure, high-temperature drying process is needed, on the other the panel faces must be absolutely parallel and have no surface flaws, so as to achieve the required optical specification of the glass.

A less expensive alternative is the manufacture of granular aerogel which consists of 1–6 mm diameter pellets loosely poured in the cavity between the panes. However, this granular form of aerogel has poorer optical and thermal properties. Reflection is increased due to the many surfaces of the spheres, which reduces transmission. In addition this type of filling scatters light and is less transparent. The spaces between the pellets also lead to a reduction in thermal insulation properties; thus a 16 mm thick granular aerogel filling achieves a U-value of under 0.8 W/m²K, a τ_{diff} of 0.41 and a g_{diff} of 0.52.

Xerogel is very similar to aerogel, but cheaper because it needs no special drying process during manufacture. As its structure is less homogeneous and the air spaces are larger, xerogel has better radiation transmission but worse thermal insulation properties than aerogel.

A comparison of the four groups of transparent insulating materials makes it clear that not only the physical properties of the material have to be taken into consideration, but also the type of use to which the material will be put and the

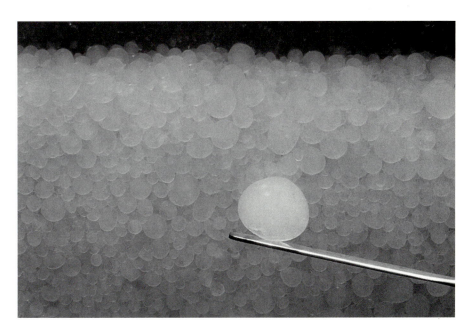

Kügelchen aus Aerogel: Basogel®.
Granular form of aerogel: Basogel®.

der Kugelzwischenräume werden auch die Wärmedämmeigenschaften schlechter; so weist eine 16 mm dicke Granulatfüllung einen k-Wert unter 0.8 W/m²K, ein τ_{diff} 0.41 und ein g_{diff} 0.52 auf.

Das Xerogel ist dem Aerogel sehr ähnlich, aber kostengünstiger, weil es ohne spezielles Trocknungsverfahren hergestellt wird. Da seine Struktur weniger homogen ist und die Luftzellen größer sind, weist das Xerogel eine bessere Strahlungstransmission, aber schlechtere Wärmedämmeigenschaften als das Aerogel auf.

Bei einem Vergleich der vier Gruppen transparenter Wärmedämmungen sind nicht nur bauphysikalische Eigenschaften maßgebend, sondern auch Überlegungen hinsichtlich Nutzung und Konstruktion zu berücksichtigen.

Heute sind Mehrfachglas- und Merhfachfoliensysteme bezüglich der Transparenz führend und damit für eine Verwendung im Durchsichtsbereich geeignet. Zudem erreichen sie k-Werte zwischen 0.7 W/m²K und 1 W/m²K. Dagegen sind die anderen Strukturen mehr oder weniger lichtstreuend und opak, was für Oberlichter und Brüstungsbereiche sowie für die passive Nutzung der Sonnenenergie durch Sonnenkollektoren und wärmespeichernde Wände geeigneter ist. Zurzeit weisen Waben- und Kapillarstrukturen eine bessere Strahlungstransmission auf als Aerogelkügelchen, obwohl ihre Einbaudicke 100 mm gegenüber den 16 mm eines Aerogelgranulats beträgt.

Eine Weiterentwicklung der monolithischen Aerogele, besonders hinsichtlich der Transparenz, ist vielversprechend. In einer Studie der Technical University of Denmark wurde geschätzt, daß die Verwendung von Aerogel-Isolierglas im Wohnungsbau eine Reduktion der Heizkosten um 20 % bewirken würde.

Transparente Wärmedämmungen sind Maßnahmen mit festen Eigenschaften. Die im Winter vorteilhaften Strahlungsdurchlässigkeits- und Wärmedämmeigenschaften entpuppen sich daher im Sommer als nachteilig. Zur Steuerung des Strahlungseinfalls im Sommer müssen Beschattungssysteme in Form von reflektierenden Geweberollos, Lamellenstoren oder Jalousien vorgesehen werden. In Zukunft könnten Systeme mit veränderbaren optischen Eigenschaften eingesetzt werden, wie thermochrome und elektrochrome Systeme.

Wenig erforscht sind bisher Wärmedämmfüllun-

way in which it is incorporated into the glazing units.

Today glazing systems comprising multiple panes of glass or plastic films lead the field in terms of transparence and thus are most suited for use where transparent glazing is needed. Moreover they reach U-values of between 0.7 W/m²K and 1 W/m²K. The other structures are more or less light-scattering and opaque, thus more suited for use in rooflights or parapets, as well as in passive solar energy measures such as solar collectors or thermal store walls. At present honeycomb and capillary structures have better radiation transmission properties than granular aerogels, although at 100 mm they are considerably thicker than the 16 mm of the granular aerogel.

The development of monolithic aerogels, particularly with regard to transparence, would seem to be very promising. In a study by the Technical University of Denmark it was estimated that the use of aerogel insulating glass in housing would lead to a 20 % reduction in heating costs.

Transparent insulation materials have fixed properties. Thus their radiation transmission and thermal insulation properties, which are so advantageous in winter, become a disadvantage in summer. To control incident solar radiation in summer, various shading systems are necessary in the form of reflecting fabric blinds or louvres. In future it could be possible to use systems with adjustable optical qualities, such as thermochromic or electrochromic systems.

Little research has so far been carried out on thermally insulating fillings with adjustable properties. For this purpose blinds with infrared-reflecting films and louvre systems with infrared-reflecting surfaces are used.

In the 1970s a system using polystyrene pellets was patented by Zomeworks, Albuquerque, USA. The antistatic granulate can, as required, either be blasted into or sucked out of an approximately 60 mm cavity between two panes of glass. As a result of the thickness of the layers a U-value of 0.6 W/m²K can be achieved. The disadvantage of this system lies in the extra space needed for the fan and the storage of the polystyrene pellets.

Fillings with Solar Shading Properties

Solar shading devices can be incorporated into the cavity between the glass panes. In summer they are intended to block direct sunlight and to prevent glare, without reducing the levels of light

gen mit veränderbaren Eigenschaften. Dafür werden Rollos mit IR-reflektierenden Folien sowie Lamellensysteme mit IR-reflektierenden Oberflächen verwendet.

In der 70er Jahren wurde ein System mit Styroporkügelchen von Zomeworks, Albuquerque, USA, patentiert. Das antistatisch behandelte Granulat wird je nach Bedarf in den etwa 60 mm breiten Scheibenzwischenraum einer Doppelverglasung eingeblasen oder abgesaugt. Aufgrund der Schichtdicke ergibt sich ein k-Wert von 0.6 W/m²K. Nachteilig ist der Platzbedarf für das Gebläse und den Kugelspeicher.

Füllungen mit sonnenschützenden Eigenschaften

Im Scheibenzwischenraum lassen sich auch Vorrichtungen zum Sonnenschutz unterbringen. Sie sollen im Sommer die direkte Strahlung und die Blendung abwehren, ohne die Raumbeleuchtung zu beeinträchtigen und ohne die Energiegewinne im Winter zu vermindern.

Sonnenschutzmaßnahmen mit festen Eigenschaften sind eingespannte Folien sowie Lamellen oder ähnliche Strukturen, welche entsprechend dem unterschiedlichen Sonnenstand ausgelegt sind. Solche Füllungen sollen keine Aufheizung des Scheibenzwischenraums verursachen, da sonst durch den wechselnden inneren Druck der Randverbund beschädigt würde.

Bei der Entwicklung von steuerbaren Sonnenschutzmaßnahmen, welche sich in den Scheibenzwischenraum einschließen lassen, versucht man, die Vorteile einer Anpassungsfähigkeit an die variablen Licht- und Wetterverhältnisse mit der Möglichkeit eines Schutzes gegen Luftverschmutzung und Witterungseinflüsse sowie einer Reduktion des Reinigungs- und Wartungsaufwands zu verbinden.

Elektrisch regelbare Beschattungssysteme, wie Rollos oder Lamellen, können samt den Elektromotoren in den Scheibenzwischenraum eingeschlossen werden. Da eine Betriebsstörung das Ersetzen der ganzen Scheibe zur Folge haben kann, wurden Produkte entwickelt, bei denen der Motor von der Seite oder von vorne entfernt werden kann.

Rollos werden mit Sonnenschutzgeweben oder -folien ausgestattet. Farbige Polyestergewebe sind an der Außenseite mit einer Aluminiumbeschichtung versehen, welche die Sonnenstrahlung reflektiert, die Wärmeabstrahlung und die Blendung vermindert (Trisolux®). Sonnenschutz-

in the room or the energy gains in winter.

Solar shading devices with fixed properties are films, louvres or similar structures positioned according to a particular angle of solar radiation. These fillings should not cause a rise in temperature in the space between the panes as this would produce varying pressures which would eventually damage the edge seal. Developments in controllable solar shading devices to be placed between panes have a three-fold aim: to exploit the advantages of systems which can adapt to variable light and weather conditions; to create the possibility of protection against pollution and weather influences; and to reduce the time and effort needed in cleaning and maintaining the devices. Electrically controlled shading systems such as blinds or louvres, together with their control mechanisms, can be incorporated in the cavity between the panes. As repairs to the mechanism would entail replacing a whole pane, products have been developed in which the motor can be removed from the side or the front. Roller blinds can be fitted with solar shading fabric layers or films. Coloured polyester blinds can have an aluminium coating on the outside to reflect radiation and to reduce thermal reradiation and glare (Trisolux®). Solar shading films are available in a variety of different reflection levels. They consist of two polyester films, each with a metal coating, which are laminated together. As the smooth surfaces would tend to act as a mirror, they have a textured surfacing (Agero®). Louvre systems offer a further possibility. In addition to the above-mentioned, fully integrated systems, products are available which can

Isolierglas mit im Scheibenzwischenraum integrierten Sonnenschutzrollos: Trisolux®.

Insulating glass with solar shading roller blinds integrated in the cavity between the panes: Trisolux®.

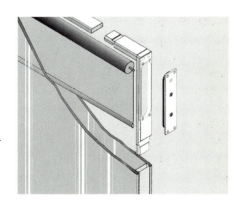

folien sind mit verschiedenen Reflexionsgraden erhältlich. Sie bestehen aus zwei Polyesterfolien, die mit einer Metallbeschichtung versehen und gegeneinander laminiert sind. Da sie glatt hochgradig spiegeln würden, werden sie mit einer Prägestruktur versehen (Agero®).

Systeme mit Lamellen stellen eine weitere Möglichkeit dar. Zusätzlich zu den obenerwähnten, vollkommen integrierten Systemen sind Produkte auf dem Markt, die mit einem elektromagnetischen Schieber von der Außenseite der Isolierscheibe verstellt werden können. Je nach Farbe, Beschichtung und Einstellungswinkel können g-Werte von 0.11 bis 0.77 erreicht werden (Luxaclair®, Velthec®).

Füllungen mit lichtumlenkenden Eigenschaften

Einen ganz anderen Lösungsansatz für den Sonnenschutz bieten Systeme zur Lichtumlenkung. Sie nutzen optische Gesetzmäßigkeiten wie Reflexion, Transmission oder Brechung, um einerseits das direkte Sonnenlicht auszublenden, andererseits das diffuse Tageslicht in den Innenraum durchzulassen oder sogar in die Raumtiefe zu lenken.

Das Sonnenschutzraster wurde von der Lichtplanung Christian Bartenbach und der Siemens AG entwickelt. Es besteht aus speziell geformten, mit Reinaluminium hochglänzend beschichteten Kunststofflamellen in Längs- und Querrichtung, die eine Struktur von eng aneinandergereihten kleinen Lichtschächten bilden. Aufgrund der Geometrie der Lamellenform und der Ausrichtung der Öffnungen nach Norden gelangt das diffuse Tageslicht ungehindert in den Innenraum, während die von Süden auftreffende direkte Sonnenstrahlung reflektiert wird.

Die Sonnenschutzraster finden hauptsächlich bei horizontalen Verglasungen Anwendung. Da die Orientierung genau der einfallenden Lichtstrahlung entsprechen muß, wird der Zuschnitt des Rasters nach Lage und Himmelsrichtung des Gebäudes durch Computerprogramme ermittelt. Der Einbau des Sonnenschutzrasters verändert den k-Wert einer Isolierverglasung kaum, und je nach Glasaufbau sind g-Werte um 0.2 erzielbar. Ein solches Sonnenschutzraster wurde für die Glasüberdachung des Kongreß- und Ausstellungsgebäudes in Linz, geplant von Herzog und Partner, 1993, verwendet. Die Tragstruktur des flachen Tonnengewölbes besteht aus besonders

be adjusted by means of a magnetic control operated from the outside of the insulating glass unit. Depending on colour, coating and angle, g-values of 0.11 to 0.77 can be achieved (Luxaclair®, Velthec®).

Fillings with Light Redirecting Properties

A completely different type of solar protection is offered by systems for light deflection. These exploit optical principles such as reflection, transmission or refraction in order to block direct sunlight on the one hand, and on the other to admit diffuse light into the interior or to deflect it into the back of the room.

The light-grid system has been developed by Lichtplanung Christian Bartenbach and Siemens AG. This device consists of specially shaped plastic louvres coated with highly reflective pure aluminium; the louvres are arranged in a regular grid pattern to create light shafts set next to each other in tight rows. The special shape of the louvres and the alignment of the openings towards the north create a situation whereby diffuse light can easily penetrate into the room while direct radiation from the south is reflected. The light-grid systems are mainly used in horizontal glazing. As the orientation must exactly correspond to the angle of the direct sunlight striking the glass panels, the grids are cut to suit the building's specific location and orientation to the sun.

Light-grid systems built into insulated glazing units have little effect on the U-value, and depending on the type of unit construction g-values of around 0.2 can be achieved.

A light-grid system for solar protection was used for the congress and exhibition hall in Linz,

Isolierglas mit im Scheibenzwischenraum integrierten verstellbaren Lamellen: Luxaclair®.
Insulating glass with integrated adjustable louvres for solar control: Luxaclair®.

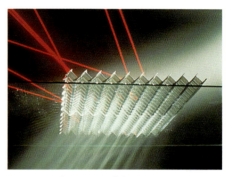

Der Sonnenschutzraster reflektiert die direkte Strahlung, läßt aber das diffuse Tageslicht durchkommen.
The light-grid system reflects direct sunlight, but allows diffuse light to penetrate.

Die Sonnenschutzraster finden hauptsächlich bei horizontalen Verglasungen Anwendung.
Kongreß- und Ausstellungshalle, Linz, Österreich, 1993, Herzog und Partner.
The light-grid systems are mainly used in horizontal glazing.
Congress and Exhibition Hall, Linz, Austria, 1993, Herzog and Partner.

Prismenplatten aus Acrylglas reflektieren die direkte Sonnenstrahlung durch Totalreflexion an der Prismenflanke. Sie werden entweder a) dem Sonnenstand nachgeführt oder b) mit einer verspiegelten Flanke fest eingebaut. Lichtlenkprismen können dagegen die diffuse Strahlung in die Raumtiefe umlenken (c).

Prismatic acrylic panes reflect all direct sunlight by total reflection on the edge of the prism. They can either a) be set to track the sun's position or b) fitted with a fixed, reflective prism edge. Light control prismatic panels allow the deflection of diffuse light c).

a

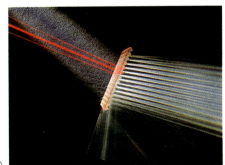
b

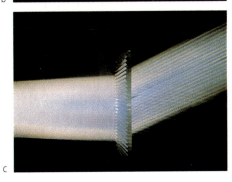
c

gefertigten bogenförmigen Kastenträgern, die eine Halle von 74 m Spannweite und 204 m Länge mit einer Scheitelhöhe von 12 m stützenfrei überdachen. Die Glaswölbung ist in der Längsrichtung in Streifenfelder unterteilt, die mit 2.70 x 0.80 m großen Isoliergläsern ausgefacht sind. Der Aufbau der Scheibe besteht aus einem innenliegenden Verbundglas (2 x 6 mm), einem Zwischenraum von 25 mm mit 16 mm hohen Spiegelrastern und einer außenliegenden 8 mm dicken low-E-beschichteten Glasscheibe. Für die notwendige Zuschnittgeometrie der einzelnen Spiegelraster mußten nicht nur der Sonnenstand und die Orientierung des Gebäudes, sondern auch ihre Lage auf dem Gewölbe berücksichtigt werden.

Eine zweite Möglichkeit stellen die Tageslichtsysteme mit Prismenplatten aus Acrylglas (PMMA) dar, wie sie von der Lichtplanung Christian Bartenbach für die Siemens AG entwickelt wurden. Die Wirkungsweise der Sonnenschutzprismen beruht auf der Totalreflexion der direkten Lichtstrahlen, die mit einem bestimmten Winkel auf die Prismenflanke eintreffen. Da der Spielbereich sehr klein ist, muß die Prismenplatte dem Sonnenstand konstant nachgeführt werden.
Dieser Winkelbereich läßt sich durch das Beschichten einer Prismenflanke mit Reinaluminium deutlich vergrößern. Damit können die Sonnenschutzprismen auch in vertikale, nicht nachführbare Verglasungen eingebaut werden, um die steil auftreffenden, direkten Lichtstrahlen zu reflektieren.
Die Umlenkung der diffusen Lichtstrahlung erfolgt durch Lichtlenkprismen. Sie werden hinter der Sonnenschutz-Prismenplatte angeordnet und lenken das diffuse Tageslicht an die Decke des Raumes, wo eine gleichmäßige Lichtverteilung durch die geeignete Gestaltung der Deckenuntersicht erzielt werden kann. Die Ausrichtung der Prismenplatten muß der Fassadenorientierung und der geographischen Lage des Gebäudes entsprechen und wird vom Computer errechnet.
Da Kunststoffe eine geringere Wärmeleitung als Luft aufweisen, sinkt der k-Wert eines normalen Isolierglases mit einer eingebauten Prismenlage auf 2.15 W/m²K, mit zwei Prismenlagen auf 1.65 W/m²K. Ein einlagiges Sonnenschutzsystem erreicht einen g-Wert von 0.13–0.15 und für eine Kombination von Sonnenschutz- und Umlenkprismen einen g-Wert von 0.15–0.17.

planned by Herzog and Partners in 1993. The support structure of the flat 204 m long barrel vault consists of specially welded box plate arched girders free-spanning 74 m across the hall and reaching an apex at 12 m. In its longitudinal direction the glass vault is divided into strips of 2.70 x 0.80 m panes of insulating glass. Each pane consists of an interior layer of laminated glass (2 x 6 mm), a 25 mm cavity with 16 mm high reflecting grids and an exterior 8 mm thick coated low-E glass pane. In calculating the exact geometry of the individual reflecting grids not only the angle of the sun and the orientation of the building had to be taken into account, but also the angle of slope of each pane on the vaulted roof.

A second possibility for daylight control is presented by prismatic systems made of acrylic panes (PMMA); one such system was developed for Siemens AG by Lichtplanung Christian Bartenbach. The way these daylight prismatic systems work is to redirect all the direct sunlight falling from a determined angle onto the edge of the prisms. As this angle of operation has very limited tolerances, the prismatic panel has to constantly track the position of the sun.
To increase the angle range available one of the prism edges can be coated with pure aluminium. This enables the solar shading prisms to be built into vertical, non-trackable glazing units, with the aim of reflecting the direct light falling from a steep angle.
The deflection of diffuse light can be achieved through light-control prismatic panels. They are placed behind the solar shading prismatic panel and deflect diffuse daylight onto the ceiling of the room which, given a suitable ceiling design, can ensure an even distribution of light across the room. The positioning of the prismatic panels must be suited to the orientation of the façades and the geographical location of the building; calculations are worked out by computer.
As plastics have a lower thermal conductivity than air, the U-value of a normal pane of insulating glass with built-in prismatic panel can be lowered to 2.15 W/m²K; if two prismatic panels are fitted, this value reaches 1.65 W/m²K. A single-layer solar protection achieves a g-value of 0.13–0.15 and in cases where solar protection and deflection prisms are used, this can reach 0.15–0.17.

Die fest eingebauten Spiegelprofile Oka-Solar® übernehmen die Funktion des Sonnenschutzes oder der Lichtumlenkung je nach Sonnenhöhe. Das System besteht aus speziell geformten Spiegellamellen, deren Profil nach den verschiedenen Einfallswinkeln der Sonnenstrahlung ausgelegt ist. Damit wird die steileinfallende direkte Lichtstrahlung im Sommer nach außen reflektiert, während die tiefliegende Strahlung im Winter durchgelassen und in die Raumtiefe umgelenkt wird. Da der Stahlungsdurchgang von der Winkeleinstellung abhängig ist, geschieht dies aber zu bestimmten Tageszeiten auch im Sommer. Das System ist sowohl für vertikale als auch für geneigte Verglasungen geeignet. Die Lamellen werden in einer für die spezielle Anwendung optimalen Winkeleinstellung in einen 16 bzw. 18 mm breiten Scheibenzwischenraum eingebaut. Sie beeinflussen den k-Wert wenig; hingegen variiert der g-Wert je nach Sonnenhöhe von 0.22 bis zu 0.51, und der τ von 0.03 bis 0.51, wobei der tiefste Wert τ_{diff} von 0.33 von Bedeutung ist (Oka-Solar® Typ 55/15).

Obwohl das System mit fest eingebauten Spiegelprofilen keine Verstellung ermöglicht, zeigt es trotzdem einen differenzierten Umgang mit der Sonnenstrahlung: Bei einer hohen Sonnenlage setzt es die Kühllasten und die Blendung herab, bei tiefliegender Einstrahlung ermöglicht es die Nutzung des Tageslichts durch die Umlenkung in die Raumtiefe.

Der Architekt Jo Coenen hat Oka-Solar® Spiegelprofile für die Fassade des Geschäftshauses Haans in Tilburg, Niederlande, 1992, verwendet. Wie beim Niederländischen Architekturinstitut in Rotterdam ist das Thema «Glaspavillon» durch einen Wasserteich, hohe freistehende Stützen und ein weit auskragendes Dach verwirklicht. Die Glasfassade ist eine Pfosten-Riegel-Konstruktion aus Aluminiumprofilen mit einem Raster von 2.4 m in der Breite und 1.05 m in der Höhe. Damit ist die geschoßhohe Verglasung bei den Großraumbüros in drei Bänder unterteilt. Im Brüstungsbereich sorgen die Spiegelprofile für eine weitgehende Ausblendung der direkten Sonnenstrahlen. Dagegen lenken sie im Deckenbereich ein Maximum an Licht in die Raumtiefe. Die Lamellen sind in Isolierscheiben mit Low-E Beschichtung und Argonfüllung eingebaut (k-Wert 1.6 W/m²K). Im Durchsichtsbereich wurden dieselben Isolierscheiben ohne Lamellen alternierend als Kippfenster und als feste Vergla-

Oka-Solar® built-in mirror profiles take on either the function of solar shading or of light deflection depending on the angle of the sun. The system consists of specially formed mirror louvres whose profile is angled to match the various incident angles of sunlight. This means that the steeply angled daylight in summer is reflected back outside, while the lower angled light in winter can penetrate into the building's interior and is deflected into the back of the room. As the level of light admitted is dependent on the angle of the mirror louvres, this occurs also in summer, depending on the time of day. The system is suited to both horizontal and vertical glazing. The louvres are built into a 16 to 18 mm cavity between two panes and set at the optimum angle suited to the particular use and situation. The louvres have little influence on the U-value, but the g-value can vary between 0.22 and 0.51 depending on the height of the sun, and the τ-value varies between 0.03 and 0.51, whereby the lowest τ_{diff} value of 0.33 is significant (Oka-Solar® Type 55/15).

Although the system with fixed, built-in mirror profiles cannot be adjusted, it reacts in an intelligent way to differing solar radiation conditions; when the sun is high it reduces cooling loads and glare, and when the sun is low, it permits the use of daylight for deflection into the depths of the room.

The architect Jo Coenen used Oka-Solar® mirror profiles for the façade of the Haans office building in Tilburg, The Netherlands, built in 1992. As with the Architectural Institute of the Netherlands in Rotterdam, the theme in this office building is also that of a glass pavilion, with pond, high free-standing support pillars and a wide cantilevered roof. The glass façade is a mullion and transom frame of aluminium profiles, spaced horizontally at 2.4 m and vertically at 1.05 m. At the office levels this gives a triple banded effect across the glazed façade. At the parapet levels the mirror profiles practically block all direct sunlight. However, at ceiling levels maximum levels of light are admitted to the back of the room. The louvres are built into insulated glazing units with a low-E coating and argon filling (U-value 1.6 W/m²K). In the transparent section the same insulating panes, but without louvres, were used either as tilting windows or fixed glazing. On the south side the 12 m high glass façade is positioned in front of the working levels with a four-

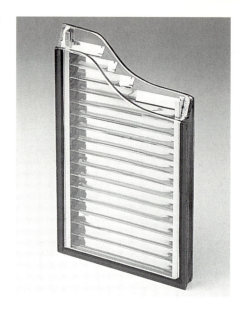

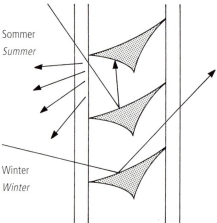

Sommer
Summer

Winter
Winter

Speziell geformte Spiegellamellen ermöglichen die Reflexion der steileinfallenden direkten Sonnenstrahlung, lenken aber die tiefliegende Strahlung in die Raumtiefe um: Oka-Solar®.
Specially shaped mirror louvres reflect steeply angled direct sunlight, but allow low-angled light to pass into the room: Oka-Solar®.

Die gebäudehohe Glasfassade ist mit Oka-Solar® Spiegelprofilen ausgestattet, und dennoch bleibt der Ausblick in die Umgebung möglich.
Geschäftshaus «Haans», Tilburg, Niederlande, 1992, Jo Coenen.
The fully glazed façade is fitted with Oka-Solar® mirror louvres which still permit a view of the surroundings.
Haans office building, Tilburg, The Netherlands, 1992, Jo Coenen.

sung eingesetzt. Auf der Südseite ist die 12 m hohe Glasfassade den Arbeitsflächen vorgelagert, so daß ein viergeschossiger offener Raum mit gestaffelten Büroetagen geschaffen wird. Die schmalen vertikalen Pfosten sind von innen gegen horizontale Lasteneinwirkung mit Stahlfachwerken verstärkt, die gegen seitliches Auskippen durch Laufstege für die Fensterreinigung stabilisiert sind.

Vorteile der festen Lichtumlenksysteme sind der Schutz vor direkter Sonnenstrahlung und die Erhöhung der Lichtverteilung in der Raumtiefe, was Kühllasten und Brennstunden der Beleuchtung reduziert.
Nachteile sind die schlechte Anpassung an die wechselnden Licht- und Wetterverhältnisse und eventuell eine gewisse Behinderung des freien Durchblicks nach außen.
Die energetischen Einsparungen decken, ökonomisch betrachtet, die hohen Investitionskosten noch nicht, dafür fallen aber die Anschaffung und der Unterhalt einer außenliegenden Sonnenschutzanlage weg.

floor high open space between them. The narrow vertical posts are braced from the inside against horizontal forces by steel framing; these steel frames are in turn stabilised against lateral shift by gantries for window cleaning and maintenance.

The advantages of the light-deflecting systems are the protection they give against direct sunlight and the increase in distribution of light into the depth of the room, which reduces both cooling loads and lighting hours.
The disadvantages are the poor adaptation to changing light and weather conditions and a certain obstruction to a clear view out of the windows.
From an economic point of view the savings in energy do not yet cover the high initial investment costs, but the costs involved in setting up and maintaining exterior sun shading devices become no longer applicable.

Die Fassade   Façades

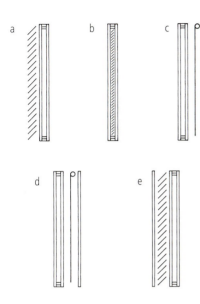

Die Vielzahl an Glasfassaden läßt sich in wenige typische Varianten einteilen: Einschalige Fassaden weisen außenliegenden (a), integrierten (b) oder innenliegenden (c) Sonnenschutz auf; bei mehrschaligen Fassaden, z. B. Abluftfassaden (d) oder zweischaligen Fassaden (e), ist der Sonnenschutz dazwischen angeordnet.

The many different types of glass façades can be broadly grouped into a few categories: single-skin façades with exterior (a), integrated (b) or interior (c) shading devices; in the case of multiple-skin façades, e. g. ventilated cavity (d) or double-skin (e) façades, the solar shading is placed between the skins.

Linke Seite: Außenliegende bewegliche Gitterstoffstoren sind Sonnenschutzmaßnahmen mit einem erhöhten Wirkungsgrad und können den Witterungsverhältnissen angepaßt werden.
IRCAM-Erweiterungsbau, Paris, 1988–89, Renzo Piano Building Workshop.
Left page: Exterior movable fabric blinds are shading devices which give effective sun protection; they can be adjusted to suit the changing weather conditions. Extension to the IRCAM building, Paris, 1988–89, Renzo Piano Building Workshop.

Die Planung einer Glasfassade umfaßt den Einsatz von verschiedenen Maßnahmen, um einerseits die Wärmeverluste niedrig zu halten, andererseits die unerwünschten Wärmegewinne durch sommerliche Sonnenstrahlung zu vermeiden. Die Vielzahl von möglichen Kombinationen läßt sich freilich in wenige typische Fassadenvarianten einteilen. Ein erstes Kriterium ist die Anzahl Verglasungsebenen, daher die Bezeichnung einschalige oder mehrschalige Fassaden. Das zweite Kriterium ist die Positionierung der Sonnenschutzmaßnahme. Es gibt einschalige Fassaden mit außenliegendem, innenliegendem oder im Luftzwischenraum der Verglasung integriertem Sonnenschutz. Bei den mehrschaligen Fassaden, z.B. Abluft- oder «Zweite Haut»-Fassaden, ist der Sonnenschutz meistens zwischen den Verglasungsebenen angeordnet.

Einschalige Fassaden

Eine Glasfassade erhält einen gewissen Sonnenschutz durch IR-reflektierende oder auch im sichtbaren Bereich absorbierende und reflektierende Beschichtungen. Da deren Eigenschaften nicht veränderbar sind, werden sowohl die Energiegewinne in kälteren Jahreszeiten verhindert als auch der Tageslichteinfall herabgesetzt. Darum ist das Anbringen von zusätzlichen, variablen Sonnenschutzmaßnahmen bei Gebäuden mit großflächiger Verglasung und hohen Klimaanforderungen unerläßlich.

Außenliegender Sonnenschutz

Diese Maßnahme weist den Vorteil eines erhöhten Wirkungsgrades auf, weil die durch direkte Sonneneinstrahlung auf dem Sonnenschutz entstehende sekundäre Wärmeabgabe außerhalb der Gebäudehülle bleibt. Ein typischer g-Wert liegt heute bei etwa 0.10. Nachteilig ist, daß der außenliegende Sonnenschutz – als Stoffstoren oder Lamellen – den Witterungseinflüssen ausgesetzt ist, was periodische Reinigungsarbeiten be-

In designing glass façades a variety of different devices are implemented to, on the one hand, keep heat losses low, and, on the other, to avoid undesired heat gains through solar radiation in summer. The range of possibilities and combinations can be broadly grouped into a few typical categories. The first main criterion is the number of glazing skins incorporated in the design – here the terms used are single-skin façades and multiple-skin façades.

The second criterion is the positioning of the solar control devices. There are single-skin façades with exterior or interior shading, or with integrated shading devices incorporated in the cavity between the panes. In the case of multiple-skin façades, e.g. ventilated cavity or double-skin façades, the solar control devices are generally placed between the glazing skins.

Single-Skin Façades

To achieve a certain level of solar control in a single-skin façade, coatings can be applied to the glass, such as infrared-reflecting coatings and/or coatings to absorb and reflect wavelengths in the visible range. As their properties are fixed, they also restrict solar gain in the colder months and reduce daylighting levels. For this reason it is necessary to provide additional adjustable solar control measures in buildings with large surface areas of façade glazing and in buildings where air conditioning requirements are strictly regulated.

Exterior Solar Control Devices

The advantage of exterior solar control devices is that the heat, resulting from reradiation from the device itself, remains on the outside of the building. A typical g-value nowadays for a façade with exterior devices is around 0.10. A disadvantage is the fact that the devices, in the form of fabric blinds or louvres, are exposed to the effects of weather, which can give rise to high costs for regular cleaning and maintenance. Exterior de-

Sonnenschutz durch ein weit auskragendes Dach.
Bibliothek der Technischen Hochschule Cranfield,
Bedfordshire, England, 1989–92, Sir Norman Foster
und Partner.
A wide projecting roof offers solar shading.
Library building of Cranfield Institute of Technology,
Bedfordshire, England, 1989–92, Sir Norman Foster
and Partners.

dingt und hohe Wartungskosten verursachen kann. Man unterscheidet zwischen starren und beweglichen Maßnahmen. Erstere sind in Form von Dachvorsprüngen und auskragenden Bauteilen, Sonnensegeln, «brise-soleils» und Lamellen allgemein bekannt. Zur zweiten Gruppe gehören ebenfalls übliche Produkte wie Gewebe- und Gitterstoffstoren sowie Jalousien und Blechlamellen. Seltener sind Lösungen mit verschiebbaren Fassadenelementen wie Paneelen, Gitterrosten oder Lichtumlenkungs-Elementen.

Ein weit auskragendes Dach charakterisiert die südliche Ansicht der neuen Bibliothek der Technischen Hochschule in Cranfield, Bedfordshire, Großbritannien, 1989–92 von Sir Norman Foster und Partnern erstellt. Als seitliche Verschattungsmaßnahme wurden gebäudehohe Module mit starren horizontalen Lamellen aus anodisiertem Aluminium verwendet.

Ein Beispiel für starre Lamellensysteme stellt die Fassade der «Hongkong und Shanghai Bank» in Honkong dar, 1979–86 ebenfalls von Sir Norman Foster und Partnern erbaut. Die schräggestellten Lamellen sind zwischen Aluminiumkonsolen eingespannt und bieten einen wirksamen Sonnenschutz, ohne den Blick nach unten zu behindern.

Als Sonnenschutzmaßnahme kann auch eine schräggestellte Fassade mit auskragenden Lamellenvordächern dienen, wie beim neuen Koordinationszentrum der British Airways, London-Heath-

vices can either be fixed or movable. Familar types of construction which fall into the first category are projecting roofs or building sections, awnings, brise-soleils and fixed-angle louvre shading. In the second category are such products as fabric blinds or screens, slatted or metal louvre blinds. A less common type are sliding façade units such as panels, screening grids and light-deflecting elements.

An example of the use of a wide projecting roof is the library building of Cranfield Institute of Technology in Bedfordshire, England, built between 1989 and 1992 by Sir Norman Foster and Partners. To shade the sides of the building, full-height modules were used with fixed horizontal louvres made of anodised aluminium.

For the "Hongkong and Shanghai" Bank in Hong Kong, built 1979–86, also by Sir Norman Foster and Partners, a solar shading device was developed with louvres fixed at an angle to the façade plane, and held between aluminium brackets. The design of this system offers effective protection without obstructing the downward view for people inside the building.

Another approach to solar control is to combine an angled façade with louvred sunshades cantilevered out beyond the façade plane. Such a design was used by Nicholas Grimshaw & Partners in 1994 for the Combined Operations Centre for British Airways at Heathrow in London. The for-

Starre Lamellensysteme bieten einen wirksamen
Sonnenschutz, ohne den Blick nach unten zu behindern.
Sitz der «Hongkong and Shanghai Bank», Hongkong,
1979–86, Sir Norman Foster und Partner.
Fixed louvre sytems offer effective solar protection
without obstructing the downward view.
Headquarters of the Hongkong and Shanghai Bank,
Hong Kong, 1979–86, Sir Norman Foster and
Partners.

row, das von Nicholas Grimshaw und Partnern 1994 fertiggestellt wurde. Die nach vorne geneigte, schräge Stellung der Fassade ist eine Maßnahme zur Vermeidung der Reflexion von Radarwellen vom nahe gelegenen Flughafen. Ihre Konstruktion besteht aus Pfosten in 3 m Achsabstand und aus Riegeln, die entsprechend der geneigten Geometrie jedes Geschoß in drei etwa 1.40 m hohe Felder unterteilen. Im Brüstungsbereich sind undurchsichtige wärmedämmende Paneele eingesetzt, welchen emailbeschichtete Gläser mit einem hellblauen Punktraster vorgelagert sind. Im Durchsichtsbereich sind schalldämmende transparente Isoliergläser eingesetzt, die aus einer 5 mm dicken äußeren Scheibe, einem 10 mm dicken innenliegenden Verbundglas und einem 17.5 mm breiten Zwischenraum bestehen. Die Lamellen werden von Konsolen aus gegossenem Aluminium getragen, die an der Spitze mit einem extrudierten Aluminiumprofil miteinander verbunden sind. Glasstreifen, die ebenfalls mit einem hellblauen Punktraster versehen sind, bilden die schräggestellten, 12 mm dicken Lamellen.

ward tilt of the façade is a measure intended to avoid the reflection of radar waves from the nearby airport. The structure of the building consists of 3 m spaced vertical mullions with a tripartite banding of each floor by means of transoms spaced at roughly 1.40 m, varying a little depending on the angled façade geometry at individual points. At parapet level the architects used thermally insulating panels, and in front of them a fritted glass with a pale blue dot pattern. At seated and standing eye levels the transparent glazing has both thermal and acoustic insulating properties. The insulating glass units consist of a 5 mm thick sheet outside, a 10 mm thick laminated glass inside and a 17.5 mm air space between the two. The louvred sunshade is supported by cast aluminium brackets joined together at the ends by extruded aluminium profiles. The 12 mm thick louvres are made of glass strips, also with a pale blue dot pattern.

Movable solar shading devices in the form of fabric blinds or screens are now quite common.

Sonnenschutz durch eine nach vorne geneigte Fassade und Glaslamellen mit einem hellblauen, emaillierten Punktraster.
Koordinationszentrum der British Airways, London-Heathrow, 1994, Nicholas Grimshaw und Partner.
Solar protection is given by an angled façade and glass louvres with a pale blue fritted dot pattern .
Combined Operations Centre for British Airways , Heathrow, London, 1994, Nicholas Grimshaw and Partners.

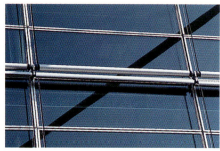

Außenliegende Gitterstoffstoren weisen den Vorteil eines erhöhten Wirkungsgrades auf, da die sekundäre Abwärme außerhalb des Gebäudes bleibt.
«Fondation Cartier», Paris, 1994, Jean Nouvel, Emmanuel Cattani und Associés.
Exterior movable fabric blinds offer effective solar protection, as the heat reradiation remains on the outside of the building.
Fondation Cartier, Paris, 1994, Jean Nouvel, Emmanuel Cattani and Associates.

Bewegliche Sonnenschutzmaßnahmen in Form von Gewebe- oder Gitterstoffstoren sind allgemein bekannt. Als Beispiele können die Glasfassade des Erweiterungsgebäudes für die IRCAM in Paris, 1988/89 vom Renzo Piano Building Workshop gebaut, oder die «Fondation Cartier», ebenfalls in Paris, von Jean Nouvel, Emmanuel Cattani et Associés 1994 fertiggestellt, dienen.

Eine spezielle Lösung für den Sonnenschutz zeigt die «Banque Populaire de l'Ouest et de l'Armorique» in Rennes, 1989 von den Architekten Odile Decq und Benoît Cornette in Zusammenarbeit mit den Spezialisten für Glaskonstruktionen Rice-Francis-Ritchie (RFR) erbaut. Vor der

Examples include the glass façade of the extension to the IRCAM building in Paris built 1988/89 by the Renzo Piano Building Workshop, or the "Fondation Cartier", Paris, completed in 1994, by Jean Nouvel, Emmanuel Cattani et Associés.

An unusual design for solar shading was realized in the "Banque Populaire de l'Ouest et de l'Armorique" in Rennes, built in 1989 by the architects Odile Decq and Benoît Cornette in collaboration with the glass construction specialists Rice-Francis-Ritchie (RFR). Two metres in front of the glazed wall is a filigree steel framework which gives both horizontal stability to the façade

Das filigrane Stahlgerüst dient gleichzeitig zur horizontalen Aussteifung der Glasfassade und zur Befestigung des Sonnenschutzes.
«Banque Populaire de l'Ouest et de l'Armorique», Rennes, Frankreich, 1989, Odile Decq und Benoît Cornette.
The filigree steel framework gives both horizontal stability to the glass façade and serves as an attachment for the external roller blinds.
Banque Populaire de l'Ouest et de l'Armorique, Rennes, France, 1989, Odile Decq and Benoît Cornette.

Bei der hängenden Glasfassade sind die oberen Scheiben in der Mitte durch einen gefederten Beschlag am Dachrand befestigt, und die nächsten Scheiben sind durch kreuzförmige Verbindungsknoten miteinander verhängt (rechts). Im Eingangsbereich wurden vorgespannte Einfachscheiben verwendet (links oben), im Bürotrakt dagegen Isolierscheiben (links unten).
«Banque Populaire de l'Ouest et de l'Armorique», Rennes, Frankreich, 1989, Odile Decq und Benoît Cornette.

In the suspended glass façade the upper row of panes is attached to the roof edge via spring assemblies at the centre. The next rows are suspended below them via cross-shaped bolted fixings (right). The glazing in the entrance area consists of toughened single panes (top left). Insulating glass units are used in the office section (bottom left). Banque Populaire de l'Ouest et de l'Armorique, Rennes, France, 1989, Odile Decq and Benoît Cornette.

Verglasung ist in einem Abstand von 2 m ein filigranes Stahlgerüst errichtet, welches gleichzeitig zur Stabilisierung der Fassade gegen Winddruck und -sog sowie zur Befestigung der Sonnenschutzrollos dient. Die 8 m hohen Masten stehen in einem Achsabstand von 12 m und werden durch horizontale Verbindungsrohre und einen darüberliegenden Fachwerkträger ausgesteift.
Die Verglasung des Eingangsbereichs besteht aus 2 x 2 m großen vorgespannten Einfachscheiben. Die obere Reihe ist in der Mitte durch einen gefederten Beschlag am Dachrand befestigt, und die nächsten Scheiben sind mittels kreuzförmigen Verbindungsknoten miteinander verhängt. Letztere sind durch runde Edelstahlstäbe mit dem außenliegenden Traggerüst verbunden, um die horizontalen Windlasten zu übertragen.
Beim Bürotrakt sind nach demselben konstruktiven Prinzip Isolierscheiben eingesetzt worden, wahrscheinlich die erste Ausführung in dieser Art überhaupt. Außen- und Innenscheibe bestehen aus 12 mm dickem vorgespanntem Glas und sind durch einen runden 15 mm dicken Abstandhalter verbunden, so daß eine punktförmige Befestigung an den kreuzförmigen Verbindungsknoten erfolgen kann.
Diese Konstruktion kann als Weiterentwicklung der Gewächshaus-Glasfront des Museums für Wissenschaft und Technik in Paris betrachtet

in terms of restraining wind pressure and suction and serves as an attachment for the external roller blinds. The 8 m high masts are spaced at 12 m and are guyed and braced with horizontal steel tube and a lattice girder on top.
The glazing in the entrance area consists of 2 x 2 m sheets of toughened single glass. The upper row is attached at the centre via spring assemblies to the roof edge, and the next rows are suspended below them via cross-shaped bolted fixings. These fixings are connected to the external support frame by means of stainless steel rods, which restrain wind loads. The same type of construction is used in the office section, with insulating glass replacing the single panes. Probably this is the first suspended glazing with double insulating glass units. Each of these has a 12 mm thick toughened glass on both inside and outside, separated by round, 15 mm spacers which enable the glass unit to be bolted to the cross-shaped fixings.
This construction can be seen as a further development of the "greenhouse" type front to the Museum of Science and Technology in Paris built in 1986 by Rice-Francis-Ritchie (RFR) for the architect Adrien Fainsilber.

Movable louvre systems can be adjusted to suit the changing levels of sunshine and do not seri-

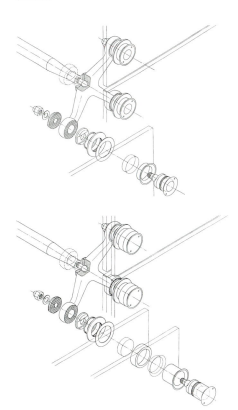

Bewegliche Lamellen ermöglichen die Anpassung an die wechselnden Sonnenstellungen und Witterungs-verhältnisse.
Gebäude «TAD», Milano-Lainate, 1989, Ottavio di Blasi und Partner.
Movable louvre systems can be adjusted in accordance with the position of the sun and the changing weather conditions.
TAD building, Milano-Lainate, 1989, Ottavio di Blasi and Partners.

Verstellbare Rohrgitterroste ermöglichen die Aus-blendung der direkten Sonnenstrahlung .
Flughafen München II, 1976–93, Hans-Busso von Busse.
A system of movable tubular grids enables the control of daylight transmission.
New Munich airport, 1976–93, Hans-Busso von Busse.

werden, welche Rice-Francis-Ritchie (RFR) für den Architekten Adrien Fainsilber 1986 ausgear-beitet haben.

Bewegliche Lamellensysteme ermöglichen die Anpassung an die wechselnde Sonnenstrahlung, ohne den Ausblick wesentlich zu behindern, wie beim Sitz der «TAD», Milano-Lainate, 1989 von den Architekten Ottavio di Blasi und Partnern er-baut.

Eine ungewöhnliche Lösung zeigt das System mit Rohrgitterrosten beim neuen Flughafen München II, von Hans-Busso von Busse, 1993. Die Konstruktion besteht aus drei übereinander liegenden Rosten aus weiß beschichteten Alumi-niumrohren von 50 mm Durchmesser. Sie sind

ously obstruct the view out of the window. One example of their use is in the "TAD" headquar-ters in Lainate, Milan, built in 1989 by Ottavio di Blasi and Partners.

A unusual system of tubular lattice grids was de-veloped for the new Munich airport, built by Professor Hans-Busso von Busse in 1993. The device is made up of three levels of grids one on top of the other; each grid is made of 50 mm diameter, white-coated aluminium tubes. The three levels are connected to each other by a swivel lever which enables the upper and lower grids to be adjusted in relation to each other, in-dependent of the middle layer, which remains fixed. Depending on how this lever is set, the di-rect solar radiation can either be admitted, or re-

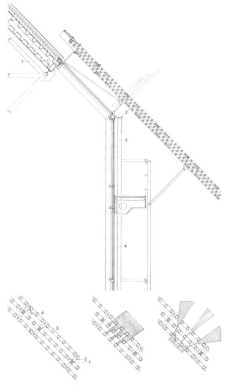

mit einem Schwenkhebel verbunden, so daß der obere und der untere Rost gegeneinander verstellt werden können, während der mittlere Rost festbleibt. Je nach Stellung wird die direkte Sonnenstrahlung entweder durchgelassen oder in verschiedene Richtungen reflektiert, während das Eintreffen des diffusen Lichts und der Ausblick weitgehend erhalten bleiben. Die Verschiebungen erfolgen durch Stellmotoren, die von einem Leitrechner zentral gesteuert werden.

Einen Sonnenschutz mittels eines verschiebbaren Fassadenteils weist der Pavillon der Siemens AG für die Expo '92 in Sevilla (1992) auf, welcher zum Büro- und Schulungszentrum umgebaut werden soll. Der von der Siemens-Architektur-abteilung mit Gunter Standke u. a. realisierte Pavillon ist mit einem gebäudehohen, in die Dach-konstruktion eingehängten, gebogenen Sonnen-schutzschild versehen. Der 17 m hohe und 28 m

flected in a number of different directions, while the admission of diffuse light remains unaffected, as does to a large extent the view to the outside. The grids are adjusted by actuators controlled from a central computer control unit.

Solar control using sliding façade elements can be seen in the example of the Siemens Pavilion at Expo '92. The building will be converted into a training and office centre. Designed by Gunter Standke and others from the Siemens architecture department, the building is fitted with a full height, curved solar shield suspended from the roof construction. The 17 m high and 28 m wide shield moves around the circular pavilion tracking the position of the sun. Mounted on the shield are movable horizontal louvres made up of 25 x 250 cm prismatic acrylic panels attached to a stainless steel frame; these panels reflect direct daylight while admitting diffuse light. A central electronic control system governs the tracking of

Der gebäudehohe Sonnenschutzschild wird, dem Lauf der Sonne folgend, um den runden Pavillon herumge-fahren. Die beweglichen horizontalen Lamellen aus Prismenplatten werden mittels Computersteuerung nach dem jeweiligen Sonnenstand ausgerichtet. Siemens-Pavillon an der Expo '92, Sevilla, 1992, Siemens-Architekturabteilung mit G. R. Standke u. a.
The full-height curved solar shield moves around the circular pavilion tracking the position of the sun. The movable horizontal louvres, made up of prismatic acrylic panels, are automatically adjusted in accordance with the position of the sun.
Siemens pavilion at Expo '92, Seville, 1992, Siemens Architecture Departement, G. R. Standke et al.

breite Bauteil wird, dem Lauf der Sonne folgend, um den runden Pavillon herumgefahren. Auf dem Schild sind bewegliche horizontale Lamellen mit Prismenplatten von etwa 25 x 250 cm auf Edelstahlrahmen befestigt, welche die direkte Sonnenstrahlung reflektieren, das diffuse Licht hingegen durchlassen. Die Nachführung des Sonnenschutzschildes und die Einstellung der Neigungswinkel der Lamellen entspricht dem Sonnenstand und wird durch einen Steuerungsrechner festgelegt. Die zur Bewegung notwendige elektrische Energie wird von Solarzellen auf dem Dach geliefert. Die kontinuierliche Umstellung der Prismenlamellen verleiht dem Pavillon ein immer wieder neues Erscheinungsbild.

Integrierter Sonnenschutz

Diese Maßnahme ist zur Zeit weniger verbreitet. Während die Reinigung besonders unproblematisch ist, kann die Wartung teuer ausfallen, wenn die Elektromotoren in den Scheibenzwischenraum eingeschlossen sind. Eine Alternative dazu sind Produkte mit magnetischem Schieber außerhalb des Isolierglases.

Die Architekten Benthem-Crouwel haben eine solche Maßnahme bei der Verglasung des Gebäudes «Mors» in Opmeer, Niederlande, 1988 eingesetzt. Die Tragkonstruktion besteht aus 10 Portalrahmen mit einer Spannweite von 21.6 m und einer Höhe von 7.6 m, welche im Achsabstand von 5.4 m angeordnet sind. Auf der Nordwestseite befinden sich die Ausstellungs- und Bürobereiche. Die doppelgeschossige Vergla-

the shield around the building, and automatically adjusts the angle of the prismatic louvres. The energy required to operate this system comes from solar cells mounted on the roof. The ever-changing position of the shield and the angle of the louvres gives the pavilion continuosly a new appearance.

Integrated Solar Control Devices

Solar control devices integrated into a glazing unit are less common at present. Costs associated with cleaning are much lower, but maintenance may be more expensive, especially in cases where the electric motors are also incorporated in the cavity between the panes. An alternative is presented by systems which make use of a magnetic control placed outside the insulating glass.

The architects Benthem-Crouwel used such an integrated solar device in the glazing of the "Mors" building in Opmeer, the Netherlands, built in 1988. The support structure consists of 10 portal frames with a span of 21.6 m, a height of 7.6 m and an axial spacing of 5.4 m. The offices and exhibition areas are located on the northwest side of the building. The double-height glazing is a mullion and transom frame construction based on a 1.8 m square grid. The insulated glazing units have a depth of 36 mm, composed of a 6 mm thick pane on the outside and inside, separated by a 24 mm cavity which incorporates the 16 mm wide, magnetically adjustable louvres.

Integrierter Sonnenschutz aus beweglichen Lamellen, die durch einen magnetischen Schieber außerhalb des Isolierglases verstellt werden können.
Gebäude «Mors», Opmeer, Niederlande, 1988, Bentem-Crouwel.
Integrated solar control device with movable louvres, which are adjusted by means of a magnetic control outside the insulating glass.
Mors building, Opmeer, The Netherlands, 1988, Bentem-Crouwel.

sung ist eine Pfosten-Riegel-Konstruktion mit einem quadratischen Raster von 1.8 m Seitenlänge. Die Isolierscheiben sind insgesamt 34 mm stark, mit je einer 6 mm dicken Scheibe außen und innen sowie einem 24 mm breiten Zwischenraum für die magnetisch verstellbaren, 16 mm breiten Lamellen.

Ein integriertes festes Lamellensystem wurde von den Architekten Jerôme Brunet und Eric Saunier für die Fassade des Hauptgebäudes der Internationalen Schule in Saint-Germain-en-Laye, Paris, 1989–92, verwendet. In den 50 mm breiten Zwischenraum der Doppelverglasung sind perforierte Aluminiumprofile eingesetzt, die als Sonnenschutzgitter nur ein gedämpftes Licht durchlassen.

Ein weiteres Beispiel mit fest eingebauten Maßnahmen stellt das Geschäftshaus «Haans» in Tilburg, Niederlande, 1992, von Architekt Jo Coenen dar, in dem lichtumlenkende Spiegelprofile Oka-Solar® zum Einsatz kommen (siehe Seite 74).

Innenliegender Sonnenschutz
Diese Maßnahme ist insofern etwas weniger wirkungsvoll, als die entstehende Wärme im Raum gefangen bleibt, was durch ein Absaugen der warmen Luft oberhalb des Sonnenschutzes zum Teil vermieden werden kann. Ein typischer g-Wert liegt bei etwa 0.30. Dafür sind Reinigung und Wartung des Sonnenschutzes wesentlich einfacher. Handelsübliche Produkte bestehen

Integrierter Sonnenschutz aus festen, perforierten Aluminiumlamellen.
Internationale Schule, Saint-Germain-en-Laye / Paris, 1989–92, J. Brunet und E. Saunier.
Integrated solar control devices with fixed perforated aluminium louvres.
International School in Saint-Germain-en-Laye / Paris, 1989–92, J. Brunet and E. Saunier.

A system with integrated, non-adjustable louvres was chosen for the façade of the main building of the International School in Saint-Germain-en-Laye, Paris, built between 1989 and 1992 by the architects Jerome Brunet and Eric Saunier. Sandwiched in the 50 mm space in the double glazing

Integrierter Sonnenschutz mit festen Lamellen, deren spezielle Profilform die flach einfallenden Sonnenstrahlen durchläßt, die steil einfallenden dagegen reflektiert.
Geschäftshaus «Haans», Tilburg, Niederlande, 1992, Jo Coenen.
Integrated solar control device with fixed louvres. Their special profile allows lower-angled sunlight to enter, but reflects steeply angled light back outside. Haans building, Tilburg, The Netherlands, 1992, Jo Coenen.

aus textilen Materialien, wie vertikale Lamellen-storen, Rollos oder Gitterstoffstoren.

Bei dem 1990 fertiggestellten Gewerbe- und Bürogebäude «Hôtel industriel Jean-Baptiste Berlier» des Architekten Dominique Perrault in Paris erfährt die übliche Monotonie einer ge-schoßhohen Verglasung durch die innenliegen-den, horizontal laufenden Sonnenschutzlamellen eine diskrete, aber sehr elegante Unterteilung. Die Fassade besteht aus 1.8 x 3.3 m großen, vor-fabrizierten Glaselementen, die jeweils an der oberen Geschoßdecke abgehängt sind. Bei der Herstellung wurden die Isolierscheiben mit Silikon auf die tragende Rahmenkonstruktion verklebt und mit mechanischen Sicherheits-klammern an den Ecken versehen. Der Glasauf-bau weist eine 6 mm dicke Außen-, eine 10 mm dicke Innenscheibe und einen Zwischenraum von 12 mm mit einer Argonfüllung auf, was einen k-Wert von 1.76, einen g-Wert von 0.52 und

are perforated aluminium profiles arranged in a grid pattern; they only admit subdued light.

A further example of fixed integrated devices is the "Haans" building in Tilburg, The Nether-lands, built in 1992 by the architect Jo Coenen. Here he makes use of Oka-Solar® light-deflecting mirror profiles (see illustration p. 74).

Interior Solar Control Devices

This type of solar control is less effective in so far as the heat produced by the solar reradiation re-mains in the room; however, this can to some ex-tent be counteracted by drawing off the warm air above these devices. A typical g-value is about 0.30. Cleaning and maintenance of interior solar control devices are considerably simpler than with the other two types mentioned above. Products generally available on the market are made of textile materials in the form of vertical blinds, roller blinds or fabric screens.

Innenliegenden Sonnenschutz können horizontal laufende Lamellen, offene Elektrokanäle und Lüftungsrohre bieten.
«Hôtel industriel Jean-Baptiste Berlier», Paris, 1986–90, Dominique Perrault.
Interior solar shading can be achieved with horizontal louvres, cable tray and air conditioning ducts. Hôtel industriel Jean-Baptiste Berlier, Paris, 1986–90, Dominique Perrault.

einen τ-Wert von 0.72 ergibt. Der innenliegende Sonnenschutz besteht aus mehreren horizontallaufenden Lamellen aus Aluminium, die wie Tablare aus Streckmetall aussehen, sowie aus dem offenen Elektrokanal und den Lüftungsröhren.

Mehrschalige Fassade

Die Anordnung des Sonnenschutzes hinter einer Deckscheibe bietet die Möglichkeit, Unterhaltskosten, Reinigungs- und Wartungsarbeiten zu reduzieren.

Beim Bürokomplex «Les Collines», in Paris-La Défense, 1990 fertiggestellt, gelang dem Architekten Jean-Pierre Buffi die Realisierung einer Fassade mit geschoßhohen Verglasungen, trotz der baurechtlichen Einschränkung durch einen zulässigen g-Wert von maximal 0.17. Dafür wurde ein starrer, gewebeartiger Sonnenschutz aus Mikrolamellen gewählt, die aus nur 1.27 mm breiten weißbeschichteten Bronzeprofilen bestehen, welche durch ein Drahtgeflecht in der Neigung von 17° gehalten werden. Sie bieten Sonnenschutz, ohne den Ausblick zu behindern. Die Pfosten-Riegel-Fassade weist einen Achsabstand von 1.35 m und eine gesamte Geschoßhöhe von 3.15 m auf, die in drei 90 cm hohe Glaselemente und ein 45 cm hohes Paneel aus Aluminium bei der Deckenstirn unterteilt ist. Die Mikrolamellen sind in die Brüstungs- und die Deckenelemente integriert. Da sie eine hohe Aufheizung der Luft hervorrufen, sind sie

An elegant example of the use of interior solar control is found in the "Hôtel industriel Jean-Baptiste Berlier", a building for small industrial activities and offices in Paris built 1986–90 by the architect Dominique Perrault; the usual monotony associated with an all-glass façade is broken up by discretely placing horizontal louvres on the inside. The façade consists of 1.8 x 3.3 m large prefabricated glass units each suspended from the floor above. During manufacture the insulating glass units were fixed with silicon to their support frames and mechanical safety clamps were attached to the corners. The insulating glass unit itself consists of a 6 mm thick outer sheet, a 10 mm thick inner sheet and a 12 mm cavity filled with argon gas; this combination produced a U-value of 1.76, a g-value of 0.52 and a τ-value of 0.72. The interior solar control device is mainly a horizontal, aluminium louvre made of expanded mesh grid; cable trays and air ventilation ducts are also used as solar control devices.

Multiple-Skin Façades

The possibility of incorporating solar control devices behind a cover pane reduces cleaning and maintenance costs.

For the "Les Collines" office complex in Paris-La Défense, built in 1990 by Jean-Pierre Buffi, the architect managed to realise his aim of a fully glazed façade despite building regulations stating a maximum permissible g-value of 0.17. To fit in with these strict requirements, a stiff, textile-like

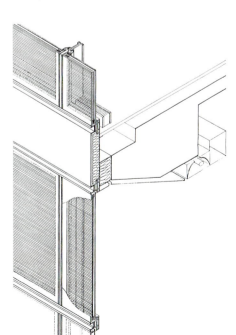

Ein starrer, gewebeartiger Sonnenschutz aus Mikrolamellen wird vor der Witterung geschützt, indem er zwischen der innenliegenden Isolierverglasung und einer außenliegenden schwarzen Einfachverglasung eingebaut wird.
Bürokomplex «Les Collines», Paris-La Défense, –1990, Jean-Pierre Buffi.
Stiff, textile-like sunshading microlouvres are protected from the weather by placing them between the interior insulating glass and an exterior black-tinted single glass pane.
Les Collines office complex, La Défense, Paris, –1990, Jean-Pierre Buffi.

zwischen die innenliegende Isolierverglasung (äußere Scheibe 6 mm, Zwischenraum 12 mm und innere Schreibe 4 mm) und eine außenliegende, schwarz eingefärbte Glasscheibe (Cool-Lite® AS 120) eingebaut. Zum Ausgleich des wegen der Aufwärmung im Scheibenzwischenraum entstehenden Drucks wurden vier Ventile eingebaut.

Ein ähnlicher Lösungsansatz ist beim «Institut du Monde Arabe», Paris, 1981–87, von Jean Nouvel mit Pierre Soria und Gilbert Lézénès, zur Anwendung gekommen. Für die Südfassade des Kulturinstituts wurde ein regulierbarer Sonnenschutz entwickelt, der sich an die traditionellen, mit Ornamenten versehenen arabischen Fenstergitter (Maschabijja) anlehnt. In die 62.4 x 26 m große Fassade wurden 27 000 Blendmechanismen aus Aluminium eingebaut, die sich elektropneumatisch, dem Einfall des Sonnenlichts entsprechend, öffnen oder schließen und damit die Tageslichttransmission von 0.10 bis 0.30 regeln. Sie sind mit photoelektrischen Zellen versehen, und die Steuerung erfolgt durch einen Computer.

layer of 1.27 mm wide, white-coated bronze profile microlouvres, held at an angle of 17° to a wire mesh support, were placed in front of the façade to give protection from the sun, but without obstructing the view outside. The mullion and transom façade has an axial spacing of 1.35 m and a total floor height of 3.15 m, divided into three 90 cm high glass units and a 45 cm high aluminium panel at the slab level. The microlouvres are integrated into the parapet and into the ceiling glass units. As these louvres give off heat to the surrounding air, they are placed between the interior insulating glass unit (6 mm outer pane, 12 mm cavity, 4 mm inner pane) and the exterior, black-tinted glass sheet (Cool-Lite® AS 120). To compensate for the change in air pressure resulting from reradiation in the additional cavity, four air vents were provided.

A similar approach was used for the "Institut du Monde Arabe" in Paris, built between 1981 and 1987 by Jean Nouvel with Pierre Soria and Gilbert Lézénès. For the south façade of this cul-

Für die große Südfassade wurde ein regulierbarer Sonnenschutz aus 27 000 Blendmechanismen entwickelt.
«Institut du Monde Arabe», Paris, 1981–87, Jean Nouvel, Pierre Soria und Gilbert Lézénès.
For the south façade an adjustable solar control device consisting of 27,000 shutter mechanisms was developed.
Institut du Monde Arabe, Paris, 1981–87, Jean Nouvel, Pierre Soria and Gilbert Lézénès.

Dem Einfall des Sonnenlichts entsprechend, öffnen und schließen sich die Blenden elektropneumatisch. Sie sind zwischen der außenliegenden Isolierverglasung und einer innenliegenden Einfachverglasung eingebaut.
«Institut du Monde Arabe», Paris, 1981–87, Jean Nouvel, Pierre Soria und Gilbert Lézénès.

The shutters open and close by means of an electropneumatic mechanism which regulates daylight transmission. The shutters are placed between the exterior insulating glass and an interior single glass pane.
Institut du Monde Arabe, Paris, 1981–87, Jean Nouvel, Pierre Soria and Gilbert Lézénès.

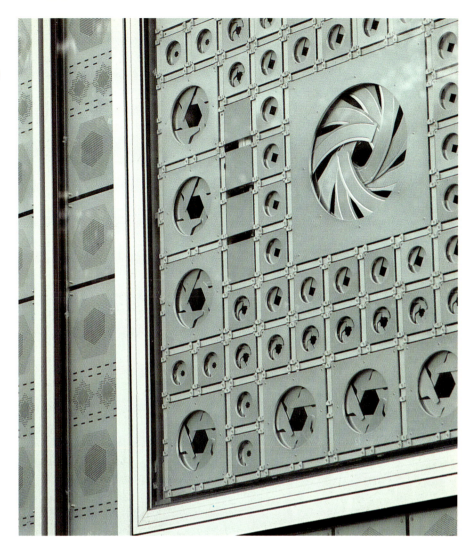

Um die empfindlichen Mechanismen zu schützen, sind die 240 quadratischen, 1.80 x 1.80 m großen Felder und die 0.40 m breiten umrahmenden Friese nach dem Prinzip eines Kastenfensters aufgebaut: außen ein festeingebautes Isolierglas, innen ein Flügel zum Öffnen aus Einscheiben-Sicherheitsglas und dazwischen die Blendmechanismen.

Trotz hohen Baukosten und gewissen Problemen mit der Funktionstüchtigkeit der Mechanismen ist es die ästhetische Anlehnung an die arabische Kultur und die Umsetzung in modernste Technologie, die diese Fassadenlösung Nouvels auszeichnet.

Beide oben aufgeführten Beispiele zeigen die Unterbringung der Sonnenschutzmaßnahmen in einem schmalen Zwischenraum, der vor oder hinter der eigentlich wärmeschützenden Isolierscheibe liegt, welcher aber keine mechanisch belüftete Raumschicht bildet.

tural institute a special, adjustable solar control device was developed, along the lines of the ornate window gratings (Maschabijja) traditionally found in the Arab world. Built into the 62.4 x 26 m façade are 27,000 aluminium shutter elements, which open and close by means of an electro-pneumatic mechanism, regulating daylight transmission between 0.10 and 0.30. They are fitted with photoelectric cells and controlled by computer. In order to protect the sensitive mechanisms the 240 square glazed areas, 1.80 x 1.80 m in size, and the 0.40 m wide framing friezes are built up according to the principle of the "box window", i.e. on the outside a fixed pane of insulating glass, and on the inside an opening sheet of single safety glass, with the shutter mechanism between the two.

Despite high construction costs and certain problems with the functional efficiency of the mechanism, this façade design by Jean Nouvel represents a modern, technological interpreta-

Abluftfassaden

Eine Abluftfassade ist durch einen breiten Luftzwischenraum gekennzeichnet, welcher durch die Anordnung einer einfachen Scheibe raumseitig vor einer mit innenliegendem Sonnenschutz versehenen Fassade entsteht. Ein Teil der Raumabluft wird durch Unterdruck in diesen Zwischenraum eingesaugt, wo er den größten Teil der im Sonnenschutz entstehenden Wärme aufnimmt und dann durch eine mechanische Entlüftung abgeführt wird. Die Luftführung erfolgt meistens geschoßweise entweder steigend oder fallend. Aus der Abluft können über einen Wärmetauscher Wärmerückgewinne erzielt werden. Für den Sonnenschutz kommen Gitterstoffstoren oder Vertikallamellen in Frage, horizontale Lamellen hingegen sind strömungstechnisch ungünstig. Die Reinigung von Zwischenraum, angrenzender Glasoberfläche und Sonnenschutzmaßnahmen erfolgt durch das Öffnen der innenliegenden Glasflügel. Der g-Wert beträgt etwa 0.15, liegt also deutlich unter einer Ausführung ohne zusätzliche Scheibe. Die Vorteile einer Abluftfassade liegen in der Minimierung der Temperaturunterschiede zwischen Raumluft und Fensteroberfläche, was zu einem erhöhten Komfort in Fensternähe führt, und in der Senkung des Energieverbrauchs für Heizung und Kühlung.

Das Museum für Kunsthandwerk in Frankfurt am Main, 1979–84 von Richard Meier erbaut, ist mit einer Abluftfassade ausgestattet. Die Raumluft wird durch einen Schlitz unter dem innenliegenden Fensterrahmen abgesaugt, an der inneren

tion of a traditional Arab device, and sets up an aesthetic link with Arab culture.

Both examples detailed above show how solar control devices can be incorporated in a narrow cavity, without mechanical ventilation, either in front of or behind the actual thermally insulating glass skin.

Mechanically Ventilated Cavity Façades

Characteristic of this kind of façade is an air cavity, which is created by adding a single glass sheet behind a façade with interior solar control device. Lower pressure in the cavity draws part of the exhaust air from the room into this space; here the air warms up, taking most of the heat from the solar control devices, and is then drawn off by means of mechanical ventilation. The air is extracted on each floor separately, either flowing upwards or downwards in the cavity. A heat exchanger may be used to reclaim energy from the exhaust air stream. The types of solar control devices which can be used in the cavity are textile blinds or vertical louvre blinds. For reasons of optimum air flow, horizontal blinds are not suitable. The blinds, the cavity and the internal glass surfaces can be cleaned by opening up the internal single sheets of glass. The g-value is approximately 0.15, which is considerably lower than if the additional, internal sheet had not been used. The advantages of ventilated cavity façades lie in the minimising of the temperature differences between the air in the room and the surface of the glass. This improves the thermal comfort conditions in the office space nearer to the win-

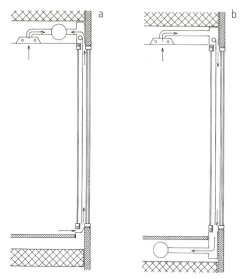

Schematische Darstellung von Abluftfassaden mit steigender (a) bzw. fallender Luftführung (b).
Diagram of a mechanically ventilated cavity façade, either with upward (a) or downward air flow (b).

Abluftfenster mit steigender Luftführung.
Museum für Kunsthandwerk, Frankfurt, 1979–84, Richard Meier.
Mechanically ventilated cavity façade with upward air flow.
Museum of Arts and Crafts, Frankfurt, 1979–84, Richard Meier.

Fläche der äußeren Isolierverglasung durch die besondere Ausbildung der Quersprossen nach oben geleitet und dort abgeführt.

Ein weiteres Beispiel ist der Hauptsitz der Lloyd's Versicherungsgesellschaft in London, 1978–86, von Richard Rogers Partnership. Hier ist die Fassade der Bürogeschosse mit Abluftfenstern versehen. Die erwärmte Raumluft wird über die Beleuchtungskörper angesaugt, womit sie deren Wärme aufnimmt, und mit einem speziell geformten Anschlußstück beim oberen Fensterriegel in den schmalen Zwischenraum der geschoßhohen Abluftfenster weitergeleitet. Dort erwärmt sich die Abluft durch die sekundäre Wärmeabgabe zusätzlich und wird schließlich im untersten Fensterbereich angesaugt und zur Klimaanlage abgeführt. Ziel der Luftführung über die Leuchte und dann von oben nach unten in den Fassadenzwischenraum ist die Nutzung eines Großteils der internen Wärmelasten, um höhere Temperaturen an der Fensteroberfläche in kälteren Jahreszeiten zu erreichen und damit einen erhöhten Komfort in Fensternähe zu gewähren. Die Fassade selbst wurde aus 1.80 x 3.35 m großen vorfabrizierten Elementen konstruiert. Ihr Aufbau weist außen ein Isolierglas, innen einen einfach verglasten Drehflügel und dazwischen einen 40 mm breiten Luftspalt auf. Die Isolierverglasung besteht aus einem 6 mm dicken Gußglas, «Lloyd's», einem 12 mm breiten Scheibenzwischenraum und einer 6 mm low-E beschichteten Scheibe Cool-Lite® SC20. Der Drehflügel besteht aus einem 6 mm dicken außenliegenden

dow and reduces energy costs for heating and cooling.

The Museum of Arts and Crafts in Frankfurt am Main, built 1979–84 by Richard Meier, has a mechanically ventilated cavity façade. The air in the room is drawn out through a slit below the inner frame of the window and then directed upwards along the inside of the outer window to be extracted at the top. This air flow is facilitated by the special design of the transverse glazing bars.

A further example is the headquarters of the Lloyd's Insurance Company in London, built 1978–86 by the Richard Rogers Partnership. The façade of the office levels has mechanically ventilated windows. The warm air in the room is extracted above the lighting units, so that the air also takes up their additional heat. Then this air is fed via specially shaped ducts at the level of the topmost transoms into the narrow cavity of the storey-height ventilated windows. Here the air is warmed further by taking up heat from reradiation of the glass, it is then taken out at the bottom of the window and drawn forward to the air conditioning system of the building. The aim in extracting the air via the lighting and then down from the top to the bottom of the cavity, is to utilise the internal heating loads as much as possible in achieving higher temperatures on the surface of the window during colder periods; this improves the thermal comfort in the office space near the windows. The façade itself is constructed of 1.80 x 3.35 m prefabricated units. On the outside is an insulating glass unit, on the inside is

Abluftfenster mit fallender Luftführung. Die Abluft wird mit einem speziell geformten Anschlußstück beim oberen Fensterriegel eingespeist und unten abgeführt.
Hauptsitz der Lloyd's Versicherungsgesellschaft, London, 1978–86, Richard Rogers Partnership.
Mechanically ventilated cavity façade with downward air flow. The exhaust air is fed via a specially shaped duct at the level of the topmost transom into the cavity and extracted at the bottom.
Headquarters of the Lloyd's Insurance Company, London, 1978–86, Richard Rogers Partnership.

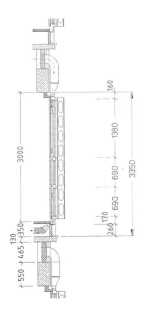

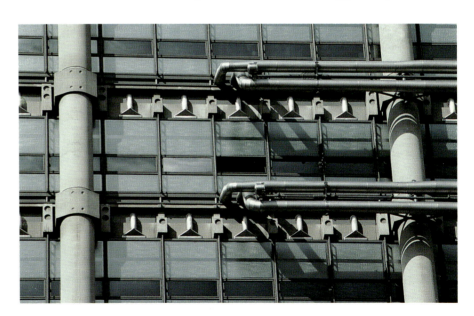

Gußglas «Lloyd's». Im Sichtbereich ist eine transparente Verglasung mit einem Isolierglas außen (6 mm Cool-Lite® SC20, 12 mm Scheibenzwischenraum, 6 mm Planilux®) und einer 6 mm dicken Planilux®-Scheibe innen eingesetzt, die jeweils alternierend fest oder beweglich als Kippflügel ausgeführt ist.

Die geplante Abluftfassade für das neue «Parliamentary Building» in Westminster, London, 1989 begonnen, wird von Michael Hopkins und Partnern entwickelt und benutzt Forschungsergebnisse des «Solar House»-Programms der Europäischen Union. Dabei sollen Erkenntnisse über das thermische Verhalten und den Energiebedarf einer Abluftfassade anhand von Computersimulationen und Prototypen gewonnen werden, um die Ergebnisse für energiesparende Gebäude zu nutzen.
Im Projekt sind die zur Straßenseite orientierten Fassaden durch Pilaster aus Sandstein und verglasten Erkern charakterisiert. Da Fenster zum

a side-hinged single glazed casement and between the two a 40 mm air cavity. The insulating glass comprises a 6 mm layer of "Lloyd's" design rolled glass outside, a 12 mm wide intermediate cavity and a 6 mm low-E coated sheet of Cool-Lite® SC20 inside. The side-hinged casement is a 6 mm pane of "Lloyd's" rolled glass. At seated eye level the glazing is transparent, with an external layer of insulating glass (6 mm Cool-Lite® SC20, 12 mm cavity, 6 mm Planilux®) and internally a 6 mm thick sheet of Planilux®; this band is designed alternately as fixed glazings or tilting sash windows.

The design for a ventilated cavity façade for the new Parliamentary Building in Westminster, London, was begun in 1989 by Michael Hopkins and Partners and utilizes results of research carried out in the "Solar House Programme" of the European Union. The aim of the project was to investigate the thermal behaviour and energy requirements of a mechanically ventilated cavity façade, using computer simulations and proto-

Städtebaulicher Kontext des neues Gebäudes und ein detailliertes Studienmodell der Abluftfassade.
«New Parliamentary Building», Westminster, London, 1989– , Michael Hopkins und Partner.
City context of the new building and detailed study model of the cavity façade.
New Parliamentary Building, Westminster, London, 1989– , Michael Hopkins and Partners.

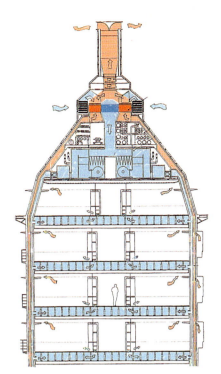

Schnitt mit Führung der Frisch- und der Abluft im Gebäude (oben); Detaillierter Schnitt durch den verglasten Erker (unten links); Luftführung und Lichtumlenkung bei einem typischen Büroraum (unten rechts). «New Parliamentary Building», Westminster, London, 1989– ,Michael Hopkins und Partner. *Section through building showing fresh air and exhaust air path (top); detailed section through glazed bay window (bottom left); system of air flow and light redirection in a typical office unit (bottom right). New Parliamentary Building, Westminster, London, 1989– , Michael Hopkins and Partners.*

Öffnen aus Schallschutz- und Sicherheitsgründen nicht möglich sind, wurde eine Abluftfassade vorgeschlagen. Ihre Konstruktion besteht aus einem außenliegenden Isolierglas – außen ein weißes Verbundglas, eine Argonfüllung im Zwischenraum, innen ein Floatglas mit einer Low-E Beschichtung – und innenliegend einem Flügel zum Öffnen aus einer vorgespannten Glasscheibe. Für den Sonnenschutz sind in den 75 mm breiten Luftzwischenraum integrierte, verstellbare Lamellen sowie ein Lichtumlenkschwert oberhalb des Erkers vorgesehen, das den nahen Fensterbereich verschattet und das direkte einfallende Tageslicht in die Raumtiefe umlenkt.

Die in der Klimaanlage aufbereitete Luft fließt von Bodenauslässen im hinteren Teil des Raumes ein und wird über Öffnungen unterhalb der Erkerverglasung sowie bei der Leuchte oberhalb des Lichtumlenkschwerts abgesaugt. Damit wird sowohl eine energiesparende Durchlüftung des Raums als auch die Beseitigung der Abwärme der Leuchte erreicht. Die Abluft wird seitlich im oberen Fensterbereich abgesaugt und entlang der Pilaster bis ins Dachgeschoß abgeführt, wo Anlagen für die Wärmerückgewinnung installiert sind.

Das Zusammenwirken der verschiedenen Maßnahmen wurde anhand eines zweigeschossigen Prototyps, erstellt im Forschungszentrum Conphoebus in der Nähe von Catania, Italien, im Sommer und Winter 1994 überprüft. Ziel ist eine Senkung des Energieverbrauchs von üblichen 270–360 kWh/m²a auf 90–110 kWh/m²a.

types, in order to test the effects for low-energy buildings. In the project, the street façade is composed of loadbearing sandstone piers and glazed bay windows. As these windows are not intended to be opened, for reasons of safety and acoustic insulation, a ventilated cavity façade was proposed. The window construction is composed of an external insulating unit (an external clear laminated glass, an argon gas filling in the cavity, and an internal float glass with a low-E coating), and internally an opening sheet of toughened glass. Solar shading is taken care of by adjustable louvre blinds integrated in the 75 mm wide cavity between the outer and inner skins, and by light shelves positioned above the bays; these shelves shade the area immediately next to the window and they are designed to reflect daylight into the back of the room. The air from the air handling plant is supplied as displacement ventilation through air vents in the floor at the back of the room and drawn off again through openings situated at the bottom of the bay windows and at the level of the lighting above the light shelf. This ensures sufficient cross ventilation in the room and it reduces the warming up caused by the lighting. In the upper window area the exhaust air is drawn off through the exhaust ducts on either side of the windows and drawn along the piers up to the roof where heat exchangers reclaim the energy from the exhaust air stream.

The combined effects of the various measures have been tested on a two-floor prototype set up at the Conphoebus test centre building near

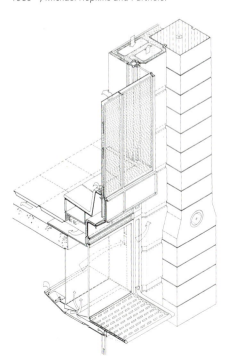

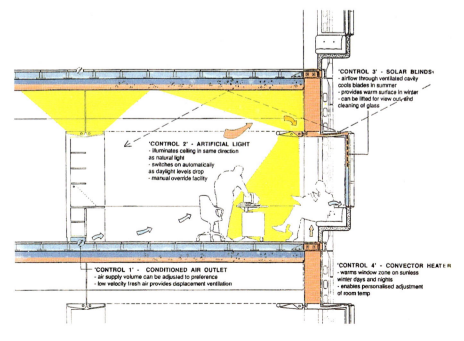

'CONTROL 3' - SOLAR BLINDS
- airflow through ventilated cavity cools blades in summer
- provides warm surface in winter
- can be lifted for view out and cleaning of glass

'CONTROL 2' - ARTIFICIAL LIGHT
- illuminates ceiling in same direction as natural light
- switches on automatically as daylight levels drop
- manual override facility

'CONTROL 1' - CONDITIONED AIR OUTLET
- air supply volume can be adjusted to preference
- low velocity fresh air provides displacement ventilation

'CONTROL 4' - CONVECTOR HEATER
- warms window zone on sunless winter days and nights
- enables personalised adjustment of room temp

«Zweite Haut»- oder zweischalige Fassade

Der Begriff «Zweite Haut»- oder zweischalige Fassade bezeichnet eine Fassade und eine Verglasung, die außen vor dem eigentlichen Raumabschluß angeordnet ist. Im Zwischenraum werden meistens die Sonnen- und Blendschutzmaßnahmen untergebracht, die so vor Witterungseinflüssen und Luftverschmutzung geschützt sind, was besonders bei hohen oder an stark befahrenen Straßen gelegenen Gebäuden von Bedeutung ist. Ein weiterer Vorteil einer zweischaligen Fassade liegt in der sommerlichen Sonnenschutzwirkung. Da die infolge der absorbierten Sonnenstrahlung entstehende Sekundärstrahlung an die Luft des Zwischenraums abgegeben wird, entsteht thermischer Auftrieb. Rechnerische und praktische Untersuchungen haben gezeigt, daß durch natürliche Luftzirkulation bis zu 25 % der im Zwischenraum in Wärme umgesetzten Sonnenstrahlung abgeführt werden kann. In der Regel können, mit entprechend ausgewählten Scheiben und Sonnenschutzmaßnahmen, g-Werte um 0.10 erreicht werden.

Aufgrund der mit steigender Höhe zunehmenden Lufttemperatur sind aber durchgehend geöffnete Zwischenräume meistens auf zwei bis drei Geschosse einzuschränken. Hinzu kommen noch technische Anforderungen an Schall- und Feuerschutz.

Durch die Verminderung des Winddrucks mit der zusätzlichen Scheibe können die Fenster auch in hochgelegenen Stockwerken geöffnet werden. Eine natürliche Lüftung der Arbeitsräume durch Frischluftzufuhr von außen steigert das Wohlbefinden der Benutzer und kann auch eine Reduktion der Investitionen für die Anlage der Gebäudetechnik und deren Energieverbrauch zur Folge haben.

Eine zweischalige Fassade vermindert auch die Wärmeverluste, weil die geringere Luftgeschwindigkeit und die erhöhte Temperatur im Zwischenraum den Wärmeübergang auf der Glasoberfläche vermindert. Damit ergeben sich höhere Oberflächentemperaturen raumseitig der inneren Verglasung, was sich auf den Komfort im Fensterbereich positiv auswirkt. Ferner besteht die Möglichkeit, über Wärmetauscher eine Energierückgewinnung aus der Abluft zu erzielen.

In konstruktiver Hinsicht kann die äußere Schale als Einfach- oder als Isolierverglasung ausgeführt werden. Für die Reinigung muß der Zwischenraum begehbar oder durch die Fenster erreichbar sein.

Catania in Italy in summer and winter 1994. The target is to reduce energy consumption from the general level of 270–360 kWh/m²a to 90–110 kWh/m²a.

Double-Skin Façades

The term "double-skin" façade refers to an arrangement with a glass skin in front of the actual building façade. Solar control devices are placed in the cavity between these two skins, which protects them from the influences of weather and air pollution, a factor of particular importance in high-rise buildings or ones situated in the vicinity of busy roads.

A further advantage of the double-skin façade is the solar shading it affords in the summer. As reradiation from absorbed solar radiation is emitted into the intermediate cavity, a natural stack effect results, which causes the air to rise, taking with it additional heat. Computer simulations and tests have shown that natural air circulation can remove up to 25 % of the heat resulting from solar radiation in the cavity. Generally, given appropriate panes of glass and solar control devices, g-values of approximately 0.10 can be achieved.

As the temperature of the air increases as it rises upwards, it is usual to restrict the height of the continuous opening to two or three floors. Technical considerations concerned with fire protection and acoustic insulation also play a role.

The reduction of wind pressure by the addition of the extra pane of glass means that the windows can be opened even in the uppermost floors of a high-rise building. Natural ventilation of offices by fresh air is much more acceptable to the building's users and it has the additional benefits of reducing investment in air handling systems and also reducing energy consumption.

A double-skin façade also reduces heat losses because the reduced speed of the air flow and the increased temperature of the air in the cavity lowers the rate of heat transfer on the surface of the glass. This has the effect of maintaining higher surface temperatures on the inside of the glass, which in turn means that the space close to the window can be better utilised as a result of increased thermal comfort conditions. An additional possibility with double-skin façades is to reclaim energy from the exhaust air stream using a heat exchanger.

Zweischalige Fassade mit einem breiten Luftzwischenraum: die steigende Außenluft nimmt die
entstehende Wärme auf und führt sie bis in Dachgeschoß; die äußere Glashaut besteht aus einem
bronzegefärbten, vorgespannten Einfachglas.
Bürogebäude Leslie und Godwin, Farnborough,
England, 1984, Arup Associates.
*Double-skin façade with wide air space: the upward
air flow absorbs the heat and draws it up to the roof;
the outer skin consists of bronze-tinted toughened
single glazing.*
*Leslie and Godwin office building, Farnborough,
England, 1984, Arup Associates.*

Einige Beispiele einer «Zweiten Haut»-Fassade
wurden schon Anfang der 80er Jahre gebaut.
Das 1984 fertiggestellte Bürogebäude Leslie
und Godwin in Farnborough, England, auch
«Briarcliff House» genannt, von Arup Associates,
weist eine zweischalige Fassade mit Wärmerückgewinnung auf. Die Verglasung erfüllt zwei
Aufgaben. Sie dient als Lärmschutz gegen Fahr-
zeug- und Flugverkehr und als Sonnenschutz
für die Büroräume, die mit Computern und
anderen wärmeerzeugenden Geräten ausgestattet sind. Sie besteht aus einem 10 mm dicken
wärmeabsorbierenden Einfachglas und ist der
inneren Fassade 120 cm vorgelagert, welche
aus geschlossenen Blechpaneelen, festen Isolier-
glasfenstern und sensorgesteuerten Lamellen
besteht.
Der breite Zwischenraum dient der Reinigung
und der Führung der vertikalen Lüftungsrohre.
Im Winter nimmt die steigende Außenluft die

The outer skin can either be made up of single
glazing or an insulating glass unit. The intermediate cavity must be accessible for cleaning, either
directly, or by opening windows.

Several examples of a double-skin façade were
built at the beginning of the 1980s. One such is
the offices of Leslie and Godwin (also called
"Briarcliff House") in Farnborough, England,
built in 1984 by Arup Associates; this building
has a double-glazed façade with an air-handling
plant to reclaim waste heat. The glazing fulfils
two functions: it serves as acoustic insulation
against noise from traffic and aircraft, and also
as solar shading for the offices, which already
have many heat-producing devices in the room,
such as computers. The outer skin is a 10 mm
thick heat-absorbing glass pane, placed 120 cm
in front of the actual building skin. This inner
façade consists of metal panels, fixed insulating

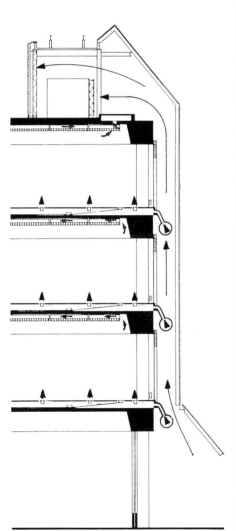

entstehende Wärme auf und führt sie zur Wärme-rückewinnungsanlage im Dachgeschoß. Im Sommer wird sie nicht weiter genutzt und durch offenstehende Lüftungsklappen direkt ins Freie geleitet.

Neuere Beispiele stellen das Haus der Wirtschaftsförderung und das Technologiezentrum in Duisburg dar, die von Sir Norman Foster und Partnern in Zusammenarbeit mit der Kaiser Bautechnik, Duisburg, 1993 fertiggestellt wurden. Sie bilden den ersten realisierten Teil eines geplanten Mikroelektronik-Parks. Die gekrümmte zweischalige Fassade des linsenförmigen Kopfbaus besteht aus einer klaren Einfachverglasung, die ca. 20 cm vor der geschoß-hohen Isolierverglasung angeordnet ist. Ihre 1.50 x 3.30 m vorgespannten, 12 mm dicken Scheiben sind mit Planar®-Bolzen in vertikale Aluminiumprofile eingehängt. Letztere sind vom Dachrand abgehängt und mit den Geschoß-decken zur Übertragung der horizontalen Lasten verbunden. Die innenliegende Fassadenschale besteht aus geschoßhohen Drehflügelfenstern

glass windows and sensor-controlled louvre blinds. The wide intermediate cavity aids cleaning and houses the vertical ventilation ducts. In winter the upward air flow absorbs the heat and draws it up to the roof where the heat energy gets reclaimed by heat exchanger system. In summer this is not necessary, and the air is directed freely via ventilation flaps to the outside.

More recent examples are the Business Promotion Centre and the Technology Centre built in Duisburg in 1993 by Sir Norman Foster and Partners in collaboration with Kaiser Bautechnik, Duisburg. These buildings form the first stage of a planned "Microelectronic Park" in Duisburg. The curved, double-skin façade of the lens-shaped building at the edge of the complex consists of clear single glazing situated 20 cm in front of the full-height insulating glass façade. The single glazing consists of 1.50 x 3.30 m toughened, 12mm thick panes suspended in vertical aluminium profiles by means of Planar® bolts. The profiles are suspended from the edge of the roof and attached to the intermediate

Die zweischalige Fassade des linsenförmigen Gebäudes besteht aus einer klaren Einfachverglasung, die der innenliegenden Isolierverglasung vorgehängt ist.
Haus der Wirtschaftsförderung, Duisburg, 1988–93, Sir Norman Foster und Partner.
The double-skin façade of the lens-shaped building consists of a clear single glazing suspended in front of the insulating glass façade.
Business Promotion Centre, Duisburg, Germany, 1988–93, Sir Norman Foster and Partners.

mit thermisch getrennten Aluminiumprofilen und einer Isolierverglasung, außen 6 mm Floatglas, innen 8 mm Verbundglas mit Low-E Beschichtung und einer Argonfüllung im Zwischenraum. Der k-Wert der gesamten Konstruktion liegt im Bereich von 1.4 W/m²K. Perforierte, computergesteuerte Aluminiumjalousien sind in den Zwischenraum eingebaut. Die Luft wird mit einem leichten Überdruck in den unteren Bereich des Zwischenraums eingeblasen. Beim Durchströmen nimmt sie die an den Lamellenstoren entstehende Abwärme auf, um schließlich durch den entstehenden Auftrieb steigend durch kleine Öffnungen am Dachrand ins Freie auszutreten.

Da das Gebäude direkt an einer stark befahrenen Straße liegt, wurde eine Vollklimatisation der Räume anderen Lösungen mit natürlicher Belüftung vorgezogen. Im Gegensatz zu Nur-Luft-Klimaanlagen, wo die Temperatur durch Zufuhr von Kalt- und Warmluft reguliert wird, ist hier eine Quellüftung eingebaut, die nur den Frischluftanteil zuführt, während für die Heizung und die Kühlung getrennte Wasserkreisläufe benutzt werden. Die Frischluft fließt durch schmale Schlitze entlang der Fensterfront ein und breitet sich, gleichsam als Frischluftsee, am Boden aus. Sie wird durch Wärmequellen – Personen oder Geräte – erwärmt und steigt zur Decke, wo sie durch Schattenfugen bei den Beleuchtungskörpern abgesaugt wird.

Für die Kühlung der Büros sind wasserdurchströmte Kühldecken eingesetzt, für die Heizung sorgt entlang der Fassade ein 60 cm breiter Streifen mit Fußbodenheizung.

floors for transfer of horizontal loading. The inner façade skin consists of storey-height side-hung windows with thermally broken aluminium profiles and insulating glass units; outside is a 6 mm float glass, inside is an 8 mm laminated glass with low-E coating and the cavity between is filled with argon gas. The U-value of the whole double-skin façade is around 1.4 W/m²K. Perforated, computer-controlled aluminium blinds are incorporated into the cavity between the two skins. Air is injected at slightly higher than ambient pressure into the lower part of this cavity and through the effects of warming a natural stack effect results. This air rises and removes heat from the louvre blinds and continues upwards to be expelled into the open air through small openings by the roof edge.

As the building is situated next to a very busy road the option of full air conditioning was preferred to other solutions with natural air ventilation. In contrast to air-only conditioning systems, in this case a displacement ventilation system is used which supplies only the required fresh air, while for heating and cooling separate water re-

Die Büroräume sind mit Quellüftung, Kühldecken und Fußbodenheizung ausgestattet (links); Sonnen- und Blendschutz erfolgen durch perforierte Lamellen (rechts); Detail des Fassadenaufbaus und Anschluß an die Geschoßdecke.
Haus der Wirtschaftsförderung, Duisburg, 1988–93, Sir Norman Foster und Partner.
The offices are supplied with displacement ventilation, chilled ceilings and underfloor heating (left); sun and glare protection is achieved through perforated blinds (right); detail of the façade construction and the connection with the floor slab.
Business Promotion Centre, Duisburg, Germany, 1988–93, Sir Norman Foster and Partners.

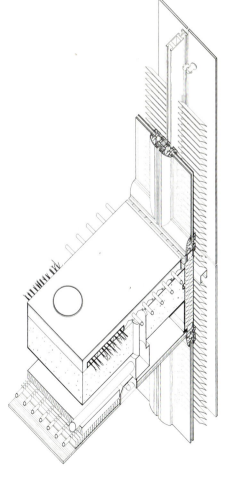

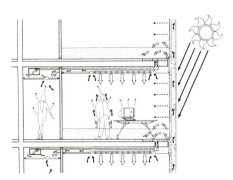
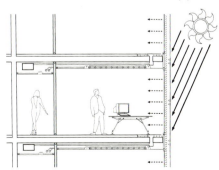

Außer für den Witterungsschutz kann eine «Zweite Haut»-Fassade auch für die natürliche Be- und Entlüftung der dahinterliegenden Räume eingesetzt werden, wie die 1995 von Architectures Jean Nouvel fertiggestellten «Galeries Lafayette» in Berlin zeigen. Die Architekten haben das geschlossene Volumen des Kaufhauses rundherum mit Büroflächen und kegelförmigen internen Atrien versehen und mit einer «Zweiten Haut»-Fassade umhüllt, die durch ihre besondere Gestaltung als Informationsträgerin und optische Attraktion dienen soll. Dafür sind die Deckenstirnen mit 55 cm hohen Leuchtschriftbändern ausgestattet, die mit Schriftzügen und Logos versehen werden können. Die Büroverglasung ist wie ein geschoßhohes Schaufenster ausgeführt, welches den Betrachtern von der Straße her eine gewisse Einsicht in die Dynamik des Innenlebens ermöglicht.

Eine weitere optische Attraktion stellt die außenliegende Wetterschutzhaut dar. Sie ist mit einer 20%igen Emailbeschichtung aus grauen Punkten

turn systems are provided. The fresh air flows in through narrow slits along the window front and spreads out along the floor forming a "fresh air pool". This air is then naturally heated by various heat sources, such as people, or equipment, and rises to the ceiling where it is extracted through vents above the lighting. To cool the offices, chilled ceilings are used, and heating is taken care of by means of a 60 cm strip of underfloor heating along the façade.

In addition to the function of weather protection a double-skin façade can be used for natural ventilation of the offices behind. An example of this is the "Galeries Lafayette" in Berlin, completed in 1995 by Architectures Jean Nouvel. The architects have ringed the closed volume of the department store with office space and conical-shaped internal atria. The whole is then enclosed in a double-skin façade, which serves additionally as an information carrier and as an optical attraction.

Modellaufnahme der abgerundeten zweischaligen Fassade bei der Straßenkreuzung.
«Galeries Lafayette», Berlin, 1991–95, Architectures Jean Nouvel.
Model photo of the curved double-skin façade at the crossroads.
Galeries Lafayette, Berlin, 1991–95,
Architectures Jean Nouvel.

Die außenliegende Glashaut besteht aus vorgespannten Einfachgläsern mit emaillierten grauen Punkten, die zunehmende Bedruckung zeichnet die Projektion der dahinterliegenden kegelförmigen Atrien nach.
«Galeries Lafayette», Berlin, 1991–95,
Architectures Jean Nouvel.
The outer skin consists of toughened single glazing with a fritted grey dot pattern; an increasing concentration of the pattern traces the outline of the conical atria inside the building.
Galeries Lafayette, Berlin, 1991–95,
Architectures Jean Nouvel.

Zeichnung der Bedruckung mit Verlaufraster; die Baustellen-Aufnahmen zeigen den Aufbau der zweischaligen Fassade mit der emaillierten grauen Bedruckung.
«Galeries Lafayette», Berlin, 1991–95,
Architectures Jean Nouvel.
Drawing of the increasing dot patern; the photos of the building site show the construction of the double-skin façade and the grey dot pattern.
Galeries Lafayette, Berlin, 1991–95,
Architectures Jean Nouvel.

versehen, wobei einige Flächen ausgespart sind, um die Projektion der kegelförmigen Atrien auf die Fassade nachzuzeichnen. Die Konturen der Atrien sind zusätzlich durch eine von 20 % auf 100 % zunehmende Bedruckung betont.

Die Wetterschutzhaut besteht aus einem 12 mm dicken vorgespannten Glas, das jeweils bei den durch den Grundriß vorgegebenen Rundungen gebogen ist, während die innenliegende wärmedämmende Verglasungsebene der Rundung polygonal folgt. Sie besteht aus 2.75 m hohen und 1.35 m breiten Fenstern, die alternierend als Festverglasung und als Dreh-Kippflügel ausgeführt sind. Das 30 mm dicke Isolierglas, außen eine 8 mm und innen eine 6 mm dicke Scheibe mit einer Low-E Beschichtung, weist eine Argonfüllung auf. Als Sonnenschutz werden perforierte Lamellenstoren aus Edelstahl in den 20 cm

Along the edge of the slab are 55 cm illuminated strips carrying advertising and logos. The glazing for the offices is like a full-height shop window, allowing passers-by to glimpse at the dynamic activity inside the offices.

The outer rain screen skin provides an additional optical attraction. It has a 20 % frit of grey dots; some areas are left clear to show the projection of the conical atria onto the façade. The contours of the atria are further emphasized by an increase from 20 % to 100 % frit cover on the edges. The weather skin consists of an outer 12 mm thick sheet of toughened glass curved to match the ground plan, while the interior insulating glass layer is more angular. It consists of 2.75 m high and 1.35 m wide windows, alternating as fixed glazing and turn-and-tilt windows. The 30 mm thick insulating glass unit has an 8 mm outer pane and a 6 mm inner pane with a low-E

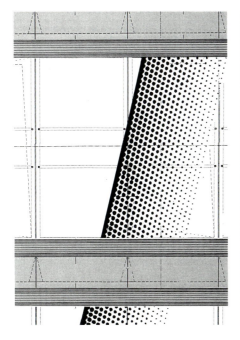

breiten Zwischenraum integriert. Die natürliche Luftzufuhr erfolgt durch 15 cm hohe Schlitze unter- und oberhalb der Wetterschutzverglasung.

Ein weiteres Beispiel für eine «Zweite Haut»-Fassade mit natürlicher Lüftung ist der 1993 von den Architekten Herzog und de Meuron fertiggestellte Sitz der Schweizerischen Unfallversicherungsanstalt, SUVA, in Basel. Die Glashülle verleiht einem bestehenden Gebäude mit einer Steinfassade und seiner neuen Erweiterung ein einheitliches Erscheinungsbild. Die Pfosten-Riegel-Konstruktion ist geschoßweise mit drei horizontalen Bändern mit Klappflügeln versehen, die verschiedene Funktionen erfüllen. Im Durchsichtsbereich sind Isoliergläser eingesetzt, die für die Frischluftzufuhr von den Benutzern manuell geöffnet werden können. Im oberen Bereich sind Isoliergläser mit integrierten Prismenplatten eingebaut. Sie werden computergesteuert dem Sonnenazimut nachgeführt, um die Büroräume vor der direkten Sonnenstrahlung zu schützen. Die unteren Klappflügel erfüllen dagegen eine klimatechnische Funktion. Im Winter sind sie meistens geschlossen und schaffen ein Luftpolster vor der Brüstung. Im Sommer sind sie offen, um die Steinfassade des älteren Baus vor Überhitzung zu bewahren und seine nächtliche Kühlung zu sichern.
Die Verstellbarkeit der Glasflügel ermöglicht eine differenzierte Anpassung der Fassade an die Wetter- und Klimaveränderungen. Sie zeigt auch, wie bestimmte Aspekte – natürliche Lüftung, Lichtumlenkung usw. – zunehmend wichtige Bestandteile einer Fassadenplanung werden. Die

coating, and argon gas filling. Perforated louvre blinds of stainless steel are integrated into the 20 cm wide cavity to protect against the sun. Air can circulate in this space through 15 cm slits above and below the glass weather skin.

A further example of a double-skin façade with natural ventilation is the headquarters of the Swiss insurance company, SUVA, in Basle, built in 1993 by the architects Herzog and de Meuron. The glass skin gives an overall unity to the existing building with its stone façade and its new extension. At each storey level the mullion and transom frame has triple horizontal banding with top-hung windows. The glazing band at window level is of clear insulating glass; these sections can be opened manually for ventilation by the rooms' occupants. The upper band consists of insulating glass with integrated prismatic panels. These glazings are computer-controlled to track the sun across the sky and thus protect the interior of the offices from direct sunlight. The top-hung windows in the lower band at each floor level, however, fulfil a different function in the energy system of the building. In winter they remain generally closed and create a buffer air zone in front of the parapet. In summer they are open, to prevent the stone façade of the old part of the building from overheating and to ensure night-cooling of this façade. This possibility of adjusting the glass panels permits a differentiated approach to changing wea-ther and climatic conditions and shows how other aspects such as natural ventilation, light deflection, etc. are becoming increasingly important components of façade

Die Zweite-Haut-Fassade ist geschoßweise durch drei horizontale Bänder mit Klappflügeln unterteilt; Detail der oberen Flügel aus Isoliergläsern mit integrierten Prismenplatten und ihrem Antriebsmechanismus. Schweizerische Unfallversicherungsanstalt, Basel, 1991–93, Herzog & de Meuron.
At each storey level the double-skin façade has triple horizontal banding with top-hung windows; detail of the upper band of insulating glass with integrated prismatic panels and the control mechanism. Headquarters of the Swiss Insurance Company, Basle, 1991–93, Herzog & de Meuron.

wachsende Komplexität der Anforderungen verlangt deshalb auch neue Arbeitsmethoden, um die Interaktion von Fassade und Gebäudetechnik zu gewährleisten.

Intelligente Glasfassaden

Das Wort «intelligent» deutet auf eine dynamische, gleichsam lebendige Fähigkeit der Fassade, sich den wechselnden Tages- und Jahreszeitverhältnissen anzupassen, was den Verbrauch von Primärenergie für Heizung, Kühlung und Belichtung reduziert und unsere Umwelt schützt. Dabei können verschiedenste energiesparende Maßnahmen, wie natürliche Belüftung, nächtliche Kühlung, natürliche Belichtung, Schaffung von Pufferzonen usw., zum Tragen kommen.

Das setzt aber eine intensive Interaktion zwischen Fassade und Gebäude voraus. Zum Beispiel muß das aero- und thermodynamische Verhalten des jeweiligen Baus erfaßt werden, weil für eine natürliche Belüftung die Luftströmungen im Fassadenzwischenraum und im Innenraum vom Winddruck oder -sog abhängig sind.

Zu diesem Zweck werden Computersimulationen, Windkanalversuche mit Gebäudemodellen und originalgroßen Musterfassaden sowie Raumströmungsversuche in Modellräumen durchgeführt.

Aufgrund der steigenden Komplexität der Zusammenhänge wird eine enge Zusammenarbeit zwischen Architekten, Fassadenplanern und beratenden Fachingenieuren unabdingbar. Diese Zusammenarbeit wird als integrale oder ganzheitliche Planung bezeichnet.

planning. The increasing complexity in façade requirements high-lights the need for new working methods to guarantee optimum interaction of façade and building services.

Intelligent Glass Façades

The word "intelligent" with respect to façades indicates an ability to respond to the changing environmental conditions according to the time of the day or year, in such a way as to reduce primary energy needs for heating, cooling and lighting, and thus to make a contribution to environmental conservation. Various energy-saving methods are employed in intelligent façades – natural ventilation, night-time thermal mass cooling, daylighting, the creation of buffer zones, etc. All these methods call for a close functional integration of façade and building.

For example, the aerodynamic and thermodynamic behaviour of the building has to be studied, because for natural ventilation the air flow in the ventilated façade cavity and in the building's interior are dependent on wind pressure and suction.

To predict this behaviour, computational fluid dynamics (CFD) methods are applied and experiments are carried out in the wind tunnel using models of the building, but also air-flow simulations with full-scale sections of façade or actual-size rooms are carried out. The increasing complexity of the relationships between these various factors means that close cooperation is necessary between architects, façade planners and building engineers. This type of cooperation is called integrated or holistic planning.

Einblick in den Windkanal mit einem zu untersuchenden Modell (links); die Luftströmungen werden durch Rauch sichtbar gemacht (rechts).
View of a wind tunnel with a model under test (left); smoke is used to give a picture of the air flow (right).

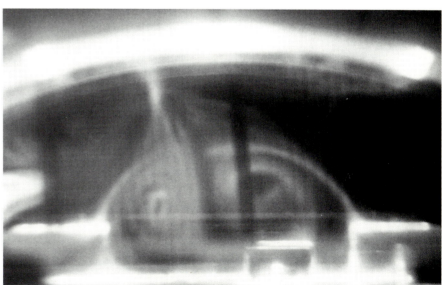

Der 1991 preisgekrönte Wettbewerbsentwurf für die Commerzbank in Frankfurt am Main, dessen Klima- und Energiekonzept von Sir Norman Foster und Partnern in Zusammenarbeit mit HL-Technik, München, erarbeitet wurde, entspricht dem Bestreben der Bauherrschaft, ein Hochhaus zu planen, das ökologischen und energiesparenden Überlegungen Rechnung trägt.

Das 60geschossige Hochhaus ist in Einheiten zu je vier Bürostockwerken und einem zugeordneten Wintergarten unterteilt, die gegeneinander spiralförmig versetzt sind. In jeder Einheit nimmt die Bürofläche zwei Seiten des leicht abgerundeten dreieckigen Grundrisses ein, der Wintergarten die dritte. Tragstruktur, Erschließung und Nebenräume sind in den Ecken angeordnet. Im Zentrum befindet sich ein gebäudehohes Atrium, das in zwölfgeschossige Abschnitte unterteilt ist.

Das Hochhaus soll während des Jahres meistens natürlich belüftet werden können, da die durch Thermik und auftretenden Wind zu erwartenden Unter- und Überdrucksituationen die dazu notwendigen Luftströmungen unterstützen.

Für die natürliche Belüftung der außenliegenden Büros wurde eine zweischalige Fassade vorge-

The 1991 prize-winning design for the Commerzbank in Frankfurt am Main, whose climatic and energy concept was developed by Sir Norman Foster and Partners in collaboration with HL-Technik of Munich, reflects the client's concern to produce an ecological, low-energy building. The 60-storey high-rise building is divided into four-storey office sections, each with a winter garden; the sections are organised spirally in relation to one another. In each unit the office space occupies two sides of the gently curved triangular floor plan, the winter garden occupies the third side. The support structure, circulation areas and ancillary rooms are located in the corners of the triangle. In the centre of the building is a full-height atrium, divided into twelve-storey sections.

For most of the year the building is expected to be naturally ventilated because thermal buoyancy and general wind conditions create the necessary low and high pressures which promote air flow. To naturally ventilate the offices facing outwards a double-skin façade is planned, with opening windows in the inner skin. Insulating glass (U-value 1.4–1.6 W/m²K) is used, and placed in the

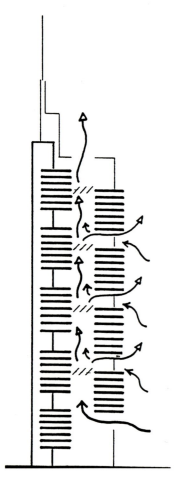

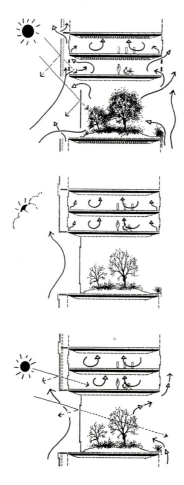

Das mehrgeschossige zentrale Atrium ermöglicht die Durchlüftung des Gebäudes und damit die natürliche Belüftung der innenliegenden Büros (links).
Bei den außenliegenden Büros wurde eine zweischalige Fassade vorgesehen (rechts); im Sommer ermöglicht sie die natürliche Belüftung der Büros durch das Öffnen der Fenster, während für den Sonnen- und Blendschutz bewegliche Lamellen vorgesehen sind; nachts und im Winter können die Lüftungsklappen geschlossen und der Zwischenraum so in eine isolierende Pufferzone umgewandelt werden.
Hauptsitz der Commerzbank, Frankfurt, 1991–97, Sir Norman Foster und Partner.

The central atrium extending over several floors enables cross-ventilation of the building and therefore the natural ventilation of the office spaces next to the atria (left).
For the offices facing outwards a double-skin façade is planned (right); in summer it allows for natural ventilation of the offices by opening windows in the inner skin, while adjustable louvres in the cavity protect against glare and direct sunlight; at night and in winter the louvred shutters can be closed, so that the cavity becomes an insulating cushion of air.
Commerzbank headquarters, Frankfurt, 1991–97, Sir Norman Foster and Partners.

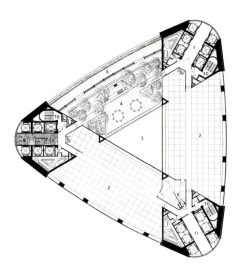

Typischer dreieckiger Grundriß mit Büroflächen und
Wintergarten; Vertikalschnitt und Photomontage des
überarbeiteten Entwurfs.
Hauptsitz der Commerzbank, Frankfurt, 1991–97,
Sir Norman Foster und Partner.

*Typical triangular floor plan with office spaces and
winter garden; vertical section and photomontage of
the developed project.*

*Commerzbank headquarters, Frankfurt, 1991–97,
Sir Norman Foster and Partners.*

sehen, deren innenliegende Fenster sich öffnen
lassen. Sie ist mit einer Wärmeschutzverglasung
(k-Wert 1.4–1.6 W/m²K) und beweglichen Lamellen für Sonnen- und Blendschutz im Zwischenraum ausgestattet. Um den Zwischenraum
bei kalter Wetterlage als isolierende Luftschicht
zu nutzen, sind verschließbare Lüftungsklappen
geplant. In der Weiterbearbeitung allerdings
wurde diese zweischalige Fassadenvariante der
Wettbewerbseingabe verschiedentlich verändert.
Die Wintergärten bilden Pufferzonen mit ausge-
glichenem Mikroklima, das für die Durchlüftung
des Gebäudes und für die natürliche Belüftung
der innenliegenden Büros genutzt wird. Wenn
die Gartenverglasung in Sommer offen ist, strömt
die Außenluft hinein und steigt oder sinkt im
mehrgeschossigen Atrium – je nach den im Garten herrschenden Temperaturen und Druckver-
hältnissen – und tritt beim nächsten Wintergarten wieder aus. Diese Durchströmung ermöglicht
die natürliche Belüftung der angrenzenden Arbeitsflächen.

In kalten Jahreszeiten ist die Verglasung weitgehend geschlossen. Dann wirkt der Garten als
Klimapuffer, indem er die eingestrahlte Sonnenenergie in Wärme umwandelt und eine tempe-

cavity are adjustable louvres to protect against
glare and direct sunlight. Louvred shutters in the
façade can be closed when temperatures drop,
so that the cavity can become an insulating cushion of air. During further development on the design, however, this particular variant of the double-skin façade underwent several changes.

The winter gardens form buffer zones with balanced micro-climates; they play a role in the
cross ventilation of the whole building and
specifically in the natural ventilation of the inward-facing offices.

In summer when the windows in the winter gardens are open, the outside air enters and either
rises or sinks in the atrium stretching over several storeys – depending on the ambient temperature and pressure conditions in the winter garden – and then this air exits at the next winter
garden. This cross ventilation enables the office
spaces facing the atria and the winter gardens to
be naturally ventilated. When the weather is colder, the glazings remain largely closed, and the
winter gardens then act as climate buffer zones,
by turning the solar radiation into heat and creating a temperate environment. In summer the ventilated thermal mass of the concrete floors, sub-

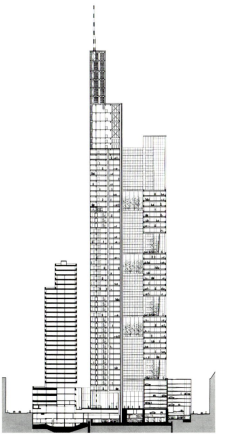

rierte Umgebung schafft. Im Sommer sollen durchlüftete, schwerspeichernde Decken, welche nachts abgekühlt werden, die tagsüber in den Büros entstehende Abwärme aufnehmen können.

Das Hochhaus befindet sich derzeit im Bau, wobei die im Wettbewerb vorgeschlagenen Maßnahmen überprüft und verfeinert werden.

Mit ähnlichen Energiekonzepten arbeitet auch das zweitrangierte Projekt des Wettbewerbs für die Commerzbank, das vom Architekten Christoph Ingenhoven, beraten vom Büro Happold, London, Prof. Frei Otto, Stuttgart, und der HL-Technik, München, eingereicht worden ist.
Das zylindrische Hochhaus weist 46 Geschosse auf, die in Abschnitte zu je 5 bis 6 Ebenen unterteilt sind. Erschließung und Nebenräume sind in

ject to night-time cooling, balances the heat produced in the offices during the day.
The project has recently gone on site and the techniques put forward are being tested and further refined.

A similar energy concept is being proposed by the second-placed project in the Commerzbank competition, a design put forward by the architect Christoph Ingenhoven, in consultation with Happold in London, Professor Frei Otto in Stuttgart and HL-Technik in Munich.
Their proposal is for a cylindrical high-rise building with 46 storeys divided into sections of 5 to 6 floors. The circulation areas and ancillary rooms are located in the central core. The round shape of the tower was selected for reasons of energy conservation. It presents a minimum sur-

Modellaufnahme des zylindrischen Hochhauses; die Form bietet eine minimale Oberfläche bei einem maximalen inneren Volumen.
Wettbewerb für den Hauptsitz der Commerzbank, Frankfurt, 1991, Christoph Ingenhoven.
Model photo of the cylindrical high-rise building; this shape presents a minimum external surface area while providing a maximum of interior space. Competition for the headquarters of the Commerzbank, Frankfurt, 1991, Christoph Ingenhoven.

Kreuzförmige Grundrißvariante mit vier Wintergärten und eine Einheit mit der Höhe von fünf Geschossen. Wettbewerb für den Hauptsitz der Commerzbank, Frankfurt, 1991, Christoph Ingenhoven.
The cross-shaped floor plan with four winter gardens and a five-storey high unit.
Competition for the headquarters of the Commerzbank, Frankfurt, 1991, Christoph Ingenhoven.

 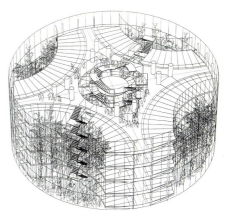

Im Winter ist die äußere Verglasung geschlossen und die Gärten wirken als Wärmepuffer; in der Übergangszeit und im Sommer ist die Verglasung weitgehend offen, und die Büros können natürlich belüftet werden; für die Beschattung sind innenliegende Screens vorgesehen.
Wettbewerb für den Hauptsitz der Commerzbank, Frankfurt, 1991, Christoph Ingenhoven.
In winter the external glazing is closed and the gardens act as an insulating buffer zone; in spring, autumn and in summer the glazings are opened and the office windows can be opened for natural ventilation; for protection against direct sunlight screens are provided.
Competition for the headquarters of the Commerzbank, Frankfurt, 1991, Christoph Ingenhoven.

einer zentralen Kernzone zusammengefaßt. Die runde Form wurde aus energetischen Überlegungen gewählt, da sie eine minimale Oberfläche bei einem maximalen inneren Volumen bietet.
Unter den verschiedenen Grundrißvarianten ist die kreuzförmige mit vier Wintergärten besonders interessant wegen der Wechselwirkung zwischen der Temperatur der Luftpolster und der natürlichen Belüftung der Büroräume.
Durch die vorgelagerten Gärten entsteht eine Art zweischalige Fassade. Bei tiefen Außentemperaturen ist die äußere Verglasung meistens geschlossen, so daß die Gärten als Wärmepuffer wirken können. Da sie infolge direkter und diffuser Strahlung von außen sowie durch die Wärmeabstrahlung der innenliegenden Fassade ausreichend temperiert werden, können die Bürofenster für eine natürliche Belüftung häufig geöffnet werden.
In der Übergangszeit und im Sommer ist die Verglasung geöffnet und die Außenluft durchströmt die Gärten aufgrund der verschiedenen Über- und Unterdrucksituationen entlang der Fassade und kann für die natürliche Belüftung der Büroräume herangezogen werden. Für die

face area to the outside but provides a maximum of interior space.
Of the various floor plan variants the cross-shaped one with four winter gardens is the most interesting one, because of the relationship between the temperature of the air cushions and the natural ventilation of the offices.
The winter gardens placed in front of the offices create a kind of double-skin façade. When the outside temperature is low, the external glazing is generally closed, and the winter garden acts as an insulating buffer zone. The temperate conditions inside this area, as a result of direct and indirect radiation from outside and reradiation from the interior façade, mean that the office windows can often be opened for natural ventilation.
In summer and in spring or autumn the façade glazings are opened, and the outside air flows through the gardens as a result of the differing low and high pressure conditions along the façade; the office windows can then be opened for natural ventilation of the interior spaces.
For protection from direct sunlight and to prevent overheating in the winter gardens, screens

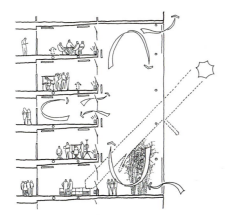 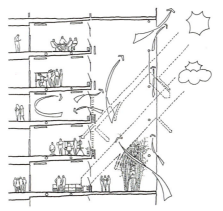 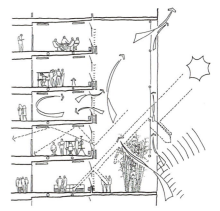

Winter / *Winter* 400 h/pa   Frühjahr und Herbst / *Spring and autumn* 1200 h/pa   Sommer / *Summer* 200 h/pa

Beschattung sind auch innenliegende Screens vorgesehen, die eine Aufheizung des Gartens verhindern. Sämtliche Decken sind als speichernde Bauteile gedacht, um eine weitgehende nächtliche Kühlung zu ermöglichen.

Die Ausleuchtung mit Tageslicht ist durch die runde Grundrißform und die Büroverteilung weitgehend gesichert. Zusätzlich sind lichtumlenkende Lamellen und eine entsprechend geformte Deckenuntersicht in der Konzeptskizze enthalten.

1991 gewann der Architekt Christoph Ingenhoven mit einem zylinderförmigen Hochhaus den Wettbewerb für die neue Hauptverwaltung der RWE AG und Ruhrkohle AG, Essen, beraten vom Büro Happold, London, der HL-Technik, München, und dem Ingenieurbüro Schalm, München. Im Grundriß sind die Büros in der Peripherie, die Nebenräume im Zentrum organisiert; der Aufzugsturm bildet einen separaten Baukörper.

Die Fassade ist eine doppelschalige Konstruktion, welche für die Nutzung mehrerer energiesparender Maßnahmen angelegt ist.

Eine natürliche Be- und Entlüftung des Fassadenzwischenraums erfolgt durch das Öffnen von Klappen im Bereich des horizontalen Deckenabschlusses. Der Fassadenzwischenraum ist 50 cm breit und sowohl horizontal bei den Geschoßdecken als auch vertikal bei den Pfosten aus akustischen und brandschutztechnischen Gründen abgeschottet. Für die natürliche Belüftung der Büros sind Schiebetüren geplant.

are placed on the inside of the outer skin. All slabs are designed to act as a thermal store, which is then subject to night-time cooling. Adequate daylight levels are guaranteed by the circular ground plan and the arrangement of the offices. The design also provides for special light-deflecting louvres and an appropriate light-reflecting ceiling surface.

In 1991 the architect Christoph Ingenhoven, in collaboration with Happold of London, HL-Technik and Schalm Engineers, both in Munich, won the competition for the new headquarters of RWE AG and Ruhrkohle AG, Essen.

Modellaufnahme des zylindrischen Hochhauses; im Grundriß sind die Büros an der Peripherie und die Nebenräume im Zentrum angeordnet, der Aufzugsturm bildet einen separaten Baukörper.
Hauptsitz der RWE AG und Ruhrkohle AG, Essen, 1991–96, Ingenhoven, Overdiek und Partner.
Model photo of the cylindrical high-rise building; the floor plan shows offices on the periphery and ancillary areas in the centre, with the lift tower as a separate element.
RWE AG and Ruhrkohle AG headquarters, Essen, Germany, 1991–96, Ingenhoven, Overdiek and Partners.

Die zweischalige Fassade weist einen 50 cm breiten Zwischenraum auf, der über zu öffnende Klappen im Deckenbereich natürlich belüftet wird; Aufnahme des zweigeschossigen Fassadenprototyps.
Hauptsitz der RWE AG und Ruhrkohle AG, Essen, 1991–96, Ingenhoven, Overdiek und Partner.

The double-skin façade presents a 50 cm deep cavity, which can be naturally ventilated by opening louvres located at the slab levels; photo of the two-storey mock-up of the façade.
RWE AG and Ruhrkohle AG headquarters, Essen, Germany, 1991–96, Ingenhoven, Overdiek and Partners.

Im Innenraum ist eine Quellüftung vorgesehen, welche die natürliche Belüftung unterstützen oder gegebenenfalls ersetzen kann. Für die Raumkühlung sind die Betondecken als Speichermasse freigelegt.
Zwecks einer natürlichen Belichtung wird für die außenliegende Einfachverglasung ein weißes Glas eingesetzt, das höchstmögliche Transparenz gestattet.
Im Zwischenraum sind für den Sonnenschutz perforierte Aluminiumlamellen geplant, die auch eine gewisse Lichtumlenkung bewirken.
Im Raum selbst soll ein Blendschutz als zusätzliche Maßnahme der Lichtkontrolle dienen.
Zurzeit wird das Projekt vom neugegründeten Büro Ingenhoven, Overdiek und Partner bearbeitet und wird 1996 fertiggestellt sein.

This design was for a cylindrical high-rise building. The typical floor plan shows offices on the periphery of the tower, with ancillary areas located in the centre; the lift tower is conceived as a separate element.
The façade is a double-skin construction designed to take advantage of several energy-saving techniques. The façade cavity can be naturally ventilated by opening the louvres located at the slab levels. The façade cavity is 50 cm wide and closed off at each floor level and also at the vertical posts, for reasons of fire safety and acoustic insulation. Sliding doors are planned for the offices, to allow natural ventilation.
In the interior displacement ventilation is planned to supplement and at times to replace natural ventilation. For cooling purposes the

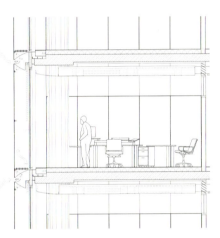

Die siegreiche Wettbewerbseingabe für den Neubau der Hessischen Landesbank HELABA in Frankfurt am Main, 1990–91, von den Architekten Schweger und Partnern – und bei der Weiterbearbeitung zusammen mit der HL-Technik, München – sah eine zweischalige Fassade für die natürliche Be- und Entlüftung der Büroräume vor. Der 35 cm breite Luftzwischenraum wird links und rechts vor jeder Stütze vertikal abgeschlossen, so daß 50geschossige, verglaste Schächte entstehen. Im Fensterbereich sind zwischen den Stützen horizontale riegelartige Abschottungen eingebaut, so daß sich Fensterkästen bilden. Wenn die Luft aufgrund der Thermik in den durchgehenden Schächten aufsteigt, wird die Raumluft über das geöffnete Fenster durch Verbindungsöffnungen zwischen den Fensterkästen und den Schächten abgesaugt. Der so im Innenraum entstehende Unterdruck hat zur Folge, daß Frischluft über Fugen in der Außenschale nachströmt.
Da der thermische Auftrieb gemäß den Berechnungen oberhalb der Gebäudemitte zu einem Überdruck in den Schächten geführt hätte, wurde

exposed concrete floors serve as a thermal store. To optimize daylight levels the external single skin consists of white glass, which gives maximum daylight transmission. In the intermediate space perforated aluminium louvres protect against direct sunlight. The louvres also serve to a certain extent to deflect light. In the offices themselves further screens are planned, to act as an additional means of controlling light levels. At present this project is being further developed by the newly formed architectural practice of Ingenhoven, Overdiek and Partner and it will be completed in 1996.

The winning competition entry for the new Hessische Landesbank building, HELABA, in Frankfurt am Main, designed in 1990–1991 by the architects Schweger and Partners (revised in collaboration with HL-Technik of Munich) also proposes a double-skin façade for the natural ventilation in the high-rise building. In the façade a 35 cm deep cavity is closed off vertically to the right and left of each support pillar, an arrangement which produces a series of 50-storey glazed

Der Luftzwischenraum der zweischaligen Fassade wird links und rechts vor jeder Stütze vertikal abgeschottet, so daß verglaste Schächte entstehen (rechts); zur Unterstützung der Unterdrucksituation in den Schächten wurde ein spezieller Dachaufsatz entwickelt (links).
Hessische Landesbank HELABA, Frankfurt/M, 1990–, Schweger und Partner.
The cavity of the double-skin façade is closed off vertically to the right and left of each support pillar, an arrangement which produces glazed shafts (right); a special roof-top was designed to promote a low-pressure situation in the shafts (left).
Hessische Landesbank HELABA building, Frankfurt/M, 1990–, Schweger and Partners.

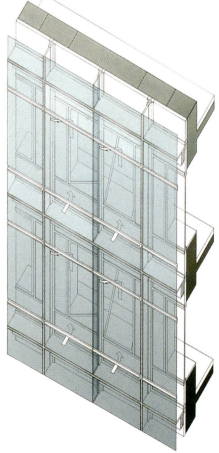

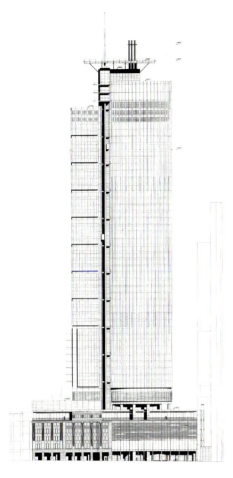

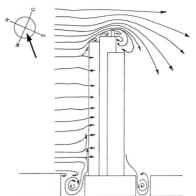

Gebäudeumströmung, Wind SW
Typical air-flow pattern, south-west wind

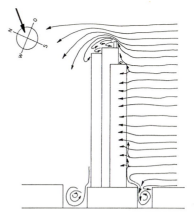

Gebäudeumströmung, Wind NO
Typical air-flow pattern, north-east wind

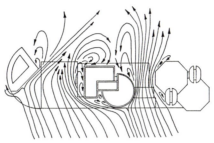

Gebäudeumströmung, Wind SW
Typical air-flow pattern, south-west wind

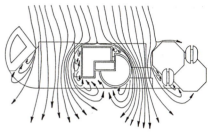

Gebäudeumströmung, Wind NO
Typical air-flow pattern, north-east wind

Fassade des Hochhauses; die Luftströmungen wurden anhand von Modelluntersuchungen im Windkanal überprüft.
Hessische Landesbank HELABA, Frankfurt/M, 1990–, Schweger und Partner.
View of the façade; air flow was tested on scale models placed in a wind tunnel.
Hessische Landesbank HELABA building, Frankfurt/M, 1990–, Schweger and Partners.

ein spezieller Dachaufsatz zur Unterstützung der Unterdrucksituation entwickelt. Da die Lösung den erwarteten Verbesserungen nur teilweise entsprach, wurde beschlossen, die Schachtfassade in Abschnitte von je vier zusammenhängenden Geschossen aufzuteilen.

Während der Entwicklung der Fassade wurden die Luftströmungen anhand von Modelluntersuchungen im Windkanal überprüft, insbesondere die bei Fensterlüftung auftretenden Innenströmungen. Dabei wurden die Luftströmungen durch Rauch sichtbar gemacht und so die typischen Strömungen entlang des Gebäudes und im Straßenraum ermittelt.

Diese Experimente dienen einerseits dazu, die ausreichende Versorgung der Räume mit Frischluft zu sichern, andererseits läßt sich ein Bild von der Immissionssituation im Fenster- und Fassadenbereich gewinnen.

Der Wettbewerb für das Hochhaus des «Düsseldorfer Stadttors» wurde 1991 von Overdiek, Petzinka und Partnern gewonnen und wird nun vom Architekturbüro Petzinka, Pink und Partner, Düsseldorf, weiterbearbeitet. Das 70 m hohe

shafts across the whole façade. Next to these shafts, horizontal panels similar to transoms divide the cavity in front of the windows into separate sections. When thermal buoyancy produces an updraught in the vertical shafts and the office windows are open, the exhaust air from the room is extracted from the individual window sections into the vertical shafts via air vents. This causes a drop of pressure and draws fresh air into the office through open joints in the outer skin of the façade. Calculations predicted that thermal buoyancy in the vertical shafts would create high pressure in the upper half of the tower. To counteract this, a special roof top was designed to promote the low-pressure situation. However, this solution only partly achieved the desired results, and so it was decided to divide the façade shafts into sections spanning four storeys.

During the design stage air flow tests were carried out on scale models placed in wind tunnels. A particular focus of the experiments was the indoor air flow produced as a result of the ventilation design. To give an exact picture of the air movements, smoke was used, which enabled the designers to see the path of air flows across the

Gebäude besteht aus zwei parallelen Bürotürmen mit 20 Stockwerken, die durch drei durchgehende Attikageschosse miteinander verbunden sind, so daß in der Mitte ein rund 50 m hohes Atrium entsteht. Das ganze Hochhaus ist mit einer Einfachverglasung aus 12 mm dickem Floatglas umhüllt, welche die Büros gegen den Verkehrslärm und die Schadstoffemissionen der Tunneleinfahrt der Rheinuferstraße abschirmt. Mit der Glashaut entsteht ein durchgehender, geschoßhoher, 95 cm bzw. 140 cm breiter Fassadenzwischenraum, der mit beweglichen Lamellen für den Sonnenschutz ausgestattet ist. Die innenliegende Fassade besteht aus Wendeflügeln mit Achsmaßen von 150 cm und einer Höhe von ca. 2.85 cm. Ihre Isolierverglasung weist einen k-Wert von 1.4 auf.

building, and at street level. These experiments help establish whether the fresh air supply to the offices is adequate, and they give a picture of the immission levels in window and façade areas.

The 1991 competition for the "Düsseldorf Stadttor" high-rise building was won by Overdiek, Petzinka and Partners, and is now undergoing further development by the architects Petzinka, Pink and Partner. The 70 m high building consists of two parallel office towers with 20 storeys, connected by three continuous attic storeys; this arrangement gives rise to an approx. 50 m high atrium in the centre. The entire building is enclosed in a 12 mm thick skin of float glass which protects the offices against the traffic noise and

Das Hochhaus besteht aus zwei parallelen Bürotürmen, die durch drei durchgehende Attikageschosse verbunden sind.
«Düsseldorfer Stadttor», Düsseldorf, 1991–97, Petzinka, Pink und Partner.
The high-rise building consists of two parallel office towers connected via three continuous attic storeys.
Düsseldorfer Stadttor building, Düsseldorf, 1991–97, Petzinka, Pink and Partners.

Die außenliegende Einfachverglasung erzeugt um die Bürotürme einen breiten, eingeschossigen Zwischenraum.
«Düsseldorfer Stadttor», Düsseldorf, 1991–97, Petzinka, Pink und Partner.
The outer single glazed skin creates a large, single-storey high cavity around the office towers.
Düsseldorfer Stadttor building, Düsseldorf, 1991–97, Petzinka, Pink and Partners.

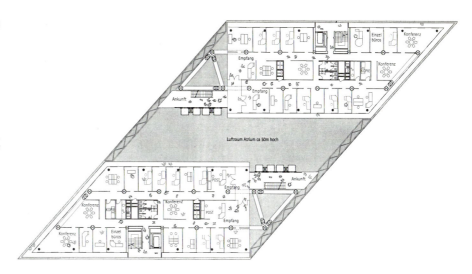

Zur natürlichen Durchlüftung des Zwischenraums ist ein System von verschließbaren Klappen vorgesehen, die in das Lüftungspaket vor der Deckenstirn eingebaut sind. Durch die ausreichende natürliche Luftdurchströmung des Zwischenraums im Sommer kann auf eine Vollklimatisierung der Büroräume verzichtet werden. Für die Kühlung können die Nutzer individuell die mit Grundwasser gekühlten Deckenelemente einschalten. Im Winter soll das große Volumen des Zwischenraums als Pufferzone wirken, so daß der Wärmebedarf und die Abstrahlug im Fensterbereich erheblich reduziert werden.

Aus dem rechnerischen Nachweis resultiert, daß in den Büros während der Betriebszeit praktisch nur ein Kältebedarf entsteht, der hauptsächlich durch Grundwasserkühlung und Desorptionsverfahren gedeckt werden kann, was die Senkung des Bedarfs an Primärenergie um mehr als 50 % ermöglicht.

the pollution from the main Rhine highway entering a tunnel at this point. The façade thus presents a floor-height continuous cavity of either 95 cm or 140 cm in depth, into which are incorporated adjustable louvres for solar shading. The interior façade layer consists of vertical pivoted windows of insulating glass with a U-value of 1.4; the axial spacing is 150 cm with a height of 2.85 m.

A system of closing louvred vents is designed to take care of natural ventilation in the cavity. This system is located in the ventilation unit in front of each slab level. Adequate natural ventilation of the façade cavity in summer means that air conditioning of the offices is not necessary. For cooling purposes the building's users can individually operate the chilled ceiling elements, which are supplied with ground water to achieve their effect. In winter the large façade cavity acts as a buffer zone, considerably reducing heat losses

Die natürliche Durchlüftung wird durch ein System von verschließbaren Klappen vor der Deckenstirn geregelt.
«Düsseldorfer Stadttor», Düsseldorf, 1991–97, Petzinka, Pink und Partner.
Natural ventilation is controlled by a system of closing louvred vents located in front of each floor slab.
Düsseldorfer Stadttor building, Düsseldorf, 1991–97, Petzinka, Pink and Partners.

Das Forschungsprojekt «Green Building» stellt einen weiteren Versuch zur Reduzierung der künstlichen Klimakontrolle dar. Der Entwurf wurde 1990 von Future Systems, Jan Kaplicky und Amanda Levete, zusammen mit den Umweltingenieuren Tom Baker, Andy Sedgwick und Mike Beaven (Ove Arup und Partner, London) erarbeitet.

Die Tragstruktur besteht aus einer dreibeinigen Konstruktion, an der die Geschoßdecken abgehängt werden; im Gebäudekern entsteht ein dreieckiges Atrium. Obwohl die zweischalige Fassade auch Schutz vor Straßenlärm und Abgasen bietet, wurde sie hauptsächlich im Hinblick auf eine natürliche Belüftung entwickelt. Aufgrund der Erwärmung durch Abstrahlung der innenliegenden Büroflächen steigt die Luft im Atrium auf und zieht frische Außenluft durch Öffnungen an der unteren Gebäudeseite nach. Gleichzeitig steigt auch im Fassadenzwischenraum die erwärmte Luft auf und entweicht durch Öffnungen an der Gebäudespitze. Damit entsteht ein Unterdruck im Fassadenzwischenraum, welcher bei Öffnung der Bürofenster die Luft aus dem Atrium nachzieht und damit die natürliche Durchlüftung der Büros ermöglicht. Diese Luftströmungen werden zusätzlich von einem Unterdruck an der Gebäudespitze, der bei Windanfall durch ihre aerodynamische Formgebung entsteht, unterstützt. In kälteren Jahreszeiten wird die unten angesaugte Außenluft mit der aus der Abluft zurückgewonnenen Wärmeenergie vorgeheizt. Die Luftströmungen in der zweischaligen Fassade sowie im Atrium wurden mit Computersimulationen eingehend untersucht.

Eine gleichmässige natürliche Belichtung in der Tiefe der Büroräume gelingt durch verstellbare lichtumlenkende Reflektoren in der innenliegenden Fassadenebene und durch speziell geformte

and radiation in the area in front of the windows. Simulations have shown that cooling needs during office hours are present practically all year round, and these needs can be met mainly by ground water cooling systems and desorption processes. The result is a 50 % reduction of energy requirements.

The research project "Green Building" represents a further attempt to reduce the need for artificial air conditioning. The design was developed in 1990 by Future Systems, Jan Kaplicky and Amanda Levete, together with the environmental engineers Tom Baker, Andy Sedgwick and Mike Beaven (Ove Arup and Partners, London). The support structure consists of a three-legged construction, like a tripod, from which the floor decks are suspended; in the core of the building is a triangular atrium. Although the double-skin façade also protects against noise and exhaust fumes from the street, it was primarily designed to optimize natural ventilation.

Reradiation from the offices causes air to warm up in the atrium; this air then rises and is replaced by fresh air entering through openings underneath the building. At the same time warmed air rises in the façade cavity and escapes through vents at the top of the building. This causes low pressure in the façade cavity, which, on opening the office windows, draws air in from the atrium producing a natural cross-ventilation

Die Tragstruktur besteht aus einer dreibeinigen Konstruktion, an der die Geschoßdecken abgehängt werden; die Gebäudeform und die zweischalige Fassade wurden im Hinblick auf eine natürliche Durchlüftung der Büros entwickelt.
«Green Building»-Forschungsprojekt, 1990, Future Systems, Jan Kaplicky und Amanda Levete.
The support structure consists of a tripod-like construction, from which the floor decks are suspended; the building shape and the double-skin façade were designed to optimize the natural ventilation of the office spaces.
Green Building research project, 1990, Future Systems, Jan Kaplicky and Amanda Levete.

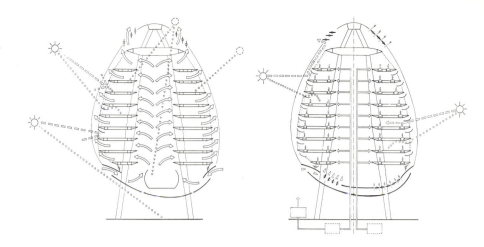

Im Fassadenzwischenraum steigt die erwärmte Luft und entweicht an der Gebäudespitze ins Freie. Damit entsteht ein Unterdruck, welcher Frischluft aus dem Atrium nachzieht (links); Heizung und Kühlung erfolgen durch separate Wasserkreisläufe (rechts).
«Green Building»-Forschungsprojekt, 1990, Future Systems, Jan Kaplicky und Amanda Levete.
Warmed air rises in the façade cavity and escapes through vents at the top of the building. This causes low pressure in the façade cavity, which draws fresh air in from the atrium (left); heating and cooling are supplied by separate water return systems (right).
Green Building research project, 1990, Future Systems, Jan Kaplicky and Amanda Levete.

Deckenelemente. Tageslicht liefert auch das Atrium im Gebäudeinneren. Sonnen- und Blendschutz werden durch individuell steuerbare Lamellen geregelt.

Für die Zwischenspeicherung der tagsüber anfallenden Wärme sind schwerspeichernde Geschoßdecken vorgesehen, die nachts die Wärme wieder an die Luft abgeben.

Obwohl der Entwurf experimentellen Charakter besitzt und in seiner extrem «organischen» Gestalt architektonische wie städtebauliche Grundfragen aufwirft, weist er exemplarisch auf die Tragweite einer integralen Planung für zukünftige energiesparende Gebäude hin.

Die zweischaligen Fassaden werden meist als konstruktive Lösungen für windausgesetzte Hochhäuser in Betracht gezogen. Doch auch bei niedrigen Gebäuden kann das Prinzip eine ener-

of the offices. These air movements are further promoted by low pressure at the top of the building, resulting from the air flow over the streamlined form. In colder weather the air drawn in from outside is heated using the thermal energy regained from the extracted air. The air movements in the double-skin façade and the atrium were closely studied using computer simulations. An even distribution of natural lighting at the back of the offices is ensured by means of adjustable light shelves in the interior façade, and specially designed ceiling elements. Daylight also enters through the atrium inside the building. Individually operating blinds are used to shade from the sun and protect from glare.

Floor decks which act as thermal stores are intended to take up excess heat in the daytime and to be cooled down again at night through natural ventilation.

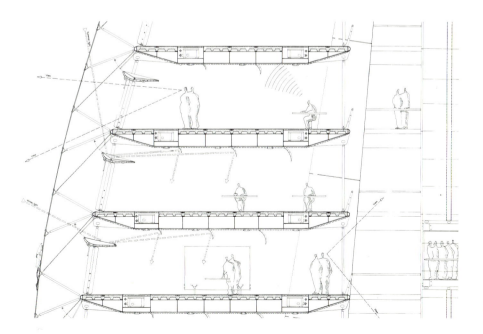

Eine natürliche Lichtverteilung in der Raumtiefe erfolgt durch verstellbare Reflektoren und speziell geformte Deckenelemente.
«Green Building»-Forschungsprojekt, 1990, Future Systems, Jan Kaplicky und Amanda Levete.
Distribution of daylight at the back of the offices is ensured by adjustable light shelves and specially designed ceiling elements.
Green Building research project, 1990, Future Systems, Jan Kaplicky and Amanda Levete.

giesparende Wirkung entfalten sowie eine Klima-
zone bilden, die als temperierte Zone zwischen
der äußeren Makro-Umwelt und der inneren
Mikro-Umwelt vermittelt.

Das seit 1988 geplante Projekt für den «Mikroelektronik-Park» in Duisburg, von Sir Norman
Foster und Partnern zusammen mit Kaiser Bautechnik, Duisburg, sieht auch zwei große Klimahallen vor, in denen neun mehrgeschossige
Bürobauten untergebracht sind. Die Lösung entspricht dem Bestreben, die Arbeitsflächen natürlich zu belüften und zu belichten – daher die
lange Fassadenabwicklung – sowie die Außenfläche wegen der Wärmeverluste auf ein Minimum zu reduzieren.
Die Klimahallen schaffen eine wettergeschützte
Zone, die als Puffer zwischen innen und außen
dient. Nach den Berechnungen soll die Temperatur in der kalten Jahreszeit wegen der Wärme-
abstrahlungen der angrenzenden Gebäudefassaden und der Isolierverglasung im Dachgewölbe
nicht unter Null sinken.
Für den Sommer sind außenliegende Rollostoren
für den Sonnenschutz sowie Klappfenster für die
Durchlüftung der Hallen vorgesehen. Somit ist

Although the design is experimental in character,
and its extremely "organic" form raises basic
questions in architecture as well as town planning, it is nevertheless a model of what can be
done in integrated planning of low-energy buildings.

The double-skin façades are often viewed as solutions for high-rise buildings exposed to the
strong effects of air flow, but the same principle
can also have beneficial effects on energy consumption in low-rise buildings, and produce a
temperate climate zone between the outer
macro-environment and the inner micro-climate.

The "Microelectronic Park" in Duisburg, designed since 1988 by Sir Norman Foster and
Partners in collaboration with Kaiser Bautechnik,
Duisburg, consists also of two large climate halls,
which accommodate nine multi-storey office
buildings.
This solution meets the wish for natural ventilation and daylighting in work areas (hence the
long façade) and the reduction of the outer surface to a minimum to reduce heat losses. Each
climate hall forms protected atria which act as a

Das gewölbte Dach der Klimahalle beherbergt drei
mehrgeschossige Bürotrakte verbunden durch zwei
verglaste Atria.
«Mikroelektronik-Park», Duisburg, 1988– ,
Sir Norman Foster und Partner.
*The curved roof of the climate hall covers three multi-
level office tracts connected by two glazed atria.
Microelectronic Park, Duisburg, Germany, 1988– ,
Sir Norman Foster and Partners.*

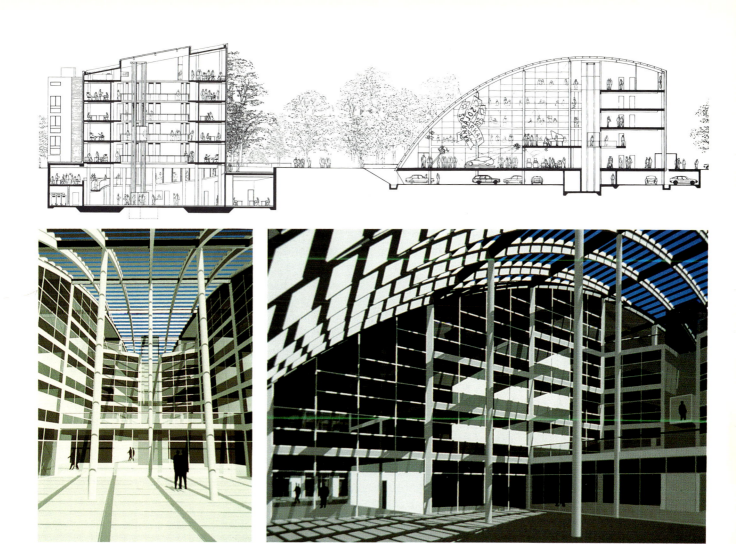

Die Klimahalle reduziert die Außenfläche der Anlage; außerdem ermöglicht sie die natürliche Belüftung und Belichtung der angrenzenden Arbeitsflächen und schafft zusätzlichen geschützten Raum.
«Mikroelektronik-Park», Duisburg, 1988– ,
Sir Norman Foster und Partner.

The climate hall reduces the external building surface. Furthermore it permits natural ventilation and daylighting in work areas and provides additional protected space.
Microelectronic Park, Duisburg, Germany, 1988– ,
Sir Norman Foster and Partners.

eine natürliche Belüftung der Büroräume weitgehend möglich. Im Sommer kann die Halle während der Nacht mit kalter Außenluft und hoher Luftwechselzahl natürlich durchlüftet werden, um die speichernden Betonmassen auszukühlen. Zur maschinellen Kühlung beziehungsweise Heizung sind Wärmepumpen im Boden vorgesehen, die entweder Wärme aus dem Erdreich nutzen oder den Wärmeüberschuß in einen breiten Wassergraben, dem sogenannten Aquifer, abführen.

Die Fassaden der Büros sind vollverglast, um eine weitgehend natürliche Belichtung zu gewährleisten. Bei der Südfassade sind im Brüstungs- und Deckenbereich Paneele mit transparenter Wärmedämmung geplant, im Durchsichtsbereich Kippfenster mit innenliegenden Lamellen. In den Hallen könnten eventuell holographisch-optische Elemente für die Lichtumlenkung verwendet werden.

Die erste Etappe ist derzeit im Bau und umfaßt eine Klimahalle mit drei Bürotrakten.

buffer zone between outside and inside. According to predictions the temperature in these zones will not fall below zero in winter, because reradiation from the surrounding building façades and the insulated glazing of the vaulted roof will keep temperatures raised.

In summer external roller blinds are used for solar shading and top-hung windows for ventilation of the atria. This ensures a high level of natural ventilation in the offices. During the night the atria can be ventilated with cold air from outside at a high rate in summer, which cools the concrete floor decks acting as thermal stores. Additional cooling and heating is provided by heat pumps, which make use of the soil heat in winter or release in the summertime excess heat into a wide water course, the "aquifer".

The façades of the office building are fully glazed, in order to guarantee maximum natural lighting conditions. On the south façade, at parapet and ceiling levels, panels with transparent thermal insulation are planned, and at seated and standing

1990 gewann der Architekt Francis Soler den ersten Preis des Wettbewerbs für das «Internationale Konferenzzentrum» in Paris. Sein Entwurf sah drei vollverglaste Pavillons vor; diese bilden große Klimahallen, in denen je nach Nutzung unterschiedliche Baukörper untergebracht sind. Der zentrale Pavillon umfaßt die Empfangshalle und die Räumlichkeiten für die Diplomaten, der linke das Pressezentrum und der rechte die Konferenzzimmer. Im Untergeschoß des rechten Pavillons befinden sich ein Pressesaal und ein großes Auditorium. Die drei Klimahallen weisen dieselbe umschließende Tragstruktur und eine außenliegende Glashülle als Wetterschutz auf, die von Nicholas Green, YRM Antony Hunt Associates, Paris, entwickelt wurde. Die 25 m hohe, 47 m breite und 97 m lange räumliche Tragkonstruktion besteht aus Vierendeelträgern, die auf einem Rastermaß von 12.5 m Achsabstand und 3.30 m Höhe aufgebaut sind, so daß ein filigranes Erscheinungsbild ohne diagonale Aussteifungen entsteht. Die außenliegende Einfachverglasung besteht aus vorgespannten 3.3 m hohen, 1.56 m breiten und 15 mm dicken Scheiben aus weißem Glas, welche an jeder Ecke mittels eines speziell entwickelten Befestigungsteils aus Edelstahl gehalten werden. Für den Sonnenschutz sind Aluminiumlamellen vorgesehen.

levels top-hung windows with integrated louvre blinds. In the atria light-deflecting holographic-optical elements are being considered.
The first stage of this project is at present under construction; it comprises one climate hall with three office tracts connected by two glazed atria.

In 1990 Francis Soler won the first prize in the competition for the International Conference Centre in Paris. His design consisted in three fully glazed pavilions: large climate halls accomodating various types of functions. The central pavilion comprises the entrance hall and the diplomats' offices; the pavilion on the left contains the press centre and the one on the right, the conference rooms. In the basement of the right-hand pavilion is a press hall and a large auditorium.
The three halls have the same support structure and are enclosed in an external glass weather-skin, developed by Nicholas Green, YRM Antony Hunt Associates, Paris. The 25 m high, 47 m wide and 97 m long space frame consists of a Vierendeel girders on a grid spacing of 12.5 m horizontally and 3.30 m vertically. Diagonal bracing is not required which gives rise to a filigree appearance. The external glazing consists of 3.3 m high, 1.56 m wide and 15 mm thick sheets of white

Die drei vollverglasten Pavillons sind Klimahallen, die verschiedene Funktionen erfüllen.
Wettbewerb «Internationales Konferenzzentrum», Paris, 1990–94, Francis Soler.
The three fully glazed pavilions are climate halls accomodating various types of functions.
International Conference Centre Competition, Paris, 1990–94, Francis Soler.

Der zentrale Pavillon beherbergt die Empfangshalle und die Räumlichkeiten für die Diplomaten (oben); die drei Klimahallen weisen dieselbe umschließende räumliche Tragstruktur und eine außenliegende Glashülle als Wetterschutz auf (links unten); beim zentralen Pavillon ist eine zweite Einfachverglasung auf der Innenseite vorgesehen (unten rechts).
Wettbewerb «Internationales Konferenzzentrum», Paris, 1990–94, Francis Soler.

The central pavilion comprises the entrance hall and the diplomats' offices (top); the three halls have the same space frame support structure and are enclosed in an external glass weather-skin (bottom left); in the central pavilion a second layer of glazing is placed on the inside of the space frame (bottom right).
International Conference Centre Competition, Paris, 1990–94, Francis Soler.

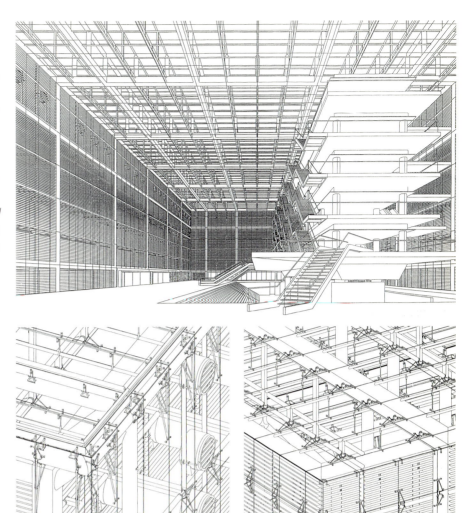

Bezüglich des innenliegenden wärmedämmenden Raumabschlusses sind die Glashallen je nach Klimaanforderung verschieden gestaltet. Für den zentralen Pavillon ist auf der Innenseite der räumlichen Tragstruktur eine zweite Einfachverglasung vorgesehen, damit die Klimahalle eine doppelte Glashülle erhält. In den Zwischenraum wird kalte oder warme Luft eingeblasen, so daß die Temperatur in der Empfangshalle konstant bleibt. Beim Pressepavillon ist keine zweite Hülle notwendig, weil der Baukörper mit einer eigenen wärmedämmenden Fassade mit Fenstern zum Öffnen ausgestattet ist. Dagegen sind die klimatechnischen Anforderung bei den Konferenz-

glass, held at the corners by specially designed stainless steel fixing bolts. Aluminium louvre blinds afford solar shading.
On the inside of the atria are different kinds of thermal insulation solutions, depending on the requirements of the particular function. In the central pavilion there is a second layer of glazing on the inside of the space frame, providing a double-skinned façade at this point. Cold or warm air is blown into the cavity to keep a constant temperature in the entrance hall. In the press pavilion no second skin is necessary because the building itself has its own insulated façade with opening windows. In the third pavi-

zimmern im dritten Pavillon sehr hoch, so daß sowohl eine Isolierverglasung als auch eine Klimaanlage vorgesehen sind.

Nach vier Jahren Planung wurde das Projekt 1994 aus politischen Gründen sistiert.

Mehrgeschossige verglaste Atrien sind auch beim «Ludwig Erhard Haus» vorgesehen (1991–95), das zurzeit von Nicholas Grimshaw und Partnern für die Industrie- und Handelskammer zu Berlin (IHK) und für den Verein Berliner Kaufleute und Industrielle eV. (VBKI) in Berlin gebaut wird. Das Gebäude weist im Erdgeschoß eine zur Fasanenstraße parallele Erschließung auf, die als Zirkulationsachse für die unterschiedlichen öffentliche Nutzungen, wie die Berliner Wertpapierbörse, ein Restaurant und ein Konferenzzentrum, dient. Darüber befinden sich die Büros von IHK und VBKI. Die Geschoßdecken dieser Büros sind von gebäudehohen, bogenförmigen Zweigelenkrahmen abgehängt, so daß das Erdgeschoß für eine maximale Flexibilität in der Nutzungsaufteilung ohne Stützen auskommt. Entlang der Fasanenstraße sind Glasfassaden geplant: Im Brüstungsbereich werden vollflächig weiß emaillierte Scheiben eingesetzt, während im

lion the high standard of comfort requirements in the conference rooms made it necessary to use both insulating glass and also to provide an artificial air conditioning system.

In 1994, after four years of planning, the project was shelved for political reasons.

Multi-storey glazed atria are also planned for the Ludwig Erhard Building (1991–95), at present under construction for the Berlin Chamber of Trade and Commerce (IHK) and the local Federation of Industrialists and Businessmen (VBKI) in Berlin. The architects are Nicholas Grimshaw and Partners. The building contains at the ground floor an internal street parallel to Fasanenstraße; this circulation axis connects together various public facilities, such as the new Berlin Stock Exchange, a restaurant and a conference centre. In the upper floors are the offices of the IHK and the VBKI. The floor decks of these offices are suspended from giant two-pin arches so that the ground floor can remain column-free and thus have maximum flexibility in planning layouts.

A kind of double-skin glass façade is planned for the Fasanenstrasse front: at parapet level white

Die Geschoßdecken sind von gebäudehohen, bogenförmigen Zweigelenkrahmen abgehängt, so daß das Erdgeschoß ohne Stütze auskommt.
«Ludwig Erhard Haus», Berlin, 1991–95, Nicholas Grimshaw und Partner.
The floor decks are suspended from giant two-pin arches, so that the ground floor can remain column-free.
Ludwig Erhard Building, Berlin, 1991–95, Nicholas Grimshaw and Partners.

Die verglasten Atrien ermöglichen eine natürliche Belüftung und die Belichtung mit Tageslicht der angrenzenden Büroräumlichkeiten.
«Ludwig Erhard Haus», Berlin, 1991–95, Nicholas Grimshaw und Partner.

The glazed roof of the atria permits natural ventilation and daylighting for the offices overlooking these spaces.
Ludwig Erhard Building, Berlin, 1991–95, Nicholas Grimshaw and Partners.

Durchsichtsbereich eine Isolierverglasung mit Dreh-Kippfenstern und drei vorgelagerten beweglichen Lamellen aus Floatglas geplant sind. Der zum Hof gerichtete Bautrakt weist zwei verglaste Atrien auf, die für die natürliche Belüftung und für die Tagesbelichtung der angrenzenden Büroräumlichkeiten sorgen. Sie sind mit einer Einfachverglasung versehen, so daß die Temperaturen im Winter freilich bis auf null Grad, aber nicht darunter sinken können. Um die Aufheizung im Sommer zu vermindern, sind Bereiche mit Glasklappen zum Öffnen vorgesehen. Das Glasdach ist auf vorfabrizierten runden Stahlbetonteilen, die zwischen die Zweigelenkbögen

colour-fritted glass panes are used, while at window level clear insulating glass is used, with turn-and-tilt windows in front of which are three adjustable float glass louvres.
The building tract facing the centre of the block has two glazed atria which take care of the natural ventilation and daylight requirements for the offices overlooking this space. The atria have single glazing, and the temperature in winter can drop to about zero, but not below.
To avoid over-heating in summer the glazing incorporates openable panes. The glass roof consists of an outer skin of approx. 1.40 m wide glass sheets which overlap in the same way as the

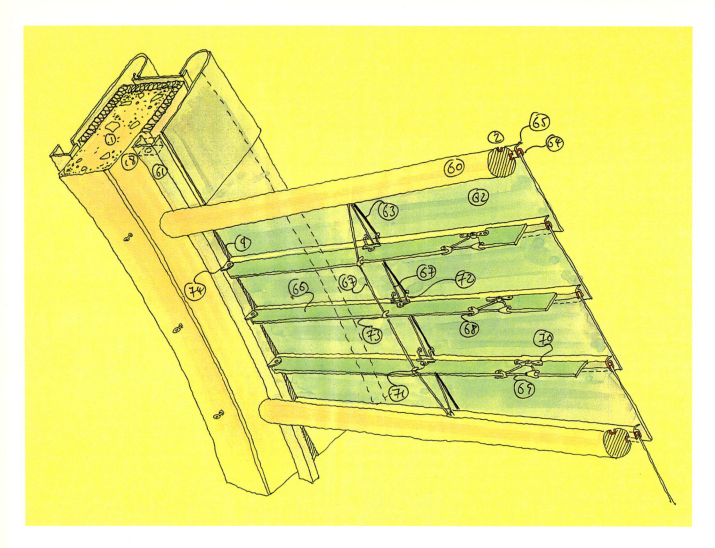

eingespannt sind, befestigt. Es besteht aus einem unterspannten Trägerrost aus Edelstahl-Zugstangen und gläsernen Druckstreifen. Die Außenhaut selbst besteht aus ca. 1.40 m breiten Glasstreifen, die sich wie bei der Londoner Waterloo Station überlappen und mit Neoprenprofilen gegen Regenwasser gedichtet werden.

Bei den zum Atrium gelegenen Bürofassaden sind im Durchsichtsbereich Dreh-Kippfenster mit Doppelverglasung und Sonnenschutzlamellen aus grünem Glas vorgesehen, im Deckenbereich Kippflügel mit Doppelverglasung. Die massiven Brüstungselemente werden mit hinterlüfteten emaillierten Glasscheiben verkleidet.

ones at the new Waterloo International Station in London; the joint is sealed against rainwater by means of a neoprene profile. These glass sheets are supported on a tensile structure of stainless steel tie rods and glass compression fins. This structure is attached to prefabricated, round reinforced concrete elements spanning between the two-pin arches.

The façades of the offices overlooking the atrium space have turn-and-tilt, double glazed windows and have louvre blinds of green glass. At ceiling level are tilting, double glazed windows. The concrete parapets are clad with ventilated fritted glass panes.

Das gewölbte Glasdach wird von einem unterspannten Trägerrost aus Edelstahl-Zugstangen und gläsernen Druckstreifen getragen. Die Außenhaut besteht aus sich überlappenden und mit Neonprofilen gedichteten Glasstreifen.
«Ludwig Erhard Haus», Berlin, 1991–95, Nicholas Grimshaw und Partner.
The curved roof is a tensile structure out of stainless steel tie rods and glass compression fins; the glass skin consists of overlapping glass bands, which are sealed against rainwater by means of a neoprene profile.
Ludwig Erhard Building, Berlin, 1991–95, Nicholas Grimshaw and Partners.

Zusammenfassung und Ausblick

Summary and Outlook

Die Idee einer hochentwickelten «polyvalenten Glashaut», die je nach Jahreszeit und Bedarf als Wärme- oder Sonnenschutz dient, war der Leitgedanke in Mike Davies' Artikel von 1981. Dieser Text steckte als Zusammenfassung einer Studie für die Firma Pilkington Glass Limited aus dem Jahre 1978 die Zukunftsziele der Glasindustrie nach der Energiekrise ab.

Solche Zielvorstellungen haben zur Entwicklung von zahlreichen neuen Glasprodukten geführt. Heute sind Glasscheiben mit einer reineren Zusammensetzung und mit hochwertigen selektiven Beschichtungen sowie Verbundgläser, Isolier- und Mehrfachisoliergläser mit verschiedenen Einlagen und Füllungen auf dem Markt erhältlich, welche differenziertere Eigenschaften für den Wärme- und Sonnenschutz aufweisen.

Trotz den vielen technologischen Fortschritten konnte die Glasindustrie aber bis heute die Vorstellung von Davies' «polyvalenter Wand» noch nicht vollständig umsetzen.

Gläser mit veränderbaren Eigenschaften, mit thermochromen und thermotropen Schichten oder mit elektrochromen Materialien wurden erst als Prototypen entwickelt. Produkte mit Flüssigkristallen sind zurzeit nur begrenzt für die Außenanwendung einsetzbar. So müssen neuere Wärme- und Sonnenschutzgläser weiterhin mit traditionellen Maßnahmen ergänzt werden.

Da aber die ökologische Zielvorstellung darin liegt, den gesamten Bedarf an Primärenergie eines Gebäudes auf ein Minimum, im Idealfall auf Null, zu senken, muß auch der Energieverbrauch im Bereich der Lüftung, Beleuchtung und Kühlung reduziert werden. Dies kann durch eine vermehrte Nutzung von natürlichen, erneuerbaren Energiequellen, wie Sonneneinstrahlung und Luftströmungen, erfolgen.

Ein besonderer Vorteil von Glasfassaden ist das Potential an Gewinnen aus der Sonnenstrahlung in Form von Wärme und Tageslicht. Obwohl in

The idea of an advanced "polyvalent glass skin" which can serve either as thermal or solar protection, according to requirements and time of the year, was the main idea in Mike Davies' article of 1981. This article, a summary of a study carried out in 1978 for Pilkington Glass Limited, set out the future goals of the glass industry in the wake of the energy crisis.

These declared aims led to the development of countless new glass products. Today a range of different glass panes are available, including glass with a purer base mix, high quality selective coatings, as well as laminated glass, insulating glass and multiple-layer insulating units with various interlayers and fillings which have different thermal and solar protection properties.

Despite the many technological advances, however, the glass industry has not yet been able to fully realise Davies' idea of a "polyvalent wall". Glass with variable properties, with thermochromic and thermotropic layers or with electrochromic materials are still at the prototype stage. Products using liquid crystals have at present only limited application on the outside of a building. Thus new types of thermal and solar protecting glass still have to be supplemented with traditional methods.

However, as the ecological goal is to reduce the total primary energy needs of a building to a minimum, ideally down to zero, then energy consumption for ventilation, heating, cooling and lighting must also be taken into consideration. This can be achieved by the increased use of natural, renewable energy sources such as solar radiation or air movements.

A particular advantage of glass façades is the energy gain from the solar radiation in the form of heat and daylight. Although the highest heat losses occur in the colder seasons, it is possible to achieve thermal gains during the day, a factor which is becoming increasingly signifi-

kälteren Jahreszeiten die höchsten Wärmeverluste erfolgen, können tagsüber Wärmegewinne erzielt werden, die durch die ständige Verbesserung der k-Werte an Bedeutung zunehmen.

Zusätzlich senken Konstruktionen wie zweischalige Fassaden die Wärmeverluste durch ihre Pufferwirkung und ermöglichen auch Wärmerückgewinne aus der Abluft. In der Übergangszeit sind die Wärmegewinne oft ausreichend, um den Heizaufwand auf Null zu reduzieren. Im Sommer sind dagegen die Kühllasten zu vermeiden, was durch einen geeigneten Sonnenschutz, eine natürliche Belüftung der Räume und eine nächtliche Kühlung der speichernden Baumasse erfolgen kann.

Eine Lichtumlenkung in die Raumtiefe trägt dazu bei, die Brennstunden der künstlichen Beleuchtung und die damit verbundene Abwärme zu reduzieren.

Auch wenn die Gesamtkosten der Gebäudetechnik in bezug auf die Investitionsausgaben bis um 15 % niedriger werden, da die Dimensionen der gebäudetechnischen Anlage reduziert werden, bleiben zweischalige Fassaden kostspielig. Ökonomisch betrachtet ist die Konstruktion zweischaliger Fassaden heute noch teurer als diejenige einschaliger; die höheren Investitionskosten werden beim derzeitigen Enwicklungsstand noch nicht durch die Einsparungen bei den Betriebskosten – Wartung, Reinigung und Energieverbrauch – wettgemacht. Dennoch besteht das Ziel darin, in naher Zukunft Gebäude mit minimalem Energieverbrauch und reduziertem Kapitaleinsatz realisieren zu können.

Für den wirkungsvollen Einsatz einer «intelligenten» Glasfassade ist die Entwicklung fortschrittlicher Gesamtenergiekonzepte notwendig, welche die Interaktion zwischen Fassade und Haustechnik ermöglichen. Das führt zu einer zunehmenden Komplexität der Entwurfsaufgabe, die nur durch eine integrale oder ganzheitliche Planung – d. h. durch eine interdisziplinäre Zusammenarbeit von Architekten, Fassadenplanern und beratenden Fachingenieuren – erfolgversprechend angegangen werden kann.

cant through the continuous improvements in U-values.

Constructions such as double-skin façades lower heat losses through their buffer effect and open up the additional possibility of regaining heat from the exhaust air. In spring and autumn the heat gains are often sufficient to reduce heating loads to zero. In summer on the other hand cooling loads have to be avoided by means of appropriate solar shading, natural ventilation of the rooms and night cooling of the thermal-store building mass.

Light deflection into the back of the rooms helps reduce the need for artificial lighting and the subsequent heat associated with it.

Even if total investment costs for heating and ventilation systems in a building were to be reduced by 15 %, simply through the need for less equipment, double-skin façades would still be expensive. Construction costs for double-skin façades are today higher than for single-skin façades and, at current development levels, the higher investment costs are also not yet compensated in savings in operating costs, in terms of servicing, cleaning and energy consumption. Nevertheless the aim is still, in the near future, to design buildings which use a minimum of energy and require reduced capital investment.

For a more effective use of "intelligent" glass façades further development is necessary in the area of more overall energy concepts which better exploit the interaction of façade and building services. This leads to an increasing complexity at the design stage which can only be successfully resolved through an integrated or holistic planning – i. e. through interdisciplinary collaboration between architects, façade planners and building engineers.

Dank   Acknowledgement

An dieser Stelle möchte ich allen, die seit Frühjahr 1994 zur Entstehung dieses Buches beige-
tragen haben, meinen verbindlichen Dank aus-
sprechen. Herr Robert Steiger vom Artemis
Verlag hat mich zu dieser Darstellung ermutigt
und den Fortgang der Arbeit mit viel Engagement
und Geduld begleitet. Frau Franziska Forter er-
leichterte mir den Vorgang des Verfassens durch
ihre intensive redaktionelle Mitarbeit entschei-
dend. Frau Ingrid Taylor, English Experts, hat mit
viel Fachwissen die Übersetzung ins Englische ge-
leistet. Herr Ueli Amacher besorgte mit Aufmerk-
samkeit die Schlußkorrektur. Herr Urs Berger-
Pecora hat das reiche Material durch ein klares
Layout aussagekräftig gestaltet.
Mein besonderer Dank gilt allen Architekten und
anderen Fachleuten sowie den Spezialfirmen,
die mir mit großzügiger Hilfsbereitschaft Infor-
mationen und Dokumentationsmaterial zur Verfügung gestellt haben, insbesondere:

I should like to record my gratitude to all those
who have helped in the creation of this book
since Spring 1994, in particular to Robert Steiger
of Artemis Publishers for his encouragement and
continued support and patience throughout the
project. Thanks also to Franziska Forter for her
assiduous editorial work which was a great help
in the writing of the texts and to Ingrid Taylor of
English Experts for the translation into English.
I am indebted also to Ueli Amacher for his meti-
culous final proofreading and to Urs Berger-
Pecora for the clear layout and presentation of
the extensive material.
My special thanks is extended to all those architects, individual experts and specialist companies
who so generously supplied information and do-
cumentary material, in particular to:

Arup Associates:
    H. Allen
Ove Arup & Partners:
    A. McDowell, A. Sedgwick
Asahi Glass Europe:
    H. Yamamoto
BASF Schweiz AG:
    W. Alig, A. Albertin
BGT Bischoff Glastechnik:
    T. Korn
J. Brunet + E. Saunier Architectes:
    J. Brunet, E. Saunier
Jean Pierre Buffi & Associés:
    J.P. Buffi, M. Buffi, B. Hassina
James Carpenter Design Associates Inc.:
    J. Carpenter
Jo Coenen:
    J. Coenen, N. Johnson, T. Kemme
Dornier Deutsche Aerospace GmbH:
    R. Braun, T. Meisel

Eckelt Glas:
    H. Esterl
EMPA-Dübendorf:
    H. Manz
Baubibliothek der ETH-Zürich:
    A. Alig, U. Häberlin, K.E. Lehmann, E. Meyer
EWI Ingenieure und Berater:
    T. Kählin
Fabrimex AG:
    W. Maag
Institut für Licht- und Bautechnik ILB,
Fachhochschule Köln:
    H. Müller, D. Wüller, P. Schuster
Sir Norman Foster and Partners:
    Sir Norman Foster, S. Behling, M. Bowmann,
    B. Haw, K. Harris, H. Turner
Fraunhofer-Institut für Solare Energiesysteme:
    H.R. Wilson
Future Systems:
    J. Kaplicky, A. Levete

Joseph Gartner & Co:
    W. Schulz
Andreas Gerber
Gesellschaft für Aerophysik mbH:
    L. Ilg
Glas Trösch:
    U. Moor, P. Beck
Nicholas Grimshaw and Partners:
    N. Grimshaw, D. Hutchinson, D. Kirkland,
    G. Stowell, S. Templeton
von Gerkan Marg und Parner:
    M. von Gerkan, V. Marg, B. Pastuschka
Herzog + Partner:
    T. Herzog, V. Hezog-Loibl
HHS Planer + Architekten:
    G. Schleiff
HL-Technik AG:
    K. Daniels, J. Stoll
Michael Hopkins and Partners:
    M. Hopkins, B. Dunster, C. Endicott, J. Pringle
Richard Horden Associates:
    R. Horden, S. Forbes-Waller, S. Kirby
Hunter Douglas Europe:
    N. Pulskens, W. Reichmut
Ingenhoven Overdiek und Partner:
    C. Ingenhoven, M. Reiss, E. Schmitz-Riol
Kaiser Bautechnik Ingenieurgesellschaft mbH:
    N. Kaiser, P.T. Benedik
Okalux Kapillarglas GmbH:
    R. Kümpers
Nippon Sheet Glass NSG Europe:
    T. Furutami, K. Maeda
Architectures Jean Nouvel:
    J. Nouvel, W. Keuthage, C. Kruk, J. Simon
Petzinka, Pink und Partner:
    K. Petzinka, T. Pink, M. Stamminger
Renzo Piano Building Workshop:
    R. Piano, J. Lelay, B. Plattner, M. Varratta

Pilkington Glass Limited:
    D. Button, R. Jennings
Ian Ritchie Architects:
    I. Ritchie, J.van den Bossche, S. Conolly,
    H. Rambow, A. Summers
Rice-Francis-Ritchie RFR:
    J.F. Blassel, H. Dutton
Richard Rogers Partnership:
    Sir Richard Rogers, M. Davies
Sabiac Sa, Saint-Gobain:
    A. Büchi, B. Giger, A. Minne
Schott Glaswerke GmbH:
    R. Langfeld, F.G.K. Baucke
Schweger + Partner:
    P. Schweger, Y. von Strachwitz
Siemens-Albis AG:
    H.M. Berger, W. Engler, R. Müller
Siemens Architekturabteilung:
    G.R. Standke, B. Engel
Francis Soler:
    F. Soler, C. Westerburg
Tuchschmid AG:
    B. Flury, W. Luessi
Lawrence Berkeley Laboratory,
University of California:
    C.M. Lampert
Labor für Bildschirmtechnik, Universität Stuttgart:
    T. Kallfass
School of Engineering, Department of Technology,
Uppsala Universitet:
    C.G. Granquist
YRM Antony Hunt Associates:
    A. Hunt, N. Green
VEGLA Vereinigte Glaswerke:
    K. Wertz
Michael Wigginton
Pieter Zaanen Architect and Associates:
    P. Zaanen, M. Snijders

Ausgewählte Bibliographie

Selected Bibliography

Allgemeines / General

Beinhauer, Benemann, Gutjahr, Müller, Hrsg.; *Fassaden der Zukunft: mit der Sonne Leben*; ILB-Fachhochschule Köln, 1992

Interpane-Gruppe; *Gestalten mit Glas*; 1990

Oswald, P., Hrsg., unter Mitarbeit Rexroth, S.; *Wohltemperierte Architektur*, C.F. Müller, Heidelberg, 1994

Balkow, D., von Bock, K., Krewinkel, H. W., Rinkens, R.; *Glas am Bau*; Deutsche Verlags-Anstalt DVA, Stuttgart, 1990

Button, D., Colvin, J., Cunliffe, J., Inmann, C., Jakson, K., Lightfoot, G., Owens, P., Pye, B., Waldron, B.; *Glass in Building*; Butterworth Architecture, Oxford, 1993

Petzold, A., Marusch, H., Schramm, B.; *Der Baustoff Glas*; 3. Auflage, K. Hofmann, Schorndorf, Verlag für Bauwesen, Berlin, 1990

Pfaender, H.G., Überarb. u. erg. von Schröder, H.; *Schott-Glaslexikon*; 4. Aufl., mvg-Moderne Verlagsgesellschaft, München, 1989

Schaal, R.; *Glas als Baumaterial*; Lehrstuhl für Architektur und Konstruktion, Schriftenreihe Nr.7, ETH-Zürich, 1989

Einführung / Introduction

Intelligentes Bauen mit Dynamischen Gebäudehüllen; in: Arch+ 99, Juli 1989, S. 71–74

Banham, R.; *The Architecture of the Well-Tempered Environment*; Architectural Press, London, 1969

Davies, M.; *A Wall for all Seasons*; in: RIBA Journal, February 1981, S. 55–57

Davies, M.; *Eine Wand für alle Jahreszeiten*; in: Arch+ 104, Juli 1990, S. 46–51

Davies, M.; *Das Ende des mechanischen Zeitalters*; in: Arch+ 113, Sept. 1992, S. 48–56

Scheerbart, P.; *Glasarchitektur*; Verlag der Sturm, Berlin, 1914

Der Werkstoff Glas / Glass, the Material

Dutton, H.; *Structural glass design from La Villette, Paris and after*; in: Symposium Proceedings, Technische Universität Delft, 1992, S. 4-0 bis 4-36

Hestnes, A.G.; *Grundlagen passiver Solarenergienutzung*; Thermische Solarenergienutzung an Gebäuden, Comett-Projekt SUNRISE, Fraunhofer-Institut für Solare Energiesysteme, Freiburg, 1994, S. 27–40

Rice, P., Dutton, H.; *Le verre structurel*; Editions du Moniteur, Paris, 1990

Ritchie, I.; *Art of Glas Architecture*; in: Fassaden der Zukunft: mit der Sonne Leben; op. cit., S. 17–38

Schulz, C., Seger, P.; *Großflächige Verglasungen*; in: Detail Nr.1, 1991, S. 13–22

Wiggington, M.; *Glass today – report and proceedings of the glass in the environment conference*; Crafts Council, London, 1986

Wiggington, M.; *Glass in architecture*; Phaidon, London, 1995

Wiggington, M.; *Daring glass applications in recent architecture*; op. cit., S. 5-0 bis 5-14

Die Glasscheibe / The Glass Pane

Fenestration 2000; Review of advanced glazing technology and study of benefit for the UK; Phase II, ETSU S 1342, Halcrow Gilbert Associates Ltd., 1992

BGT-Bischoff Glastechnik, Hrsg.; *Konstruieren und Gestalten mit Glas*; Bretten, 1/1993

Glas Trösch, Hrsg.; *Modernes Sonnenschutzglas mit zeitloser Ästhetik*; Bützberg, 1994

Glas Trösch, Hrsg.; *Silverstar®: Technologievorsprung auf Glas*; Bützberg, 1994

Button, D.A., Dunning, R.; *Fenestration 2000: an investigation into the long-term requirements for glass*; Phase I, Pilkington Glass Ltd. and the UK Department of Energy, St Helens, July 1989

Dolden, M.; *James Carpenter Profile*; in: Progressive Architecture, 3/1988, S. 113–117

Lampert, C.M., Yan-ping Ma; *Advanced glazing*

material study; Phase III, ETSU S 1215, Pilkington Glass plc, St Helens, 1992

Ortmanns, G.; *Die Bedeutung von Schichten für das moderne Funktionsisolierglas*; in: Glasforum, Nr.6, 1990, S. 38–42

Ortmanns, G.; *Hochwärmedämmendes Isolierglas*; in: Glasforum, Nr.1, 1992, S. 42–47

Ortmanns, G.; *Klimasteuerung durch Glasbeschichtungen*; in: Wohltemperierte Architektur, op. cit., S. 112–115

Pepchinski, M.; *Verwandlung des Raumes durch Licht und Glas: Arbeiten von James Carpenter*; in: Glasforum, Nr.5, 1990, S. 18–23

Das Verbundglas / Laminated Glass

Glas und Sonnenschutz; in: Arch+ 100/101, Oktober 1989, S. 109–113

Benson, D., Tracy, E.; *Wanted: smart windows that save energy*; in: NREL In Review, June 1992, S. 12–14

Baucke, F.G.K; *Electrochromic applications*; in: Materials, Science and Engineering, B10, 1991, S. 285–292

Benson, D.K., Tracy, C.E., Ruth, M.R.; *Solid-state electrochromic switchable window glazing FY 1984 progress report*; Solar Research Institute, Colorado, USA, April 1986

Burg, M., Müller, H., Wüller, D; *Eine «Intelligente» Solarfassade*; in: HLH, Nr.10, 1993, S. 592–595

Dietrich, U.; *Partly transparent shading systems based on holografic-optical elements*; in: Solar Energy in Architecture and Urban Planning, 3. European Conference CEC, H. S. Stephens and Associates, May 1993, S. 246–249

Eicker, U., Pfisterer, F.; *Semi-Transparente Photovoltaikfassaden*; in: Fassaden der Zukunft: op. cit., S. 315–320

Granqvist, C. G.; *Electrochromic coatings for smart Windows: a status report*; in: Renewable Energy; 2nd world renewable energy congress, Vol. 1, Pergamon Press, Oxford, 1992, S. 115–123

Granqvist, C.G.; *Electrochromic oxides: a bandstructure approach*; in: Solar Energy Materials and Solar Cells 32, Amsterdam, 1994, S. 369–382

Granqvist, C. G.; *Electrochromic tungsten-oxide-based thin films; physics, chemistry and technology*; in: Academic Press Inc., 1993, S. 301–370

Gutjahr, J.; *Die Anwendung Holographisch-Optischer Elemente in Gebäudefassaden*; in: Fassaden der Zukunft: op.cit., S. 167–168

Häberlin, H.; *Photovoltaik*; AT Verlag, 1991

Hegger-Luhnen, D., Hegger, M.; *Multifunktionale Glashaut mit lichtlenkenden Hologrammen und Solarzellen*; in: Fassaden der Zukunft: op. cit., S. 187–200

Meisel, T.; *Elektrochrome Schichten: Anwendung und Technik*; Dornier GmbH, Friedrichshafen, 1993

Meisel, T., Braun, R.; *Large scale electrochromic devices for smart windows and absorbers*; in: SPIE 1728, 1992

Nagai, J.; *Recent development in electrochromic glazings*; in: SPIE 1728, 1992

Müller, H., Gutjahr, J.; *Tageslichtbeleuchtung in Büroräumen*; in: Deutsche Bauzeitschrift, DBZ, Nr.2, 1992

Müller, H.; *Lichtlenkung mit Hologrammen*; in: Fassaden der Zukunft: op. cit., S. 175–186

Susemihl, I., Chehab, O.; *Die Energieaktive Fassade: Fassadenelemente mit integrierten Solarzellen*; in: Fassaden der Zukunft: op. cit., S. 299–314

Wilson, H.R, Raicu, A., Rommel, M., Nitz, P.; *Überhitzungsschutz mit thermotropen Schichten*; 9. Internationales Sonnenforum '94 in Stuttgart, Tagungsband DGS

Wilson, H.R.; *Potential of thermotropic layers to prevent overheating*; SPIE 2255, 1994

Das Isolierglas / Insulating Glass

Braun, P. O.; *Transparente Wärmedämmung von Gebäudefenstern*; in: Thermische Solarenergienutzung an Gebäuden, op. cit., S. 121–143

Grimme, F. W.; *Wärmeschutz*; in: Thermische Solarenergienutzung an Gebäuden, op. cit., S. 87–115

Herzog, T. Schrade, H. J.; *Lichtdach in Linz*; in: Fassaden der Zukunft: op. cit., S. 201–206

Platzer, W.; *Fenster und Verglasungen*; in: Thermische Solarenergienutzung an Gebäuden, op. cit., S. 45–80

Platzer, W.J.; *Licht und Wärme; Entwicklungslinie bei TWD Materialien*; in: Sonnenenergie, Nr.2, April 1992, S. 3–8

Sick, F.; *Tageslichtnutzung*; in: Thermische Solarenergienutzung an Gebäuden, op. cit., S. 149–182

Svendsen, S., und Jensen, K.I.; *Development of evacuated windows based on monolithic silika aerogel spacers*; in: Solar Energy in Architecture and Urban Planning, op. cit., S. 165–167

Die Fassade / Façades

Achstetter, G.; *Sonnenschutz*; Wohltemperierte Architektur,.op. cit., S.104–111

Daniels, K.; *Skin Technology*; Werkbericht 10, HL-Technik AG, München-Zürich, März 1992

Daniels, K., Stoll, J., Pültz, G., Schneider J.; *Hochhäuser natürlich belüftet?* Werkbericht 11, HL-Technik AG, München-Zürich, Juli 1992

Daniels, K.; *Gebäudetechnik für die Zukunft – «weniger ist mehr»*; Werkbericht 12, HL-Technik AG, München-Zürich, 1994

Daniels, K.; *Integrale Planungskonzepte: Ein Muß für die Zukunft?* Werkbericht 13, HL-Technik AG, München-Zürich, 1994

Daniels, K.; *Gebäudetechnik: Ein Leitfaden für Architekten und Ingenieure*; R. Oldenbourg Verlag, München, Verlag der Fachvereine an den schweiz. Hochschulen und Techniken, Zürich, 1992

Meyer, K.H.; *Energiesparende Lüftung und Kühlung*; in: Wohltemperierte Architektur, op. cit., S. 78–83

Michael Hopkins and Partners; *Engineering research and prototype development for low-energy buildings*; Commission of the European Communities, CEC DGXII, Joule-II Programme, Interim Report, March 1994

Müller, H.; *Fenster und Fassaden*; in: Deutsche Bauzeitschrift, DBZ, Nr.2, 1991. S. 261–264

Müller, H., Balkowski, M.; *Abluftfenster in Bürogebäuden*; in: HLH 34/10, S. 412–417

Oswalt, P.; *Die Architektur intelligenter Gebäude*; in: Wohltemperierte Architektur, op. cit., S. 94–99

Schaal, R.; *Klimafassaden*; Auszug vom 2. Bauphysik-Kongress, VDI Berichte Nr.316, Düsseldorf, 1978

Schwab, A., Heusler, W., und Ernst, J.; *Zweite Haut-Fassaden im Wohnungs- und Verwaltungsbau*; in: Fassade, Nr.6, 1993, S. 36–45

Schöning, W., Oswalt, P.; *Zweischalige Klimafassaden*; in: Wohltemperierte Architektur, op. cit., S. 128–143

Stoll, J.; *Großflächige Verglasungen: Sonnenschutz und Lüftung*; in: Fassaden der Zukunft: op. cit., S. 67–89

Bildnachweis   Illustration Credits

o = oben/top; m = mitte/middle;
u = unten/bottom; l = links/left; r = rechts/right

Umschlagphotos / Cover photos:	
	Ingenhoven Overdiek und Partner, Düsseldorf
8	Mike Davies, Richard Rogers Partnership, London
12/o	Jan Dvorak, Umzeichnung aus: Button, D., Pye, B.; *Glass in building*, Butterworth Architecture, Oxford, 1993, S. 40
12/m	Jan Dvorak, Umzeichnung aus: Balkow, D., von Bock, K., Krewinkel, H.W., Rinkens, R.; *Glas am Bau*; DVA-Stuttgart, 1990, S. 49
12/u	Jan Dvorak, Umzeichnung aus: *Glass in building*, op. cit., S.163
15	Hermann Forster AG, Arbon
16/ol	Hermann Forster AG, Arbon
16/or	Hueck Swiss, Münchenstein
18/or	Sir Norman Foster and Partners, London
18/m, u	Pilkington Glass Limited, St Helens
19/ol, ml	Rice Francis Ritchie RFR, Paris
20	Richard Davies, London
21	Jan Dvorak, Umzeichnung aus; *Werkbericht Nr.10*, März 1992, HL-Technik, München-Zürich, S.16
22	Jan Dvorak, Umzeichnung aus: *Glass in Building*, op. cit., S. 163
23/o	Jan Dvorak, Umzeichnung aus: *Glass in Building*, op. cit., S. 64
23/u	Jan Dvorak, Umzeichnung aus: *Glass in Building*, op. cit., S. 162
25/o	Nicholas Grimshaw and Partners, London
26/l	Joceline van den Bossche, London
26/r	Ian Ritchie Architects, London
27	Jo Reid and John Peck, London
28/l	Jo Reid and John Peck, London
28/r	Nicholas Grimshaw and Partners, London
29/l	P & G Morisson, Den Haag
30	James Carpenter, New York
31	Jan Dvorak, Umzeichnung aus: Lampert, C.M., Yan-ping Ma: *Fenestration 2000; Advanced glazing material study; Phase III*, ETSU S 1215, Pilkington Glass plc, 1992, S. 41
32	Jan Dvorak, Umzeichnung aus: *Glass in building*, op. cit., S. 168
33	Glas Trösch, Bützberg
34	Jan Dvorak, Umzeichnung aus: *Glass in Building*, op. cit., S. 133
35	James Carpenter, New York
36	Balthazar Korab, New York
37/o	Glas Trösch, Bützberg
38	Rice Francis Ritchie RFR, Paris
39	Bruno Flury, Tuchschmid AG, Frauenfeld
42	Bruno Flury, Tuchschmid AG, Frauenfeld
44	Hans Georg Esch, Köln
45	Nippon Sheet Glass NSG Europe, Themse
46	Institut für Licht- und Bautechnik ILB, Fachhochschule Köln
47/o	Institut für Licht- und Bautechnik ILB, Fachhochschule Köln
47/u	HHS Planer + Architekten, Kassel
48/m	HHS Planer + Architekten, Kassel
49	Willi Maag, Fabrimex, Schwerzenbach
51	Jan Dvorak, Umzeichnung aus: *Fenestration 2000;* op. cit., S. 43
53	Vegla Vereinigte Glaswerke GmbH, Aachen
54/o	C. G. Granqvist, Uppsala
54/u	Dornier, Deutsche Aerospace, Friedrichshafen